ZEPHYR BOOKS

A Library of British and American Authors

VOL. 60

THE ZEPHYR BOOK

OF

ENGLISH VERSE

THE ZEPHYR BOOK OF ENGLISH VERSE

An Anthology Chosen by
Margaret and Ronald Bottrall

ZEPHYR
BOOKS

The Continental Book Company AB
STOCKHOLM / LONDON

PREFACE

In compiling this selection we have had as our principal aim the provision of a body of verse representative of English poetry in all its main aspects. We have attempted to give a historical survey of the growth and development of English poetry and at the same time to select poems of outstanding merit. We have not limited ourselves to songs and lyrics, but have included examples of dramatic, heroic, metaphysical, satirical and humorous verse, as being no less than the lyric typical of the English poetical genius, whose colloquial line, through Chaucer, Skelton, Wyatt, Donne, Herbert, Dryden, Pope, Byron, Browning, Hopkins, Hardy and T. S. Eliot, is one of its most persistent strengths. We have therefore extracted passages from plays and long poems to a much greater extent than has been usual in anthologies of comparable length.

An anthology by its very nature must contain certain vicious aspects. Giving so much space to this author or that, selecting one poem and rejecting another, is an invidious task, calling for the most stringent exercise of value judgments, which must at no time be allowed to relax to the level of accepting a piece because it has so often been anthologized. At the same time an urge to produce novelties may lead to a falsification of standards. In making the present selection we have taken due note of the contents of Palgrave's *Golden Treasury*, *The Oxford Book of English Verse* and *The Albatross Book of Living Verse*, as being the three anthologies most widely read. Where it has been possible to select poems equally representative and distinguished, we have avoided repetition, but in no case have we excluded an important poem on the grounds that it has appeared in one or all of the other three selections.

We have attempted to preserve, whenever considerations of length have not precluded this, poems intact as their authors wrote them. Many anthologists seem to have considered it as their prerogative to omit lines and stanzas, or to transpose them, without even indicating that such impertinences have been committed. We have preferred to assume that where a poem is of such high merit as to be included, the author is sufficient master of his craft to arrange the lines and stanzas in their proper order. Where omissions have been made, and this we have only done, reluctantly, for reasons of limitation of space, these are clearly indicated by dots both before and after the cuts. Where we have made extracts from long poems we have given the reference to the book or section from which the extract has been taken. Poems of middle length have given the greatest trouble. Only one such poem, *The Ancient Mariner,* has been printed in its entirety, and we have been able only by extracts to indicate the quality of such poems as *Of the Progress of the Soul, The Vanity of Human Wishes, A Song to David, Adonais* and *The Wreck of the Deutschland.* We have omitted translations from other languages.

The poems have been arranged in chronological order according to the dates of birth of the authors. A number of ballads have been placed arbitrarily in the book in the middle of the sixteenth century. Contemporary spelling has been preserved up to the time of Spenser and modernised thereafter.

As this book has a companion volume of American poetry we have not included poems by American authors. By so doing we have had to omit poems by such important writers as Ezra Pound and Laura Riding, who have written extensively in England and had a considerable influence on contemporary British poetry. We have omitted poems by Dominion poets, owing to our ignorance of this field.

At the request of the publishers, two of my own poems have been included.

R. B.

ACKNOWLEDGEMENTS

For permission to use copyright poems the editors and publishers are greatly indebted to the following authors: W. H. Auden, Edmund Blunden, Roy Campbell, T. S. Eliot, William Empson, Robert Graves, Lionel Johnson, Cecil Day Lewis, Walter de la Mare, John Masefield (and the Society of Authors), Wilfred Owen, Isaac Rosenberg, Siegfried Sassoon, Edith Sitwell, Stephen Spender, Dylan Thomas; to the literary executors of Lewis Carroll, Sir W. S. Gilbert (Miss Nancy McIntosh), G. M. Hopkins (the poet's family), Thomas Hardy (the Trustees of the Hardy Estate), A. E. Housman (the Society of Authors as literary representative of the Trustees of the Estate of the late A. E. Housman), D. H. Lawrence (Mrs. Lawrence), Harold Monro (Mrs. Monro and the Poetry Bookshop), Edward Thomas (Mrs. Thomas), W. B. Yeats (Mrs. Yeats); and to the following publishers in respect of the poets enumerated: Messrs. Allen & Unwin, Ltd. (Lionel Johnson), Messrs. G. Bell & Sons, Ltd. (Coventry Patmore), Messrs. Burns & Oates, Washbourne, Ltd. (Francis Thompson), Messrs. Jonathan Cape, Ltd. (A. E. Housman: *Collected Poems*), Messrs. Cassell & Co., Ltd. (Robert Graves: *Collected Poems, 1938*, and *Poems, 1938—45*), Messrs. Chatto & Windus (William Empson, Wilfred Owen, and Isaac Rosenberg), Messrs. J. M. Dent & Sons, Ltd. (Dylan Thomas), Messrs. Gerald Duckworth & Co., Ltd. (Edith Sitwell: *Collected Poems*), Messrs. Faber & Faber, Ltd. (W. H. Auden: *Charade, The Orators*, and *Look, Stranger;* Roy Campbell: *Adamastor;* T. S. Eliot: *Collected Poems;* Walter de la Mare: *Collected Poems;* Stephen Spender: *Poems;* Edward Thomas: *Collected Poems*), Messrs. Wm. Heinemann, Ltd. (D. H. Lawrence: *Collected Poems;* John Masefield: *Collected Poems;* A. C. Swinburne: *Collected Poems*), The Hogarth Press (Cecil Day Lewis), Messrs. Macmillan & Co., Ltd. (Lewis Carroll: *Alice through the Looking Glass;* Sir W. S. Gilbert: *The Savoy Operas;* Thomas Hardy: *Collected Poems;* W. B. Yeats: *Collected Poems*), The Oxford University Press (Robert Bridges: *The Poetical Works of Robert Bridges;* G. M. Hopkins: *Poems*).

TABLE OF CONTENTS

JOHN OF FORNSETE (?)

(c. 1225)

CUCKOO SONG

Sumer is icumen in,
   Lhude sing cuccu;
Groweth sed and bloweth med
   And springth the wude nu.
       Sing cuccu!
Awe bleteth after lomb,
   Lhouth[1] after calve cu;
Bulluc sterteth, bucke verteth[2];
   Murie sing cuccu.
      Cuccu, cuccu,
   Wel singes thu, cuccu,
   Ne swik[3] thu naver nu.

WILLIAM LANGLAND

(c. 1360)

COVETOUSNESS

... And thanne cam Covetyse; I can him not descryve,
So hungri and so holwe Sire Hervy him loked.
He was bitel-browed and baber-lipped[4] also
With two blered eyen as a blynde hagge;

[1] loweth. [2] harbours in the green. [3] ceae. [4] thick-lipped.

And as a letherne purs lolled his chekes,
Well sydder[1] than his chyn thei chiveled[2] for elde;
And as a bondman of his bacon his berde was bidraveled[3].
With a hode on his hed, a lousi hatte above,
And in a tauny tabarde of twelve winter age,
Al to-torne and baudy[4] and ful of lys crepynge;
But if that a lous couthe have lopen[5] the bettre,
She sholde not wandre on that welch[6], so was it thred-bare ...

The Vision of Piers Plowman, Passus V.

GLUTTONY

... He myghte neither steppe ne stonde til he his staffe hadde;
And thanne gane he go lyke a glemannes bicche[7],
Som tyme aside and som tyme a-rere,
As who-so leyth lynes for to lacche foules.[8]

And whenne he drow to the dore, thanne dymmed his eyen;
He stumbled on the thresshewolde and threw to the erthe.
Clement the cobelere cauhte hym by the myddel,
For to lifte hym alofte, and leyde hym on his knees;
And Glotoun was a gret cherl, and a grym in the liftyinge,
And coughed up a caudel[9] in Clementes lappe;
That the hungriest hound of Hertforde-shire
Ne durst lape of the levynges, so unlovely thei smauhte.[10]

With al the wo of this world his wyf and his wenche
Baren hym home to his bedde, and brouhte hym therinne.
And after al this excesse he had an accidie[11],
That he slepte Saterday and Sonday til sonne went to reste ...

The Vision of Piers Plowman, Passus V

[1] lower. [2] shivered. [3] slobbered. [4] dirty. [5] run away. [6] flannel. [7] a gleeman's bitch. [8] like one who lays nets to catch birds. [9] mess. [10] tasted. [11] a fit of sloth.

A DREAM

...And thus I went wide-where, walking myn one[1],
By a wilde widerness and by a wode-syde.
Blisse of the briddes abyde me made,
And under a lynde[2] uppon a launde[3] lened I a stounde
For to leorne the layes that lovely foules made.
Murthe of her murye mouthes made me there to slepe;
The merviloste meetying mette I me thenne
That ever dremed wyhte in world, as I wene.

A muche man, me thouhte, and lyke to my-selve,
Come and called me by my kynde[4] name.
'What art thou,' quod I, 'that my name knowest?'
'That wost thou, Wille', quod he, 'and no wyghte bettere.'

'Wot I what thou art?' 'Thought,' seide he thenne,
'I have suwed[5] thee this seven yere, seith thou me no rather[6]?

'Art thou Thought!' quod I tho, 'const thou me telle
Where that Do-wel dwelleth, and do me that to knowe?'

'Do-wel and Do-bet and Do-best the thridde,' quod he,
'Aren three faire vertues, and beth not far to fynde...'

The Vision of Piers Plowman, Passus VIII.

GEOFFREY CHAUCER
(1340?—1400)

MERCILES BEAUTE

Your yen[7] two wol slee me sodenly;
    I may the beauté of hem not sustene,
So woundeth hit throughout my herte kene.

[1] widely wandering, walking by myself. [2] lime-tree. [3] meadow.
[4] usual. [5] followed. [6] saw thou me no sooner. [7] eyes.

And but your word wol helen hastily
My hertes wounde, whyl that hit is grene,
   Your yen two wol slee me sodenly;
   I may the beauté of hem not sustene.

Upon my trouthe I sey yow feithfully,
That ye ben of my lyf and deeth the quene;
For with my deeth the trouthe shal be sene.
   Your yen two wol slee me sodenly;
   I may the beauté of hem not sustene,
   So woundeth hit throughout my herte kene.

LAK OF STEDFASTNESSE

Som tyme this world was so stedfast and stable,
That mannes word was obligacioun,
And now hit is so fals and deceivable,
That word and deed, as in conclusioun,
Ben nothyng oon, for turned up so doun
Is al this world throgh mede and wilfulnesse,
That al is lost for lak of stedfastnesse.

What maketh this world to be so variable,
But lust that folk have in dissensioun?
Among us now a man is holde unable,
But if he can, by som collusioun,
Don his neighbour wrong or oppressioun.
What causeth this, but wilful wrecchednesse,
That al is lost, for lak of stedfastnesse?

Trouthe is put doun, resoun is holden fable;
Vertu hath now no dominacioun,
Pitee exyled, no man is merciable.

Through covetyse is blent[1] discrecioun;
The world hath mad a permutacioun
Fro right to wrong, fro trouthe to fikelnesse.
That al is lost, for lak of stedfastnesse.

L'ENVOY TO KING RICHARD

O prince, desire to be honourable,
Cherish thy folk and hate extorcioun!
Suffre no thyng, that may be reprevable,
To thyn estat, don in thy regioun.
Shew forth thy swerd of castigacioun,
Dred God, do law, love throuthe and worthynesse,
and wed thy folk ageyn to stedfastnesse.

THE ASSUMPTION OF TROILUS

. . . And whan that he was slayn in this manere,
His lighte goost ful blisfully is went
Up to the holownesse of the seventh spere,
In convers letinge[2] every element;
And ther he saugh, with ful avysement,
The erratik sterres, herkeninge armonye
With sownes fulle of hevenish melodye.

And doun from thenns faste he gan avyse
This litel spot of erthe, that with the see
Enbraced is, and fully gan despyse
This wrecched world, and held al vanitee
To respect of the pleyn felicitee
That is in hevene above; and at the laste,
Ther he was slayn, his loking doun he caste;

[1] blinded. [2] leaving.

And in him-self he lough right at the wo
Of hem that wepten for his deeth so faste;
And dampned al our werk that folweth so
The blinde lust, the which that may not laste,
And sholden al our herte on hevene caste.
And forth he wente, shortly for to telle,
Ther as Mercurie sorted him to dwelle.—

Swich fyn[1] hath, lo, this Troilus for love,
Swich fyn hath al his grete worthinesse;
Swich fyn hath his estat real above,
Swich fyn his lust, swich fyn hath his noblesse;
Swich fyn hath false worldes brotelnesse.
And thus bigan his loving of Criseyde,
As I have told, and in this wyse he deyde.

O yonge fresshe folkes, he or she,
In which that love up groweth with your age,
Repeyreth hoom from worldly vanitee,
And of your herte up-casteth the visage
To thilke god that after his image
Yow made, and thinketh al nis but a fayre
This world, that passeth sone as floures fayre.

And loveth him, the which that right for love
Upon a cros, our soules for to beye,
First starf,[2] and roos, and sit in hevene a-bove;
For he nil falsen no wight, dar I seye,
That wol his herte al hoolly on him leye.
And sin he best to love is, and most meke,
What nedeth feyned loves for to seke?

[1] end. [2] died.

Lo here, of Payens corsed olde rytes,
Lo here, what alle hir goddes may availle;
Lo here, these wrecched worldes appetytes;
Lo here, the fyn and guerdon for travaille
Of Jove, Apollo, of Mars, of swich rascaille!
Lo here, the forme of olde clerkes speche
In poetrye, if ye hir bokes seche.—

O moral Gower, this book I directe
To thee, and to the philosophical Strode,
To vouchen sauf, ther nede is, to corecte,
Of your benignitees and zeles gode.
And to that sothfast Crist, that starf on rode
With al myn herte of mercy ever I preye;
And to the lord right thus I speke and seye:

Thou oon, and two, and three, eterne on-lyve,
That regnest ay in three and two and oon,
Uncircumscript, and al mayst circumscryve,
Us from visible and invisible foon
Defende; and to thy mercy, everychoon,
So make us, Jesus, for thy grace, digne,
For love of mayde and moder thyn benigne! Amen.

Troilus and Criseyde.

THE CLERK OF OXENFORD

...A Clerk ther was of Oxenford also,
That un-to logik hadde longe y-go.
As lene was his hors as is a rake,
And he nas nat right fat, I undertake;
But loked holwe, and ther-to soberly,
Ful thredbar was his overest courtepy;[1]

[1] Short coat.

For he had geten him yet no benefyce,
Ne was so worldly for to have offyce.
For him was lever have at his beddes heed
Twenty bokes, clad in blak or reed,
Of Aristotle and his philosophye,
Than robes riche, or fithele, or gay sautrye.
But al be that he was a philosophre,
Yet hadde he but litel gold in cofre;
But al that he mighte of his freendes hente,[1]
On bokes and on lerninge he it spente,
And bisily gan for the soules preye
Of hem that yaf him wher-with to scoleye.
Of studie took he most cure and most hede.
Noght o word spak he more than was nede,
And that was seyd in forme and reverence,
And short and quik, and ful of hy sentence.
Souninge[2] in moral vertu was his speche,
And gladly wolde he lerne, and gladly teche...

Prologue to the Canterbury Tales.

ALISOUN

...Fair was this yonge wyf, and ther-with-al
As any wesele hir body gent and smal.
A ceynt she werede barred al of silk,
A barmclooth[3] eek as whyt as morne milk
Up-on hir lendes,[4] ful of many a gore.
Whyt was hir smok and brouded al bifore
And eek bihinde, on hir coler aboute,
Of col-blak silk, with-inne and eek withoute.
The tapes of hir whyte voluper[5]
Were of the same suyte of hir coler;

[1] get. [2] tending to. [3] apron. [4] loins. [5] cap.

Hir filet brood of silk, and set ful hye:
And sikerly she hadde a likerous yë.
Ful smale y-pulled were hir browes two,
And tho were bent, and blake as any sloo.
She was ful more blisful on to see
Than is the newe pere-jonette tree;
And softer than the wolle is of a wether.
And by hir girdel heeng a purs of lether
Tasseld with silk, and perled with latoun.[1]
In al this world, to seken up and doun,
There nis no man so wys, that coude thenche[2]
So gay a popelote, or swich a wenche.
Ful brighter was the shyning of hir hewe
Than in the tour the noble y-forged newe.
But of hir song, it was loude and yerne[3]
As any swalwe sittinge on a berne.
Ther-to she coude skippe and make game,
As any kide or calf folwinge his dame.
Hir mouth was swete as bragot[4] or the meeth,
Or hord of apples leyd in hey or heeth.
Winsinge she was, as is a joly colt,
Long as a mast, and upright as a bolt.
A brooch she baar up-on hir lowe coler,
As brood as is the bos of a bocler.
Hir shoes were laced on hir legges hye;
She was a prymerole, a pigges-nye[5]
For any lord to leggen in his bedde,
Or yet for any good yeman to wedde . . .

The Milleres Tale.

[1] metal. [2] imagine. [3] lively. [4] sweetened ale. [5] dear little thing.

CHASING THE FOX

This sely widwe, and eek hir doghtres two,
Herden thise hennes crye and maken wo,
And out at dores sterten they anoon,
And syen the fox toward the grove goon,
And bar upon his bak the cok away;
And cryden, 'Out! harrow! and weylaway!
Ha, ha, the fox!' and after him they ran,
And eek with staves many another man;
Ran Colle our dogge, and Talbot, and Gerland,
And Malkin, with a distaf in hir hand;
Ran cow and calf, and eek the verray hogges
So were they fered for berking of the dogges
And shouting of the men and wimmen eke,
They ronne so, hem thoughte hir herte breke.
They yelleden as feendes doon in helle;
The dokes cryden as men wolde hem quelle;
The gees for fere flowen over the trees;
Out of the hyve cam the swarm of bees;
So hidous was the noyse, a! *benedicite!*
Certes, he Jakke Straw, and his meynee,
Ne made never shoutes half so shrille,
Whan that they wolden any Fleming kille,
As thilke day was maad upon the fox...

The Nonne Preestes Tale

QUEST FOR DEATH

...Thise ryotoures three, of which I telle,
Longe erst er pryme rong of any belle,
Were set hem in a taverne for to drinke;

And as they satte, they herde a belle clinke
Biforn a cors, was caried to his grave;
That oon of hem gan callen to his knave,
'Go bet,' quod he, 'and axe redily,
What cors is this that passeth heer forby;
And look that thou reporte his name wel.'
    'Sir,' quod this boy, 'it nedeth never-a-del.
It was me told, er ye cam heer, two houres;
He was, pardee, an old felawe of youres;
And sodeynly he was y-slayn to-night,
For-dronke, as he sat on his bench upright;
Ther cam a privee theef, men clepeth Deeth,
That in this contree al the peple sleeth,
And with his spere he smoot his herte a-two,
And wente his wey with-outen wordes mo.
He hath a thousand slayn this pestilence:
And, maister, er ye come in his presence,
Me thinketh that it were necessarie
For to be war of swich an adversarie:
Beth redy for to mete him evermore.
Thus taughte me my dame, I sey na-more.'
'By seinte Marie,' seyde this taverner,
'The child seith sooth, for he hath slayn this yeer,
Henne[1] over a myle, with-in a greet village,
Both man and womman, child and hyne,[2] and page
I trowe his habitacioun be there;
To been avysed greet wisdom it were,
Er that he dide a man a dishonour.'
'Ye, goddes armes,' quod this ryotour,
'Is it swich peril with him for to mete?

[1] hence. [2] servant.

I shal him seke by wey and eek by strete,
I make avow to goddes digne bones!
Herkneth, felawes, we three been al ones;
Lat ech of us holde up his hond til other,
And ech of us bicome otheres brother,
And we wol sleen this false traytour Deeth;
He shal be slayn, which that so many sleeth,
By goddes dignitee, er it be night.'

Togidres han thise three her trouthes plight,
To live and dyen ech of hem for other,
As though he were his owene y-boren brother.
And up they sterte al dronken, in this rage,
And forth they goon towardes that village,
Of which the taverner had spoke biforn,
And many a grisly ooth than han they sworn,
And Cristes blessed body they to-rente—
'Deeth shal be deed, if that they may him hente.'

Whan they han goon nat fully half a myle,
Right as they wolde han troden over a style,
An old man and a povre with hem mette.
This olde man ful mekely hem grette
And seyde thus, 'now, lordes, god yow see!'

The proudest of thise ryotoures three
Answerde agayn, 'what? carl, with sory grace,
Why artow al forwrapped save thy face?
Why livestow so longe in so greet age?'

This olde man gan loke in his visage,
And seyde thus, 'for I ne can nat finde
A man, though that I walked in-to Inde,
Neither in citee nor in no village,
That wolde chaunge his youthe for myn age;

And therfore moot I han myn age stille,
As longe time as it is goddes wille.

Ne deeth, allas! ne wol nat han my lyf;
Thus walke I, lyk a restelees caityf,
And on the ground, which is my modres gate,
I knokke with my staf, bothe erly and late,
And seye, 'leve moder, leet me in!
Lo, how I vanish, flesh, and blood, and skin!
Allas! whan shul my bones been at reste?
Moder, with yow wolde I chaunge my cheste,
That in my chambre longe tyme hath be,
Ye! for an heyre clout to wrappe me!'
But yet to me she wol nat do that grace,
For which ful pale and welked[1] is my face.

But, sirs, to yow it is no curteisye
To speken to an old man vileinye,
But he trespasse in worde, or elles in dede.
In holy writ ye may your-self wel rede,
'Agayns an old man, hoor[2] upon his heed,
Ye sholde aryse;' wherfor I yeve yow reed,
Ne dooth un-to an old man noon harm now,
Na-more than ye wolde men dide to yow
In age, if that ye so longe abyde;
And god be with yow, wher ye go or ryde.
I moot go thider as I have to go.'

'Nay, olde cherl, by god, thou shalt nat so,'
Seyde this other hasardour anon;
'Thou partest nat so lightly, by seint John!
Thou spak right now of thilke traitour Deeth,
That in this contree alle our frendes sleeth.

[1] withered. [2] white-haired.

Have heer my trouthe, as thou art his aspye,
Tel wher he is, or thou shalt it abye,
By god, and by the holy sacrament!
For soothly thou art oon of his assent,
To sleen us yonge folk, thou false theef!'
   'Now, sirs,' quod he, 'if that yow be so leef
To finde Deeth, turne up this croked wey,
For in that grove I lafte him, by my fey,
Under a tree, and ther he wol abyde;
Nat for your boost he wol him no-thing hyde.
See ye that ook? right ther ye shul him finde.
God save yow, that boghte agayn mankinde,
And yow amende!'—thus seyde this olde man.
And everich of thise ryotoures ran,
Til he cam to that tree, and ther they founde
Of florins fyne of golde y-coyned rounde
Wel ny an eighte busshels, as hem thoughte.
No lenger thanne after Deeth they soughte,
But ech of hem so glad was of that sighte,
For that the florins been so faire and brighte,
That doun they sette hem by this precious hord ...

The Pardoner's Tale.

JOHN LYDGATE

(1370?—1450?)

LIKE A MIDSUMMER ROSE

... Lat noman booste of konnying nor vertu,
  Of tresour, richesse nor of sapience,
Of worldly support, for al comyth of Jesu,
  Connsayl, confort, discrecioun and prudence,

Provision, forsight and providence,
  Like as the Lord of grace list dispoose;
Som man hath wisdom, som man hath elloquence,
  Al stant on chaung[1] lyke a mydsomyr roose.

Holsom in smellying be the soote fflourys,
  Ful delitable outward to the sight;
The thorn is sharp curyd with fresh colouris,
  Al is nat gold that outward shewith bright,
A stokfyssh boon[2] in dirknesse yevith a light,
  Twen fair and foul as God list dispoose
A difference atwix day and nyght;
  Al stant on chaung lyke a mydsomyr roose.

Floures open upon every grene,
  Whan the larke the messager of day
Salveth the uprist of the sonne shene
  Moost amerously in Apryl and in May,
And Aurora ageyn the morwe gray
  Causith the dayeseye hir crowne to uncloose;
Worldly gladnesse is medlyd with affray;
  Al stant on chaung lyke mydsomyr roose.

Atwen the Cokkow and the Nightyngale
  Ther is a maner straunge difference;
On fressh braunchys syngyth the woode wale,
  Jayes in musyk have smal experyence,
Chateryng pyes when they come in presence
  Moost malapert there verdite to purpoose;
Al thyng hath favour, breffly in sentence,
  Of soffte or sharp lyke a mydsomyr roose...

              The Fall of Princes.

[1] change. [2] bone.

ROBERT HENRYSON
(1425—1500)

CRESSEID'S LAMENT

... Thy lufe, thy lawtie, and thy gentilnes,
I countit small in my prosperitie,
So elevait I was in wantones,
And clam[1] upon the fickill quheill[2] sa hie;
All Faith and Lufe, I promissit to thee,
Was in the self fickill and frivolous:
O, fals Cresseid! and trew knicht Troilus!

For lufe of me thou keipt gude continence,
Honest and chaste in conversatioun,
Of all Wemen protectour and defence
Thou was, and helpit thair opinioun:
My mynd in fleschlie foull affectioun
Was inclynit to Lustis Lecherous:
O, fals Cresseid! O, trew Knicht Troilus!

Lovers, beware, and tak gude heid about
Quhome that ye lufe, for quhome ye suffer paine;
I lat you wit, thair is richt few thairout
Quhome ye may traist to have trew lufe agane;
Preif[3] quhen ye will, your labour is in vaine;
Thairfoir, I reid[4] ye tak thame as ye find,
For thay ar sad[5] as Widdercock in Wind.

---

[1] climbed. [2] wheel. [3] prove. [4] advise. [5] steady.

Becaus I knaw the greit unstabilnes,
Brukkill as glas, into my self I say,
Traisting in other als greit unfaithfulnes,
Als unconstant, and als untrew of fay;
Thocht sum be trew, I wait[1] richt few are thay;
Quha findis treuth, lat him his Lady ruse[2]:
Nane but my self, as now, I will accuse...

The Testament of Cresseid.

UNKNOWN

ADAM LAY IBOUNDEN

Adam lay ibounden,
  Bounden in a bond;
Four thousand winter
  Thoght he not too long;
And all was for an appil,
  An appil that he tok,
As clerkes finden
  Wreten in here[3] book.
Ne hadde the appil take ben,
  The appil taken ben,
Ne hadde never our lady
  A ben hevene quene.
Blessed be the time
  That appil take was.
Therefore we moun[2] singen
  'Deo gracias.'

---

[1] know. [2] praise. [3] their. [4] may.

CAROL

I sing of a maiden
   That is makeles[1],
King of all kinges
   To her sone sche ches.[2]
He cam also stille
   There his moder was,
As dew in Aprille
   That falleth on the grass.
He cam also stille
   To his moderes bour,
As dew in Aprille
   That falleth on the flour.
He cam also stille
   There his moder lay,
As dew in Aprille
   That falleth on the spray.
Moder and maiden
   Was never non but sche;
Well may swich a lady
   Godes moder be.

HOLLY AND IVY

Nay, nay, Ivy!
It may not be, iwis,
For Holly must have the mastry
As the maner is.

Holly bereth beris,
   Beris rede enough;

[1] without a match. [2] chose.

The thristilcok, the popingay
   Daunce in every bough.
Welaway, sory Ivy!
   What fowles hast thou,
But the sory howlet
   That singeth 'How how'?

Ivy bereth beris
   As blak as any sloe.
There commeth the woode colver[1],
   And fedeth her of tho[2];
She lifteth up her taill
   And she cakkes or she go
She wold not for an hundred pound
   Serve Holly so.

Holly with his mery men
   They can daunce in hall;
Ivy and her jentell women
   Can not daunce at all,
But like a meine[3] of bullokes
   In a water fall,
Or on a hot somers day
   Whan they be mad all.

Holly and his mery men
   Sitt in cheires of gold;
Ivy and her jentell women
   Sitt without in fold,

[1] pigeon. [2] them. [3] company.

With a paire of kibed[1]
Heles caught with cold.
So wold I that every man had
That with Ivy will hold!

THE SHEPHERDS AT BETHLEHEM

Primus Pastor

Hail, comly and clene,
  Hail, yong child!
Hail, maker, as I meene,
  Of a maden so milde!
Thou has wared,[2] I weene,
  The warlo[3] so wilde;
The fals giler of teen,
  Now goes he begilde.
    Lo! he merys,
Lo! he laghes, my sweting.
A welfare meting!
I have holden my heting[4].
    Have a bob of cherys!

Secundus Pastor

Hail, sufferan Savioure,
  For thou has us soght!
Hail, frely[5] foyde[6] and floure,
  That all thing has wroght!
Hail, full of favoure,
  That made all of noght!

---

[1] covered with chilblains. [2] cursed. [3] warlock. [4] promise. [5] nobl[e]
[6] child.

Hail! I kneel and I cowre.
  A bird have I broght
    To my barne.
Hail, litel tine mop[1]!
Of oure crede thou art crop;
I wold drink on thy cop,
    Litel day starne.

Tertius Pastor

Hail, derling dere,
  Full of godhede!
I pray thee be nere
  When that I have nede.
Hail! Swete is thy chere;
  My hart wolde blede
To see thee sitt here
  In so poore wede,
    With no pennys.
Hail! Put furth thy dall[2]!
I bring thee bot a ball;
Have and play thee with all,
    And go to the tenis!

QUIA AMORE LANGUEO

In a valey of this restles minde
  I soughte in mounteine and in mede,
Trustinge a trewe love for to finde.
  Upon an hill than I took hede;
  A voice I herde, and neer I yede,[3]

[1] baby. [2] hand. [3] went.

In huge dolour complaininge tho,
  'See, dere soule, how my sides blede,
Quia amore langueo.'

Upon this hill I fond a tree,
  Under the tree a man sittinge;
From heed to foot wounded was he;
  His herte blood I segh bledinge;
  A semely man to ben a king,
A graciouse face to loken unto.
  I askede why he had peininge.
He seide '*Quia amore langueo.*

'I am true love that fals was nevere;
  My sister, mannes soule, I loved her thus;
Because we wolde in no wise discevere,
  I lefte my kingdom glorious.
  I purveide for her a paleis precious;
Sche fleith, I folowe, I soughte her so;
  I suffrede this peine piteuous,
Quia amore langueo.

'I crowned her with bliss, and sche me with thorn;
  I ledde her to chaumber, and sche me to die;
I broughte her to worschipe, and sche me to scorn;
  I dide her reverence, and sche me vilonie.
  To love that loveth is no maistrie.
Her hate made nevere my love her fo.
  Axe me no questioun why,
Quia amore langueo.

'I wole abide till sche be redy;
  I wole her sue if sche seie nay;

If sche be recheless, I wole be gredy,
   And if sche be daungerus, I wole her praie.
   If sche wepe, that hide I ne may,
Mine armes her hired to clippe her me to,
   Crie oones, 'I come;' now, soule, asay!
Quiu amore langueo.

'I sitte on this hill for to see fer;
   I loke into the valey my spouse to see;
Now renneth sche awayward, yet come sche me neer,
   For out of my sighte may sche not flee.
   Summe waite her pray to make her to flee;
I renne bifore, and fleme[1] her fo.
   Returne, my spouse, ayen to me,
Quia amore langueo.

Fair love, lete us go pleye!
   Apples ben ripe in my gardine
I schal thee clothe in a newe aray;
   Thy mete schall be milk, hony, and win.
   Fair love, lete us go digne!
Thy sustenaunce is in my crippe, lo!
   Tarie thou not, my faire spouse mine,
Quia amore langueo.

'If thou be foul, I schall thee make clene;
   If thou be sik, I schall thee hele;
If thou moorne ought, I schall thee meene.
   Why wolt thou not, fair love, with me dele?
   Foundest thou evere love so leel?

---

[1] put to flight.

What woldest thou, spouse, that I schulde do?
  I may not unkindely thee appele,
Quia amore langueo.

'What schall I do with my fair spouse,
  But abide her of my gentilness,
Till that sche loke out of her house
  Of fleischly affeccioun? Love mine sche is.
  Her bed is made, her bolster is bliss,
Her chaumber is chosen; is there none mo?
  Loke out on me at the window of kindeness,
Quia amore langueo.

'My love is in her chaumber. Hold youre pees;
  Make ye no noise, but lete her slepe.
My babe I wolde not were in disese;
  I may not heere my dere child wepe.
  With my pap I schall her kepe.
Ne merveille ye not though I tend her to.
  This hole in my side had nevere be so depe
But *quia amore langueo.*

'Longe thou for love nevere so high,
  My love is more than thine may be;
Thou wepest, thou gladest, I sitte thee by,
  Yet woldest thou oones, leef, loke unto me!
  Schulde I alwey fede thee
With children mete? Nay, love, not so!
  I wole preve thy love with adversité,
Quia amore langueo.

'Wexe not wery, mine owne wife!
  What mede is it to live evere in coumfort?

In tribulacioun I regne moore rife
   Oftetimes than in disport.
   In wele and in wo I am ay to supporte.
Mine owne wife, go not me fro!
   Thy meede is marked whan thou art mort,
   Quia amore langueo.'

WESTERN WIND

Western wind, when will thou blow,
   That the smal rain down can rain?
Christ, that my love were in my arms
   And I in my bed again!

JOHN SKELTON
(1460?—1529)

TO MISTRESS MARGERY WENTWORTH

With margerain[1] gentle,
   The flower of goodlihead,
Embroidered the mantle
   Is of your maidenhead.

Plainly I cannot glose,
   Ye be as I divine
The pretty primrose,
   The goodly columbine.

[1] marjoram.

With margerain gentle,
  The flower of goodlihead,
Embroidered the mantle
  Is of your maidenhead.

Benign, courteous, and meek,
  With words well devised,
In you who list to seek
  Be virtues well comprised.

With margerain gentle,
  The flower of goodlihead,
Embroidered the mantle
  Is of your maidenhead.

TO MISTRESS MARGARET HUSSEY

Merry Margaret,
As midsummer flower,
Gentle as falcon
  Or hawk of the tower,
With solace and gladness,
Much mirth and no madness;
All good and no badness,
So joyously,
So maidenly,
So womanly,
Her demeaning
In every thing
Far far passing

That I can endite
Or suffice to write
Of merry Margaret,
  As midsummer flower,
Gentle as falcon
  Or hawk of the tower.

As patient and as still,
And as full of good will,
As fair Isaphill,
Coliander,
Sweet pomander,
Good Cassander,
Steadfast of thought,
Well made, well wrought.
Far may be sought
Erst that ye can find
So courteous, so kind,
As merry Margaret,
  This midsummer flower,
Gentle as falcon
  Or hawk of the tower.

SALUTATION TO CARDINAL WOLSEY

... Prepayre you, Parrot, bravely your passage to take,
  Of Mercury under the trynall aspecte,
And sadlye salute ower sullen syre Sydrake,[1]
  And shewe hym that all the world doth conjecte.
  How the matters he mellis in com to small effecte;

[1] Cardinal Wolsey.

For he wantythe of hys wyttes that all wold rule alone;
It is no lytyll burden to bere a grete mylle stone:

To bryng all the see into a cherryston pytte,
　　To number all the sterrys in the fyrmament,
To rule nyne realmes by one mannes wytte
　　To such thynges impossybyll reason cannot consent:
　　Much money, men say, there madly he hath spent:
Parrot, ye may prate thys under protestation
Was never such a senatour synce Crystes incarnation . . .

Speke, Parrot.

WORLDLY PRELATES

　　　　. . . They occupye them so
　　With syngyng *Placebo,*
　　They wyll no farther go:
　　They had lever to please,
　　And take their worldly ease,
　　Than to take on hande
　　Worsshepfully to withstande
　　Such temporall warre and bate,
　　As nowe is made of late
　　Agaynst holy Churche estate,
　　Or to maynteyne good quarelles.
　　The lay men call them barrelles
　　Full of glotony
　　And of hypocrysy,
　　That counterfaytes and payntes
　　As they were very sayntes:
　　In matters that they lyke
　　They shewe them polytyke,

Pretendyng gravyte
And sygnoryte,
With all solemptnyte,
For theyr indemptnyte;
For they wyll have no losse
Of a peny nor of a crosse
Of theyr predyall landes[1],
That cometh to theyr handes,
And as farre as they dare set,
All is fysshe that cometh to net:
Buyldyng royally
Theyr mancyons curyously,
With turrettes and with toures,
With halles and with boures,
Stretchynge to the starres,
With glasse wyndowes and barres;
Hangynge aboute the walles
Clothes of golde and palles,
Arras of ryche array,
Fresshe as flours in May;
With dame Dyana naked;
How lusty Venus quaked,
And howe Cupid shaked
His darte, and bent his bowe
For to shoote a crowe
At her tyrly tyrlowe;
And how Parys of Troy
Daunced a lege de moy,[2]
Made lusty sporte and ioy
With dame Helen the quene . . .

Colyn Clout.

[1] farm-lands. [2] dance like a saraband.

WILLIAM DUNBAR
(1465—1520?)

IN HONOUR OF THE CITY OF LONDON

London, thou art of townes *A per se.*
  Soveraign of cities, seemliest in sight,
Of high renoun, riches and royaltie;
  Of lordis, barons, and many a goodly knyght;
  Of most delectable lusty ladies bright;
Of famous prelatis, in habitis clericall;
  Of merchauntis full of substaunce and of myght:
London, thou art the flour of Cities all.

Gladdith[1] anon, thou lusty Troynovaunt,[2]
  Citie that some tyme cleped was New Troy;
In all the erth, imperiall as thou stant,
  Pryncesse of townes, of pleasure and of joy,
  A richer restith under no Christen roy;
For manly power, with craftis naturall,
  Fourmeth none fairer sith[3] the flode of Noy:
London, thou art the flour of Cities all.

Gemme of all joy, jasper of jocunditie,
  Most myghty carbuncle of vertue and valour;
Strong Troy in vigour and in strenuytie;
  Of royall cities rose and geraflour;[4]
  Empress of townes, exalt in honour;

---

[1] rejoice. [2] Troja nova or Trinovantum. [3] since. [4] gillyflower.

In beawtie beryng the crone imperiall;
  Swete paradise precelling in pleasure;
London, thou art the flour of Cities all.

Above all ryvers thy Ryver hath renowne,
  Whose beryall stremys, pleasaunt and preclare
Under thy lusty wallys renneth down,
  Where many a swan doth swymme with wyngis fair;
  Where many a barge doth saile and row with are;[1]
Where many a ship doth rest with top-royall.
  O, towne of townes! patrone and not compare,[2]
London, thou art the flour of Cities all.

Upon thy lusty Brigge of pylers white
  Been merchauntis full royall to behold;
Upon thy stretis goeth many a semely knyght
  In velvet gownes and in cheynes of gold.
  By Julyus Cesar thy Tour founded of old
May be the hous of Mars victoryall,
  Whose artillary with tonge may not be told:
London, thou art the flour of Cities all.

Strong be thy wallis that about thee standis;
  Wise be the people that within thee dwellis;
Fresh is thy ryver with his lusty strandis;
  Blith be thy chirches, wele sownyng be thy bellis;
  Rich be thy merchauntis in substaunce that excellis;
Fair be their wives, right lovesom, white and small,[3]
  Clere be thy virgyns, lusty under kellis:[4]
London, thou art the flour of Cities all.

---

[1] oar. [2] compeer. [3] slender. [4] hoods, head-dresses.

Thy famous Maire, by pryncely governaunce,
  With sword of justice thee ruleth prudently.
No Lord of Parys, Venyce, or Floraunce
  In dignitye or honour goeth to hym nigh.
  He is exampler, loode-ster, and guye;
Principall patrone and rose orygynalle,
  Above all Maires as maister most worthy:
London, thou art the flour of Cities all.

LAMENT FOR THE MAKARIS

I that in heill[1] was and gladnès
Am trublit now with great sickness
And feblit with infirmitie:—
  Timor Mortis conturbat me.

Our plesance here is all vain glory,
This fals world is but transitory,
The flesh is bruckle,[2] the Feynd is slee[3]:—
  Timor Mortis conturbat me.

The state of man does change and vary,
Now sound, now sick, now blyth, now sary,
Now dansand[4] mirry, now like to die:—
  Timor Mortis conturbat me.

No state in Erd here standis sicker;[5]
As with the wynd wavis the wicker[6]
So wannis[7] this world's vanitie:—
  Timor Mortis conturbat me.

---

[1] health. [2] brittle, feeble. [3] sly. [4] dancing. [5] sure. [6] willow. [7] wanes

Unto the ded gois all Estatis,
Princis, Prelatis, and Potestatis,
Baith rich and poor of all degree:—
 Timor Mortis conturbat me.

He takis the knichtis in to the field
Enarmit under helm and scheild;
Victor he is at all mellie:[1]—
 Timor Mortis conturbat me.

That strong unmerciful tyrand
Takis, on the motheris breast sowkand,[2]
The babe full of benignitie:—
 Timor Mortis conturbat me.

He takis the campion[3] in the stour,[4]
The captain closit in the tour,
The lady in bour full of bewtie:—
 Timor Mortis conturbat me.

He spairis no lord for his piscence,[5]
Na clerk for his intelligence;
His awful straik[6] may no man flee:—
 Timor Mortis conturbat me.

Art-magicianis and astrologgis,
Rethoris, logicianis, and theologgis,
Them helpis no conclusionis slee:—
 Timor Mortis conturbat me.

[1] mellay. [2] sucking. [3] champion. [4] fight. [5] puissance. [6] stroke.

In medecine the most practicianis,
Leechis, surrigianis, and physicianis,
Themself fra ded may not supplee:[1]—
    Timor Mortis conturbat me.

I se that makaris[2] amang the lave[3]
Plays here their padyanis,[4] syne gois to grave;
Sparit is nocht their facultie:—
    Timor Mortis conturbat me.

He has done petuously devour
The noble Chaucer, of makaris flour,
The Monk of Bury, and Gower, all three:—
    Timor Mortis conturbat me.

The good Sir Hew of Eglintoun,
Ettrick, Heriot, and Wintoun,
He has tane out of this cuntrie:—
    Timor Mortis conturbat me.

That scorpion fell has done infeck
Maister John Clerk, and James Afflek,
Fra ballat-making and tragedie:—
    Timor Mortis conturbat me.

Holland and Barbour he has berevit;
Alas! that he not with us levit
Sir Mungo Lockart of the Lee:—
    Timor Mortis conturbat me.

---

[1] save. [2] poets. [3] the leave, the rest. [4] pageants.

Clerk of Tranent eke he has tane,
That made the anteris[1] of Gawaine;
Sir Gilbert Hay endit has he:—
Timor Mortis conturbat me.

He has Blind Harry and Sandy Traill
Slain with his schour[2] of mortal hail
Quhilk Patrick Johnstoun might nought flee:—
Timor Mortis conturbat me.

He has reft Merseir his endite,[3]
That did in luve so lively write,
So short, so quick, of sentence hic:—
Timor Mortis conturbat me.

He has tane Rowll of Aberdene,
And gentill Rowll of Corstorphine;
Two better fallowis[4] did no man se:—
Timor Mortis conturbat me.

In Dumfermline he has done roun
With Maister Robert Henrysoun;
Sir John the Ross enbrast has he:—
Timor Mortis conturbat me.

And he has now tane, last of a,
Good gentil Stobo and Quintin Shaw,
Of quhom all wichtis[5] hes pitie:—
Timor Mortis conturbat me.

---

[1] adventures. [2] shower. [3] inditing. [4] fellows. [5] wights, person.

Good Maister Walter Kennedy
In point of Death lies verily;
Great ruth it were that so suld be:—
    Timor Mortis conturbat me.

Sen he has all my brether tane,
He will naught let me live alane;
Of force I man[1] his nex prey be:—
    Timor Mortis conturbat me.

Since for the Death remeid is none,
Best is that we for Death dispone,[2]
After our death that live may we:—
    Timor Mortis conturbat me.

UNKNOWN

SIR PATRICK SPENS

The king sits in Dunfermline town
    Drinking the blude-red wine;
'O whare will I get a skeely[3] skipper
    To sail this new ship o'mine?'

O up and spake an eldern knight,
    Sat at the king's right knee;
'Sir Patrick Spens is the best sailor
    That ever sail'd the sea.'

The king has written a braid letter,
    And seal'd it with his hand,

---

[1] must. [2] make disposition. [3] skilful.

And sent it to Sir Patrick Spens,
  Was walking on the strand.

'To Noroway, to Noroway,
  To Noroway o'er the faem;
The king's daughter o' Noroway,
  Tis thou must bring her hame.'

The first line that Sir Patrick read
  A loud laugh laughèd he;
The neist line that Sir Patrick read
  The tear blinded his e'e.

'O wha is this has done this deed
  And tauld the king o' me,
To send us out, at this time o' year,
  To sail upon the sea?

'Be it wind, be it weet, be it hail, be it sleet,
  Our ship must sail the faem;
The king's daughter o' Noroway,
  'Tis we must fetch her hame.'

They hoysed their sails on Monenday morn
  Wi' a' the speed they may;
And they hae landed in Noroway
  Upon a Wodensday.

They hadna been a week, a week,
  In Noroway, but twae.
When that the lords o' Noroway
  Began aloud to say.

'Ye Scottishmen spend a' our King's goud,
  And a' our queenis fee!'
'Ye lee, ye lee, ye liars loud!
  For' loud I hear ye lee!

'For I brought as much white monie,
  As gane my men and me,
And I brought a half-fou o' gude red goud
  Out o'er the sea wi'me.

'Mak ready, mak ready, my merry men a'!
  Our gude ship sails the morn.'
'Now ever alack, my master dear,
  I fear a deadly storm.

'I saw the new moon late yestreen
  Wi' the auld moon in her arm;
And if we gang to sea, master,
  I fear we'll come to harm.'

They hadna sail'd a league, a league,
  A league but barely there,
When the lift[1] grew dark, and the wind blew loud,
  And gurly grew the sea.

The ankers brak, and the topmast lap,[2]
  It was sic a deadly storm:
And the waves cam owre the broken ship
  Till a' her sides were torn.

'Go fetch a web o' the silken claith,
  Another o' the twine,

---

[1] sky. [2] sprang.

And wap them into our ship's side,
   And let nae the sea come in.'

They fetch'd a web o' the silken claith,
   Another o' the twine,
And they wapp'd them round that gude ship's side,
   But still the sea came in.

O laith, laith were our gude Scots lorus
   To wet their cork-heel'd shoon,
But lang or a' the play was play'd
   They wat their hats aboon.

And mony was the feather bed
   That flatter'd[1] on the faem;
And mony was the gude lord's son
   That never mair cam hame.

O lang, may the ladies sit,
   Wi' their fans into their hand,
Before they see Sir Patrick Spens
   Come sailing to the strand.

And lang, lang may the maidens sit
   Wi' their gowd kames[2] in their hair,
A-waiting for their ain dear loves!
   For them they'll see nae mair.

O forty miles off Aberdeen,
   'Tis fifty fathoms deep;
And there lies gude Sir Patrick Spens,
   Wi' the Scots lords at his feet.

[1] tossed afloat. [2] combs.

TRUE THOMAS

True Thomas lay on Huntlie bank;
  A ferlie[1] he spied wi' his e'e;
And there he saw a ladye bright
  Come riding down by the Eildon Tree.

Her skirt was o' the grass-green silk,
  Her mantle o' the velvet ſyne;
At ilka tett[2] o' her horse's mane,
  Hung fifty siller bells and nine.

True Thomas he pu'd aff his cap,
  And louted low down on his knee:
'Hail to thee, Mary, Queen of Heaven!
  For thy peer on earth could never be.'

'O no, O no, Thomas,' she said,
  'That name does not belang to me;
I'm but the Queen o' fair Elfland,
  That am hither come to visit thee.

'Harp and carp,[3] Thomas,' she said,
  'Harp and carp along wi' me;
And if ye dare to kiss my lips,
  Sure of your bodie I will be.'

'Betide me weal, betide me woe,
  That weird shall never daunten me.'
Syne he has kiss'd her rosy lips,
  All underneath the Eildon Tree.

[1] marvel. [2] tuft, lock. [3] play and sing.

'Now ye maun go wi' me,' she said,
  'True Thomas, ye maun go wi' me;
And ye maun serve me seven years,
  Thro' weal or woe as may chance to be.'

She's mounted on her milk-white steed,
  She's ta'en true Thomas up behind;
And aye, whene'er her bridle rang,
  The steed gaed swifter than the wind.

O they rade on, and farther on,
  The steed gaed swifter than the wind;
Until they reach'd a desert wide,
  And living land was left behind.

'Light down, light down now, true Thomas,
  And lean your head upon my knee;
Abide ye there a little space,
  And I will show you ferlies three.

'O see ye not yon narrow road,
  So thick beset wi' thorns and briers?
That is the Path of Righteousness,
  Though after it but few inquires.

'And see ye not yon braid, braid road,
  That lies across the lily leven?[1]
That is the Path of Wickedness,
  Though some call it the Road to Heaven

'And see ye not yon bonny road
  That winds about the fernie brae?

[1] lawn.

That is the Road to fair Elfland,
  Where thou and I this night maun gae.

'But, Thomas, ye sall haud your tongue,
  Whatever ye may hear or see;
For speak ye word in Elfyn-land,
  Ye'll ne'er win back to your ain countrie.'

O they rade on, and farther on,
  And they waded rivers abune the knee;
And they saw neither sun nor moon,
  But they heard the roaring of the sea.

It was mirk, mirk night, there was nae starlight,
  They waded thro' red blude to the knee;
For a' the blude that's shed on the earth
  Rins through the springs o' that countrie.

Syne they came to a garden green,
  And she pu'd an apple frae a tree:
'Take this for thy wages, true Thomas;
  It will give thee the tongue that can never lee.'

'My tongue is my ain,' true Thomas he said;
  'A gudely gift ye wad gie to me!
I neither dought[1] to buy or sell
  At fair or tryst where I might be.

'I dought neither speak to prince or peer,
  Nor ask of grace from fair ladye!'—
'Now haud thy peace, Thomas,' she said,
  'For as I say, so must it be.'

---

[1] could.

He has gotten a coat of the even cloth,
   And a pair o' shoon of the velvet green;
And till seven years were gane and past,
   True Thomas on earth was never seen.

CLERK SAUNDERS

Clerk Saunders and may Margaret
   Walk'd owre yon garden green;
And sad and heavy was the love
   That fell thir twa between.

'A bed, a bed,' Clerk Saunders said,
   'A bed for you and me!'
'Fye na, fye na,' said may Margaret,
   Till anes we married be;

'For in may come my seven bauld brothers,
   Wi' torches burning bright;
They'll say, we hae but ae sister,
   And behold, she's wi'a knight!'

'Then I'll take the sword frae my scabbard
   And slowly lift the pin;
And you may swear, and save your aith,
   Ye ne'er let Clerk Saunders in.

'Take you a napkin in your hand,
   And tie up baith your bonnie e'en,
And you may swear, and save your aith
   Ye saw me na since late yestreen.'

It was about the midnight hour,
　When they asleep were laid,
When in and came her seven brothers,
　Wi' torches burning red:

When in and came her seven brothers,
　Wi' torches burning bright:
They said, 'We hae but one sister,
　And behold her lying with a knight!'

Then out and spake the first o' them,
　'I bear the sword shall gar him die.'
And out and spake the second o' them,
　'His father has nae mair but he.'

And out and spake the third o' them,
　'I wot that they are lovers dear.'
And out and spake the fourth o' them,
　'They hae been in love this mony a year.'

Then out and spake the fifth o' them,
　'It were great sin true love to twain.'
And out and spake the sixth o' them,
　'It were shame to slay a sleeping man.'

Then up and gat the seventh o' them,
　And never a word spake he;
But he has striped[1] his bright brown brand
　Out through Clerk Saunders' fair bodye

Clerk Saunders he started, and Margaret she turn'd
　Into his arms as asleep she lay;

---

[1] thrust.

And sad and silent was the night
  That was atween thir twae.

And they lay still and sleepit sound
  Until the day began to daw';
And kindly she to him did say,
  'It is time, true love, you were awa'.'

But he lay still, and sleepit sound,
  Albeit the sun began to sheen;
She look'd atween her and the wa',
  And dull and drowsie were his e'en.

Then in and came her father dear;
  Said, 'Let a' your mourning be;
I'll carry the dead corse to the clay,
  And I'll come back and comfort thee.'

'Comfort weel your seven sons,
  For comforted I will never be:
I ween 'twas neither knave nor loon
  Was in the bower last night wi' me.'

The clinking bell gaed through the town,
  To carry the dead corse to the clay;
And Clerk Saunders stood at may Margaret's window,
  I wot, an hour before the day.

'Are ye sleeping, Margaret?' he says,
  'Or are ye waking presentlie?
Give me my faith and troth again,
  I wot, true love, I gied to thee.'

'Your faith and troth ye sall never get,
   Nor our true love sall never twin,[1]
Until ye come within my bower,
   And kiss me cheik and chin.'

'My mouth it is full cold, Margaret;
   It has the smell, now, of the ground;
And if I kiss thy comely mouth,
   Thy days of life will not be lang.

'O cocks are crowing a merry midnight;
   I wot the wild fowls are boding day;
Give me my faith and troth again,
   And let me fare me on my way.'

'Thy faith and troth thou sallna get,
   And our true love sall never twin,
Until ye tell what comes o' women,
   I wot, who die in strong traivelling?'

'Their beds are made in the heavens high,
   Down at the foot of our good Lord's knee,
Weel set about wi' gillyflowers;
   I wot, sweet company for to see.

'O cocks are crowing a merry midnight;
   I wot the wild fowls are boding day;
The psalms of heaven will soon be sung,
   And I, ere now, will be miss'd away.'

Then she has taken a crystal wand,
   And she has stroken her troth thereon;

[1] part in two.

She has given it him out at the shot-window,
   Wi' mony a sad sigh and heavy groan.

'I thank ye, Marg'ret; I thank ye, Marg'ret;
   And ay I thank ye heartilie;
Gin ever the dead come for the quick,
   Be sure, Marg'ret, I'll come for thee.'

It's hosen and shoon, and gown alone,
   She climb'd the wall, and follow'd him,
Until she came to the green forest,
   And there she lost the sight o' him.

'Is there ony room at your head, Saunders?
   Is there ony room at your feet?
Or ony room at your side, Saunders,
   Where fain, fain, I wad sleep?'

'There's nae room at my head, Marg'ret,
   There's nae room at my feet;
My bed it is fu' lowly now,
   Amang the hungry worms I sleep.

'Cauld mould is my covering now,
   But and my winding-sheet;
The dew it falls nae sooner down
   Than my resting-place is weet.

'But plait a wand o' bonny birk,
   And lay it on my breast;
And shed a tear upon my grave,
   And wish my saul gude rest.'

Then up and crew the red, red cock,
    And up and crew the gray:
"Tis time, 'tis time, my dear Marg'ret,
    That you were going away.

'And fair Marg'ret, and rare Marg'ret,
    And Marg'ret o' veritie,
Gin e'er ye love another man,
    Ne'er love him as ye did me.'

EDWARD

'Why does your brand sae drop wi' blude,
    Edward, Edward?
Why does your brand sae drop wi' blude,
    And why sae sad gang ye, O?
'O I hae kill'd my hawk sae gude,
    Mither, mither;
O I hae kill'd my hawk sae gude,
    And I had nae mair but he, O.'

'Your hawk's blude was never sae red,
    Edward, Edward;
Your hawk's blude was never sae red,
    My dear son, I tell thee, O.'
'O I hae kill'd my red-roan steed,
    Mither, mither;
O I hae kill'd my red-roan steed,
    That erst was sae fair and free, O.'

'Your steed was auld, and ye hae got mair,
    Edward, Edward;

Your steed was auld, and ye hae got mair;
    Some other dule ye dree,[1] O.'
'O I hae kill'd my father dear,
    Mither, mither;
O I hae kill'd my father dear,
    Alas, and wae is me, O!'

'And whatten penance will ye dree for that,
    Edward, Edward?
Whatten peance will ye dree for that?
    My dear son, now tell me, O.'
'I'll set my feet in yonder boat,
    Mither, mither;
I'll se my feet in yonder boat,
    And I'll fare over the sea, O.'

'And what will ye do wi' your tow'rs and your ha',
    Edward, Edward?
And what will ye do wi' your tow'rs and your ha',
    That were sae fair to see, O?'
'I'll let them stand till they doun fa',
    Mither, mither;
I'll let them stand till they doun fa',
    For here never mair maun I be, O.'

'And what will ye leave to your bairns and your wife,
    Edward, Edward?
And what will ye leave to your bairns and your wife,
    When ye gang owre the sea, O?'
'The warld's room: let them beg through life,
    Mither, mither;

[1] grief you suffer.

The warld's room: let them beg through life;
    For them never mair will I see, O.'

'And what will ye leave to your ain mither dear,
    Edward, Edward?
And what will ye leave to your ain mither dear,
    My dear son, now tell me, O?'
'The curse of hell frae me sall ye bear,
    Mither, mither,
The curse of hell frae me sall ye bear:
    Sic counsels ye gave to me, O!'

THE TWA CORBIES

As I was walking all alane
I heard twa corbies[1] making a mane:
The tane unto the tither did say,
Whar sall we gang and dine the day?'

'—In behint yon auld fail[2] dyke
I wot there lies a new-slain knight;
And naebody kens that he lies there
But his hawk, his hound, and his lady fair.

'His hound is to the hunting gane,
His hawk to fetch the wild-fowl hame,
His lady's ta'en anither mate,
So we may mak our dinner sweet.

'Ye'll sit on his white hause[3]-bane,
And I'll pike out his bonny blue e'en:

[1] ravens. [2] turf. [3] neck.

Wi' ae lock o' his gowden hair
We'll theek[1] our nest when it grows bare.

'Mony a one for him maks mane,
But nane sall ken whar he is gane:
O'er his white banes, when they are bare,
The wind sall blaw for evermair.'

WALY, WALY

O waly, waly, up the bank,
   And waly, waly, doun the brae,
And waly, waly, yon burn-side,
   Where I and my Love wont to gae!
I lean'd my back unto an aik,
   I thocht it was a trustie tree;
But first it bow'd and syne it brak—
   Sae my true love did lichtlie me.

O waly, waly, gin love be bonnie
   A little time while it is new;
But when 'tis auld it waxeth cauld,
   And fades awa' like morning dew.
O wherefore should I busk my heid,
   Or wherefore should I kame my hair?
For my true Love has me forsook,
   And says he'll never lo'e me mair.

Now Arthur's Seat sall be my bed,
   The sheets sall ne'er be 'filed by me;
Saint Anton's well sall be my drink;
   Since my true Love has forsaken me.

[1] thatch.

Marti'mas wind, when wilt thou blaw,
   And shake the green leaves aff the tree?
O gentle Death, when wilt thou come?
   For of my life I am wearie.

'Tis not the frost, that freezes fell,
   Nor blawing snaw's inclemencie,
'Tis not sic cauld that makes me cry,
   But my Love's heart grown cauld to me.
When we cam in by Glasgow toun,
   We were a comely sicht to see;
My Love was clad in the black velvèt,
   And I myself in cramasie.[1]

But had I wist, before I kist,
   That love had been sae ill to win,
I had lock'd my heart in a case o' gowd.
   And pinn'd it wi' a siller pin.
And O! if my young babe were born,
   And set upon the nurse's knee;
And I mysel were dead and gane,
   And the green grass growing over me!

SIR THOMAS WYATT
(1503—1542)

REMEMBRANCE

They flee from me, that sometime did me seek
   With naked foot, stalking in my chamber.
I have seen them gentle, tame, and meek,

[1] crimson.

That now are wild, and do not remember
That sometime they put themselves in danger
  To take bread at my hand; and now they range
  Busily seeking with a continual change.

Thanked be fortune it hath been otherwise
  Twenty times better; but once, in special,
In thin array, after a pleasant guise,
  When her loose gown from her shoulders did fall,
  And she me caught in her arms long and small,
    Therewith all sweetly did me kiss
    And softly said, 'Dear heart how like you this?'

It was no dream; I lay broad waking:
  But all is turned, thorough my gentleness,
Into a strange fashion of forsaking;
  And I have leave to go of her goodness,
  And she also to use newfangleness.
    But since that I so kindly am served,
    I would fain know what she hath deserved.

TO HIS LUTE

My lute, awake! perform the last
Labour that thou and I shall waste,
  And end that I have now begun;
For when this song is sung and past,
  My lute, be still, for I have done.

As to be heard where ear is none,
As lead to grave in marble stone,
  My song may pierce her heart as soon.

Should we then sigh, or sing, or moan?
No, no, my lute, for I have done.

The rocks do not so cruelly
Repulse the waves continually,
    As she my suit and affection;
So that I am past remedy,
    Whereby my lute and I have done.

Proud of the spoil that thou hast got
Of simple hearts thorough love's shot,
    By whom, unkind, thou hast them won,
Think not he hath his bow forgot,
    Although my lute and I have done.

Vengeance shall fall on thy disdain,
That makest but game on earnest pain;
    Think not alone under the sun
Unquit to cause thy lovers plain,
    Although my lute and I have done.

Perchance thee lie withered and old,
The winter nights that are so cold,
    Plaining in vain unto the moon;
Thy wishes then dare not be told.
    Care then who list, for I have done.

And then may chance thee to repent
The time that thou hast lost and spent
    To cause thy lovers sigh and swoon;
Then shalt thou know beauty but lent,
    And wish and want as I have done.

Now cease, my lute! this is the last
Labour that thou and I shall waste,
    And ended is that we begun;
Now is this song both sung and past.
    My lute, be still, for I have done.

STEADFASTNESS

Forget not yet the tried intent
Of such a truth as I have meant;
My great travail so gladly spent
        Forget not yet!

Forget not yet when first began
The weary life ye know, since whan
The suit, the service, none tell can;
        Forget not yet!

Forget not yet the great assays,
The cruel wrong, the scornful ways,
The painful patience in denays,
        Forget not yet!

Forget not yet, forget not this,
How long ago hath been, and is,
The mind that never meant amiss
        Forget not yet!

Forget not then thine own approved,
The which so long hath thee so loved,
Whose steadfast faith yet never moved;
        Forget not this!

FAREWELL

What should I say,
    Since faith is dead,
And truth away
    From you is fled?
    Should I be led
        With doubleness?
        Nay, nay mistress!

I promised you,
    And you promised me,
To be as true,
    As I would be.
    But since I see
        Your double heart,
        Farewell my part!

Though for to take
    It is not my mind,
But to forsake
    One so unkind,
    And as I find
        So will I trust,
        Farewell, unjust!

Can ye say nay,
    But that you said
That I alway
    Should be obeyed?
    And thus betrayed,
        Or that I wist,
        Farewell, unkissed!

HENRY HOWARD, EARL OF SURREY
(1516—1547)

THE SEAFARER

O happy dames, that may embrace
  The fruit of your delight,
Help to bewail the woeful case
  And eke the heavy plight
Of me, that wonted to rejoice
The fortune of my pleasant choice;
Good ladies, help to fill my mourning voice.

In ship, freight with rememberance
  Of thoughts and pleasures past,
He sails that hath in governance
  My life while it will last;
With scalding sighs, for lack of gale,
Furthering his hope, that is his sail,
Toward me, the sweet port of his avail.[1]

Alas! how oft in dream I see
  Those eyes that were my food;
Which sometime so delighted me,
  That yet they do me good;
Wherewith I wake with his return,
Whose absent flame did make me burn:
But when I find the lack, Lord, how I mourn!

When other lovers in arms across
  Rejoice their chief delight,

[1] disembarking.

Drowned in tears, to mourn my loss
   I stand the bitter night
In my window, where I may see
Before the winds how the clouds flee.
Lo! what a mariner love hath made me!

And in green waves when the salt flood
   Doth rise by rage of wind,
A thousand fancies in that mood
   Assail my restless mind.
Alas! now drencheth[1] my sweet foe,
That with the spoil of my heart did go,
And left me; but, alas! why did he so?

And when the seas wax calm again
   To chase fro me annoy,
My doubtful hope doth cause me plain;[2]
   So dread cuts off my joy.
Thus is my wealth mingled with woe,
And of each thought a doubt doth grow;
' Now he comes! Will he come? Alas, no, no!'

THOMAS SACKVILLE, EARL OF DORSET
(1536—1608)

THE APPROACH OF WINTER

... The wrathful winter, 'proaching on apace,
   With blustering blasts had all ybared the treen,
And old Saturnus, with his frosty face,

[1] drowns. [2] to lament.

With chilling cold had pierced the tender green;
The mantles rent, wherein enwrapped been
    The gladsome groves that now lay overthrown,
    The tapets[1] torn, and every bloom down blown.

The soil, that erst so seemly was to seen,
    Was all despoiled of her beauty's hue;
And soote[2] fresh flowers, wherewith the summers' queen
    Had clad the earth, now Boreas' blasts down blew;
    And small fowls flocking in their song did rue
      The winter's wrath, wherewith each thing defaced
      On woeful wise bewailed the summer past.

Hawthorn had lost his motley livery,
    The naked twigs were shivering all for cold,
And dropping down the tears abundantly;
    Each thing, methought, with weeping eye me told
    The cruel season, bidding me withhold
      Myself within; for I was gotten out
      Into the fields, whereas I walked about.

When lo! the night with misty mantles spread
    'Gan dark the day and dim the azure skies;
And Venus in her message Hermes sped
    To bloody Mars, to will him not to rise,
    While she herself approached in speedy wise;
      And Virgo, hiding her disdainful breast,
      With Thetis now had laid her down to rest.

Whiles Scorpio, dreading Sagittarius' dart,
    Whose bow prest bent in fight the string had slipped,

---

[1] tapestries. [2] sweet.

Down slid into the ocean flood apart;
  The Bear, that in the Irish seas had dipped
  His grisly feet, with speed from thence he whipped;
    For Thetis, hasting from the Virgin's bed,
    Pursued the Bear, that ere she came was fled.

And Phaethon now, near reaching to his race
  With glistering beams, gold streaming where they bent,
Was prest[1] to enter in his resting place.
  Erythius, that in the cart first went,
  Had even now attained his journey's stent;[2]
    And, fast declining, hid away his head,
    While Titan couched him in his purple bed.

And pale Cynthia, with her borrowed light,
  Beginning to supply her brother's place,
Was past the noonstead six degrees in sight,
  When sparkling stars amid the heaven's face
  With twinkling light shone on the earth apace,
    That, while they brought about the nightes chare,[3]
    The dark had dimmed the day ere I was ware.

And sorrowing I to see the summer flowers,
  The lively green, the lusty leas, forlorn,
The sturdy trees so shattered with the showers,
  The fields so fade that flourished so beforn,
  It taught me well all earthly things be born
    To die the death, for nought long time may last;
    The summer's beauty yields to winter's blast.

Then looking upward to the heaven's leams,[4]
  With nightes stars thick powdered everywhere,

<hr />

[1] ready. [2] close. [3] chariot. [4] lights.

Which erst so glistened with the golden streams
 That cheerful Phoebus spread down from his sphere,
Beholding dark oppressing day so near;
  The sudden sight reduced to my mind
  The sundry changes that in earth we find:

That musing on this worldly wealth in thought,
 Which comes and goes more faster than we see
The flickering flame that with the fire is wrought,
 My busy mind presented unto me
Such fall of peers as in this realm had be,
  That oft I wished some would their woes descrive,
  To warn the rest whom fortune left alive . . .

       The Mirror for Magistrates.

EDMUND SPENSER
(1552?—1599)

ELISA

Ye dainty nymphs, that in this blessed brook
  Do bathe your breast,
Forsake your watery bowers, and hither look,
  At my request;
And eke you virgins, that on Parnasse dwell,
Whence floweth Helicon the learned well,
  Help me to blaze
  Her worthy praise,
Which in her sex doth all excel.

Of fair Elisa be your silver song,
  That blessed wight;

The flower of virgins, may she flourish long,
　　In princely plight.
For she is Syrinx' daughter without spot,
Which Pan the shepherds' God of her begot:
　　　So sprang her grace
　　　Of heavenly race,
No mortal blemish may her blot.

See, where she sits upon the grassy green,
　　(O seemly sight)
Yclad in scarlet like a maiden Queen,
　　And ermines white,
Upon her head a cremosin coronet,
With damask roses and daffodillies set:
　　　Bay-leaves between,
　　　And primroses green
Embellish the sweet violet.

Tell me, have ye seen her angelic face,
　　Like Phoebe fair?
Her heavenly haviour, her princely grace,
　　Can you well compare?
The red rose medled[1] with the white yfere[2]
In either cheek depeincten lively cheer.
　　　Her modest eye,
　　　Her majesty,
Where have you seen the like, but there?

I saw Phoebus thrust out his golden head,
　　Upon her to gaze:
But when he saw, how broad her beams did spread,
　　It did him amaze.

[1] mingled. [2] together.

He blushed to see another sun below,
Ne durst again his fiery face outshow:
    Let him, if he dare,
    His brightness compare
With hers, to have the overthrow.

Shew thyself, Cynthia, with thy silver rays,
    And be not abashed;
When she the beams of her beauty displays,
    O how art thou dashed?
But I will not match her with Latona's seed;
Such folly great sorrow to Niobe did breed.
    Now she is a stone,
    And makes daily moan,
Warning all other to take heed.

Pan may be proud, that ever he begot
    Such a bellibone,[1]
And Syrinx rejoice, that ever was her lot
    To bear such an one.
Soons as my younglings cryen for the dam,
To her will I offer a milkwhite lamb:
    She is my goddess plain,
    And I her shepherds' swain,
Albeit forswonk[2] and forswat[3] I am.

I see Calliope speed her to the place,
    Where my goddess shines;
And after her the other Muses trace,
    With their violins.

[1] goodly one. [2] tired. [3] sweaty.

Been they not bay branches, which they do bear,
All for Elisa in her hand to wear?
    So sweetly they play,
    And sing all the way,
That it a heaven is to hear.

Lo, how finely the Graces can it foot
    To the instrument;
They dancen deftly, and singen soote,[1]
    In their merriment.
Wants not a fourth Grace, to make the dance even?
Let that room to my lady be yeven:[2]
    She shall be a Grace,
    To fill the fourth place,
And reign with the rest in heaven.

And whither runs this bevy of ladies bright,
    Ranged in a row?
They been all ladies of the lake behight,
    That unto her go.
Chloris, that is the chiefest nymph of all,
Of olive branches bears a coronal:
    Olives been for peace,
    When wars do surcease;
Such for a princess been principal.

Ye shepherds' daughters, that dwell on the green,
    Hie you there apace;
Let none come there, but that virgins been,
    To adorn her grace.
And when you come, whereas she is in place,

[1] sweet. [2] given.

See, that your rudeness do not you disgrace:
    Bind your fillets fast,
    And gird in your waist,
For more fineness, with a tawdry lace.

Bring hither the pink and purple columbine,
    With gillyflowers;
Bring coronations, and sops in wine,
    Worn of paramours.
Strew me the ground with daffadowndillies,
And cowslips, and kingcups, and loved lilies:
    The pretty paunce,
    And the chevisaunce,
Shall match with the fair flower delice.

Now rise up Elisa, decked as thou art,
    In royal array;
And now ye dainty damsels may depart
    Each one her way,
I fear, I have troubled your troops too long;
Let Dame Elisa thank you for her song.
    And if you come hither,
    When damsons I gather,
I will part them all you among.

The Shepheardes Calender, April.

STANZAS FROM 'EPITHALAMION'

... Now cease, ye damsels, your delights forepast;
Enough is it, that all the day was yours.
Now day is done, and night is nighing fast;
Now bring the bride into the bridal bowers.

Now night is come, now soon her disarray,
And in her bed her lay;
Lay her in lilies and in violets,
And silken curtains over her display,
And odoured sheets, and Arras coverlets.
Behold how goodly my fair love does lie
In proud humility;
Like unto Maia, when as Jove her took,
In Tempe, lying on the flowery grass,
'Twixt sleep and wake, after she weary was,
With bathing in the Acidalian brook.
Now it is night, ye damsels may be gone,
And leave my love alone,
And leave likewise your former lay to sing;
The woods no more shall answer, nor your echo ring.

Now welcome, night, thou night so long expected,
That long day's labour dost at last defray,
And all my cares, which cruel love collected,
Hast summed in one, and cancelled for aye:
Spread thy broad wing over my love and me,
That no man may us see,
And in thy sable mantle us enwrap,
From fear of peril and foul horror free.
Let no false treason seek us to entrap,
Nor any dread disquiet once annoy
The safety of our joy:
But let the night be calm and quietsome,
Without tempestuous storms or sad affray;
Like as when Jove with fair Alcmena lay,
When he begot the great Tirynthian groom;

Or like as when he with thyself did lie,
And begot majesty.
And let the maids and young men cease to sing;
Ne let the woods them answer, nor their echo ring.

Let no lamenting cries, nor doleful tears,
Be heard all night within nor yet without;
Ne let false whispers, breeding hidden fears,
Break gentle sleep with misconceived doubt.
Let no deluding dreams nor dreadful sights
Make sudden sad affrights;
Ne let housefires, nor lightning's helpless harms,
Ne let the Puck, nor other evil sprights,
Ne let mischievous witches with their charms,
Ne let hobgoblins, names whose sense we see not,
Fray us with things that be not.
Let not the screech owl, nor the stork be heard;
Nor the night raven that still deadly yells,
Nor damned ghosts called up with mighty spells,
Nor grisly vultures make us once affeared:
Ne let th' unpleasant quire of frogs still croaking
Make us to wish their choking.
Let none of these their dreary accents sing;
Ne let the woods them answer, nor their echo ring ...

EASTER

Most glorious Lord of Life! that, on this day,
Didst make Thy triumph over death and sin;
And, having harrow'd hell, didst bring away
Captivity thence captive, us to win:

This joyous day, dear Lord, with joy begin;
And grant that we, for whom thou diddest die,
Being with Thy dear blood clear washt from sin,
May live for ever in felicity!
And that Thy love we weighing worthily,
May likewise love Thee for the same again;
And for Thy sake, that all lyke dear didst buy,
With love may one another entertain!
    So let us love, dear Love, like as we ought,
    —Love is the lesson which the Lord us taught.

THE BOWER OF BLISS

... Eftsoons they heard a most melodious sound,
    Of all that mote[1] delight a dainty ear,
Such as at once might not on living ground,
    Save in this paradise, be heard elsewhere:
    Right hard it was, for wight, which did it hear,
To read, what manner music that mote be;
    For all that pleasing is to living ear,
Was there consorted in one harmony,
Birds, voices, instruments, winds, waters, all agree.

The joyous birds, shrouded in cheerful shade
    Their notes unto the voice attempered sweet;
Th' angelical soft trembling voices made
    To th' instruments divine respondence meet;
    The silver sounding instruments did meet
With the bass murmur of the waters' fall;
    The waters' fall with difference discreet,
Now soft, now loud, unto the wind did call;
The gentle warbling wind low answered to all.

[1] might.

There, whence that music seemed heard to be,
   Was the fair witch herself now solacing,
With a new lover, whom through sorcery
   And witchcraft she from far did thither bring:
   There she had him now laid a-slumbering,
In secret shade, after long wanton joys;
   Whilst round about them pleasantly did sing
Many fair ladies, and lascivious boys,
That ever mixed their song with light licentious toys.

And all that while, right over him she hung,
   With her false eyes fast fixed in his sight,
As seeking medicine, whence she was stung,
   Or greedily depasturing delight:
   And oft inclining down with kisses light,
For fear of waking him, his lips bedewed,
   And through his humid eyes did suck his spright,
Quite molten into lust and pleasure lewd;
Wherewith she sighed soft, as if his case she rued.

The whiles some one did chant this lovely lay:
   'Ah see, whoso fair thing dost fain to see,
In springing flower the image of thy day;
   Ah see the virgin rose, how sweetly she
   Doth first peep forth with bashful modesty,
That fairer seems, the less ye see her may;
   Lo see soon after, how more bold and free
Her bared bosom she doth broad display;
Lo see soon after, how she fades, and falls away.

'So passeth, in the passing of a day,
   Of mortal life the leaf, the bud, the flower,

Ne more doth flourish after first decay,
   That erst was sought to deck both bed and bower,
   Of many a lady, and many a paramour:
Gather therefore the rose, whilst yet is prime,
   For soon comes age, that will her pride deflower;
Gather the rose of love, whilst yet is time,
Whilst loving thou mayst loved be with equal crime.'

He ceased, and then 'gan all the quire of birds
   Their diverse notes t' attune unto his lay,
As in approvance of his pleasing words.
   The constant pair heard all, that he did say,
   Yet swerved not, but kept their forward way,
Through many covert groves, and thickets close,
   In which they creeping did at last display
That wanton lady, with her lover loose,
Whose sleepy head she in her lap did soft dispose.

Upon a bed of roses she was laid,
   As faint through heat, or dight to pleasant sin,
And was arrayed, or rather disarrayed,
   All in a veil of silk and silver thin,
   That hid no whit her alabaster skin,
But rather shewed more white, if more might be:
   More subtle web Arachne cannot spin,
Nor the fine nets, which oft we woven see
Of scorched dew, do not in th' air more lightly flee.

Her snowy breast was bare to ready spoil
   Of hungry eyes, which n'ote[1] therewith be filled

[1] could not.

And yet through languor of her late sweet toil,
  Few drops, more clear then nectar, forth distilled,
  That like pure orient pearls adown it trilled,
And her fair eyes, sweet smiling in delight,
  Moistened their fiery beams, with which she thrilled
Frail hearts, yet quenched not; like starry light
Which, sparkling on the silent waves, does seem
                        more bright.

The young man sleeping by her seemed to be
  Some goodly swain of honourable place,
That certès it great pity was to see
  Him his nobility so foul deface:
  A sweet regard, and amiable grace,
Mixed with manly sternness did appear,
  Yet sleeping, in his well proportioned face;
And on his tender lips the downy hair
Did now but freshly spring, and silken blossoms bear.

His warlike arms, the idle instruments
  Of sleeping praise, were hung upon a tree,
And his brave shield, full of old monuments,
  Was foully razed, that none the signs might see;
  Ne for them, ne for honour cared he,
Ne ought, that did to his advancement tend,
  But in lewd loves, and wasteful luxury,
His days, his goods, his body he did spend:
O horrible enchantment, that him so did blend!...

                    The Faerie Queene, II. xii.

MUTABILITY

... When I bethink me on that speech whilere
Of Mutability, and well it weigh,
Meseems that though she all unworthy were
Of the heav'n's rule, yet very sooth to say
In all things else she bears the greatest sway:
Which makes me loathe this state of life so tickle,
And love of things so vain to cast away;
Whose flowering pride, so fading and so fickle,
Short Time shall soon cut down with his consuming sickle.

Then gin I think on that which Nature said;
Of that same time when no more Change shall be,
But steadfast rest of all things firmly stayed
Upon the pillars of Eternity,
That is contrare to Mutability;
For all that moveth doth in Change delight:
But thenceforth all shall rest eternally
With Him that is the God of Sabbaoth hight:
O that great Sabbaoth God, grant me that Sabbaoth's sight! ..

The Faerie Queene, VII. viii

SIR WALTER RALEIGH
(1552?—1599)

THE LIE

Go, soul, the body's guest,
    Upon a thankless arrant;
Fear not to touch the best;

The truth shall be thy warrant.
　Go, since I needs must die,
　And give the world the lie.

Say to the court, it glows
　And shines like rotten wood;
Say to the church, it shows
　What's good, and doth no good:
　　If church and court reply,
　　Then give them both the lie.

Tell potentates, they live
　Acting by others' action,
Not loved unless they give,
　Not strong but by their faction:
　　If potentates reply,
　　Give potentates the lie.

Tell men of high condition
　That manage the estate,
Their purpose is ambition,
　Their practice only hate:
　　And if they once reply,
　　Then give them all the lie.

Tell them that brave it most,
　They beg for more by spending,
Who, in their greatest cost,
　Seek nothing but commending:
　　And if they make reply,
　　Then give them all the lie.

Tell zeal it wants devotion;
　Tell love it is but lust;
Tell time it is but motion;
　Tell flesh it is but dust:
　　And wish them not reply,
　　For thou must give the lie.

Tell age it daily wasteth;
　Tell honour how it alters;
Tell beauty how she blasteth;
　Tell favour how it falters:
　　And as they shall reply,
　　Give every one the lie.

Tell wit how much it wrangles
　In tickle points of niceness;
Tell wisdom she entangles
　Herself in over-wiseness:
　　And when they do reply,
　　Straight give them both the lie.

Tell physic of her boldness;
　Tell skill it is prevention;
Tell charity of coldness;
　Tell law it is contention:
　　And as they do reply,
　　So give them still the lie.

Tell fortune of her blindness;
　Tell nature of decay;
Tell friendship of unkindness;

Tell justice of delay:
   And if they will reply,
   Then give them all the lie.

Tell arts they have no soundness
   But vary by esteeming;
Tell schools they want profoundness,
   And stand too much on seeming:
     If arts and schools reply,
     Give arts and schools the lie.

Tell faith it's fled the city;
   Tell how the country erreth;
Tell, manhood shakes off pity;
   Tell, virtue least preferreth:
     And if they do reply,
     Spare not to give the lie.

So when thou hast, as I
   Commanded thee, done blabbing,
Although to give the lie
   Deserves no less than stabbing,
     Stab at thee he that will,
     No stab the soul can kill.

THE PASSIONATE MAN'S PILGRIMAGE

Give me my scallop-shell of quiet,
My staff of faith to walk upon,
My scrip of joy, immortal diet,
My bottle of salvation,

My gown of glory, hope's true gage,
And thus I'll take my pilgrimage.

Blood must be my body's balmer,
No other balm will there be given,
Whilst my soul like a white palmer
Travels to the land of heaven,
Over the silver mountains,
Where spring the nectar fountains;
And there I'll kiss
The bowl of bliss,
And drink my everlasting fill
On every milken hill.
My soul will be a-dry before,
But after it shall thirst no more.

And by the happy blissful way
More peaceful pilgrims I shall see,
That have shook off their gowns of clay
And go apparelled fresh like me.
I'll take them first
To slake their thirst,
And then to taste of nectar suckets,
At the clear wells
Where sweetness dwells,
Drawn up by saints in crystal buckets.

And when our bottles and all we
Are filled with immortality,
Then the holy paths we'll travel,
Strewed with rubies thick as gravel,

Ceilings of diamonds, sapphire floors,
High walls of coral and pearl bowers.

From thence to heaven's bribeless hall
Where no corrupted lawyers brawl,
No conscience molten into gold,
Nor forged accusers bought and sold,
No cause deferred, nor vain-spent journey,
For there Christ is the King's Attorney,
Who pleads for all, without degrees,
And he hath angels, but no fees.

When the grand twelve million jury
Of our sins with dreadful fury
'Gainst our souls black verdicts give,
Christ pleads his death, and then we live.
Be thou my speaker, taintless pleader,
Unblotted lawyer, true proceeder;
Thou won'st salvation even for alms,
Not with a bribed lawyer's palms.

And this is my eternal plea
To him that made heaven, earth, and sea:
Seeing my flesh must die so soon,
And want a head to dine next noon,
Just at the stroke when my veins start and spread,
Set on my soul an everlasting head.
Then am I ready, like a palmer fit,
To tread those blest paths which before I writ.

SIR PHILIP SIDNEY
(1554—1586)

SONNETS

(i)

With how sad steps, O Moon, thou climb'st the skies!
  How silently, and with how wan a face!
  What! may it be that even in heavenly place
That busy archer his sharp arrows tries?
Sure, if that long-with-love-acquainted eyes
  Can judge of love, thou feel'st a lover's case;
  I read it in thy looks; thy languished grace
To me, that feel the like, thy state descries.
Then, even of fellowship, O Moon, tell me,
  Is constant love deemed there but want of wit?
Are beauties there as proud as here they be?
  Do they above love to be loved, and yet
    Those lovers scorn whom that love doth possess?
    Do they call virtue there ungratefulness?

(ii)

Come, sleep, O sleep, the certain knot of peace,
  The baiting place of wit, the balm of woe,
The poor man's wealth, the prisoner's release,
  Th' indifferent judge between the high and low;
With shield of proof shield me from out the prease[1]
  Of those fierce darts despair at me doth throw;
O make me in those civil wars to cease;
  I will good tribute pay, if thou do so.

[1] crowd.

Take thou of me smooth pillows, sweetest bed,
A chamber deaf to noise and blind to light,
A rosy garland and a weary head;
And if these things, as being thine by right,
Move not thy heavy grace, thou shalt in me,
Livelier than elsewhere, Stella's image see.

(iii)

Leave me, O Love, which reachest but to dust;
And thou, my mind, aspire to higher things;
Grow rich in that which never taketh rust;
Whatever fades but fading pleasure brings.
Draw in thy beams, and humble all thy might
To that sweet yoke where lasting freedoms be;
Which breaks the clouds and opens forth the light,
That doth both shine and give us sight to see.
O take fast hold; let that light be thy guide
In this small course which birth draws out to death,
And think how evil becometh him to slide,
Who seeketh heaven, and comes of heavenly breath.
Then farewell, world; thy uttermost I see;
Eternal Love, maintain thy life in me.

STREPHON AND KLAIUS

Strephon

Ye Goat-herd Gods, that love the grassy mountains,
Ye Nymphs that haunt the springs in pleasant valleys,
Ye Satyrs joy'd with free and quiet forests,
Vouchsafe your silent ears to plaining music,
Which to my woes give still an early morning,
And draws the dolour on till weary evening.

Klaius

O Mercury, foregoer to the evening,
O heavenly huntress of the savage mountains,
O lovely star, entitled of the morning,
While that my voice doth fill the woeful valleys,
Vouchsafe your silent ears to plaining music,
Which oft hath Echo tir'd in secret forests.

Strephon

I that was once free burgess of the forests,
Where shade from sun and sports I sought at evening,
I that was once esteem'd for pleasant music,
Am banish'd now among the monstrous mountains
Of huge despair, and foul affliction's valleys,
Am grown a screech-owl to myself each morning.

Klaius

I that was once delighted every morning,
Hunting the wild inhabitants of forests;
I that was once the music of these valleys,
So darken'd am, that all my day is evening,
Heart broken so, that molehills seem high mountains,
And fill the vales with cries instead of music.

Strephon

Long since, alas, my deadly swannish music
Hath made itself a crier of the morning,
And hath with wailing strength clim'd highest mountains;
Long since my thoughts more desert be than forests;
Long since I see my joys come to their evening,
And state thrown down to overtrodden valleys.

Klaius

Long since the happy dwellers of these valleys
Have pray'd me leave my strange exclaiming music,
Which troubles their day's work and joys of evening;
Long since I hate the night, more hate the morning;
Long since my thoughts chase me like beasts in forests,
And make me wish myself laid under mountains.

Strephon

Meseems I see the high and stately mountains
Transform themselves to low dejected valleys;
Meseems I hear in these ill-changed forests
The nightingales do learn of owls their music;
Meseems I feel the comfort of the morning
Turn'd to the mortal serene of an evening.

Klaius

Meseems I see a filthy cloudy evening,
As soon as sun begins to climb the mountains;
Meseems I feel a noisome scent, the morning
When I do smell the flowers of these valleys;
Meseems I hear, when I do hear sweet music,
The dreadful cries of murder'd men in forests.

Strephon

I wish to fire the trees of all those forests,
I give the sun a last farewell each evening,
I curse the fiddling finders-out of music;
With envy I do hate the lofty mountains,
And with despite despise the humble valleys;
I do detest night, evening, day and morning.

Klaius

Curse to myself my prayer is, the morning;
My fire is more than can be made with forests;
My state more base than are the basest valleys;
I wish no evenings more to see, each evening;
Shamed I hate myself in sight of mountains,
And stop my ears, lest I grow mad with music.

Strephon

For she whose parts maintained a perfect music,
Whose beauty shin'd more than the blushing morning,
Who much did pass in state the stately mountains,
In straightness passed the cedars of the forest,
Hath cast me wretch into eternal evening,
By taking her two suns from these dark valleys.

Klaius

For she, to whom compar'd, the Alps are valleys,
She, whose least word brings from the spheres their music
At whose approach the sun rose in the evening,
Who where she went bare in her forehead morning,
Is gone, is gone, from these our spoiled forests,
Turning to deserts our best pastur'd mountains.

Strephon

These mountains witness shall, so shall these valleys,
These forests eke, made wretched by our music.

Klaius

Our morning hymn is this, and song at evening.

Certain Sonnets: Arcadia

A LITANY

Ring out your bells, let mourning shows be spread;
For Love is dead.
  All Love is dead, infected
With plague of deep disdain;
    Worth, as nought worth, rejected,
And Faith fair scorn doth gain.
  From so ungrateful fancy,
  From such a female franzy,
    From them that use men thus,
    Good Lord, deliver us!

Weep, neighbours, weep! do you not hear it said
That Love is dead?
  His death bed, peacock's folly;
His winding-sheet is shame;
  His will, false-seeming holy;
His sole executor, blame.
  From so ungrateful fancy,
  From such a female franzy,
    From them that use men thus,
    Good Lord, deliver us!

Let dirge be sung and trentals[1] rightly read,
For Love is dead.
  Sir Wrong his tomb ordaineth
My mistress Marble-heart,
  Which epitaph containeth,
'Her eyes were once his dart.'

[1] masses for the dead.

From so ungrateful fancy,
From such a female franzy,
 From them that use men thus,
 Good Lord, deliver us!

Alas! I lie, rage hath this error bred;
Love is not dead.
 Love is not dead, but sleepeth
In her unmatched mind,
 Where she his counsel keepeth,
Till due desert she find.
 Therefore from so vile fancy,
 To call such wit a franzy,
  Who Love can temper thus,
  Good Lord, deliver us!

JOHN LYLY

(1554?—1606)

PAN'S SONG

Pan's Syrinx was a girl indeed,
Though now she's turned into a reed;
From that dear reed Pan's pipe does come,
A pipe that strikes Apollo dumb;
Nor flute, nor lute, nor gittern can
So chant it, as the pipe of Pan;
Cross-gartered swains, and dairy girls,
With faces smug, and round as pearls,
When Pan's shrill pipe begins to play,
With dancing wear out night and day;

The bagpipe's drone his hum lays by,
When Pan sounds up his minstrelsy;
His minstrelsy! O base! This quill,
Which at my mouth with wind I fill,
Puts me in mind, though her I miss,
That still my Syrinx' lips I kiss.

Midas.

FULKE GREVILLE, LORD BROOKE
(1554—1628)

MYRA

I, with whose colours Myra dressed her head,
  I, that ware posies of her own hand making,
I, that mine own name in the chimneys read
  By Myra finely wrought ere I was waking;
    Must I look on, in hope time coming may
    With change bring back my turn again to play?

I, that on Sunday at the church-stile found
  A garland sweet, with true-love knots in flowers,
Which I to wear about mine arm was bound,
  That each of us might know that all was ours;
    Must I now lead an idle life in wishes,
    And follow Cupid for his loaves and fishes?

I, that did wear the ring her mother left,
  I, for whose love she gloried to be blamed,
I, with whose eyes her eyes committed theft,
  I, who did make her blush when I was named;
    Must I lose ring, flowers, blush, theft, and go naked,
    Watching with sighs, till dead love be awaked?

I, that, when drowsy Argus fell asleep,
  Like jealousy o'erwatched with desire,
Was ever warned modesty to keep,
    While her breath, speaking, kindled Nature's fire;
      Must I look on a-cold, while others warm them?
      Do Vulcan's brothers in such fine nets arm them?

Was it for this that I might Myra see
  Washing the water with her beauties white?
Yet would she never write her love to me;
    Thinks wit of change, while thoughts are in delight?
      Mad girls must safely love, as they may leave;
      No man can print a kiss; lines may deceive.

Caelica.

CHANGE

The world, that all contains, is ever moving;
  The stars within their spheres for ever turned;
Nature, the queen of change, to change is loving,
  And form to matter new is still adjourned.
Fortune, our fancy-god, to vary liketh;
  Place is not bound to things within it placed;
The present time upon time passed striketh;
  With Phoebus' wandering course the earth is graced.
The air still moves, and by its moving cleareth;
  The fire up ascends, and planets feedeth;
The water passeth on, and all lets weareth;
  The earth stands still, yet change of changes breedeth.
Her plants, which summer ripes, in winter fade;
  Each creature in unconstant mother lieth;

Man made of earth, and for whom earth is made,
   Still dying lives, and living ever dieth.
   Only, like fate, sweet Myra never varies,
   Yet in her eyes the doom of all change carries.

Caelica.

CHORUS SACERDOTUM

  ... O wearisome condition of humanity!
Born under one law, to another bound:
Vainly begot, and yet forbidden vanity;
Created sick, commanded to be sound:
What meaneth nature by these diverse laws?
Passion and reason self-division cause:
Is it the mark or majesty of power
To make offences that it may forgive?
Nature herself doth her own self deflower,
To hate those errors she herself doth give.
For how should man think that he may not do
If nature did not fail, and punish too?
Tyrant to others, to herself unjust,
Only commands things difficult and hard;
Forbids us all things which it knows is lust,
Makes easy pains, unpossible reward.
If nature did not take delight in blood,
She would have made more easy ways to good.
We that are bound by vows and by promotion,
With pomp of holy sacrifice and rites,
To teach belief in good and still devotion,
To preach of heaven's wonders and delights,
Yet when each one of us in his own heart looks
He finds the God there, far unlike his books ...

Mustapha.

GEORGE PEELE
(1557?—1596)

A FAREWELL TO ARMS: TO QUEEN ELIZABETH

His golden locks time hath to silver turned;
　　O time too swift, O swiftness never ceasing!
His youth 'gainst time and age hath ever spurned,
　　But spurned in vain; youth waneth by increasing:
Beauty, strength, youth, are flowers but fading seen;
Duty, faith, love, are roots, and ever green.

His helmet now shall make a hive for bees;
　　And, lovers' sonnets turned to holy psalms,
A man-at-arms must now serve on his knees,
　　And feed on prayers, which are age's alms:
But though from court to cottage he depart,
His saint is sure of his unspotted heart.

And when he saddest sits in homely cell,
　　He'll teach his swains this carol for a song:
'Blest be the hearts that wish my sovereign well,
　　Curst be the souls that think her any wrong.'
Goddess, allow this aged man his right,
To be your beadsman now, that was your knight.

BETHSABE'S SONG

Hot sun, cool fire, tempered with sweet air,
Black shade, fair nurse, shadow my white hair:
Shine, sun; burn, fire; breathe, air, and ease me;

Black shade, fair nurse, shroud me and please me:
Shadow, my sweet nurse, keep me from burning,
Make not my glad cause cause of mourning.
> Let not my beauty's fire
> Inflame unstaid desire,
> Nor pierce any bright eye
> That wandereth lightly.

David and Bethsabe.

ROBERT GREENE
(1558—1592)

THE SHEPHERD'S WIFE'S SONG

Ah! what is love? It is a pretty thing,
As sweet unto a shepherd as a king,
> And sweeter too;
For kings have cares that wait upon a crown,
And cares can make the sweetest love to frown.
> Ah then, ah then,
If country loves such sweet desires gain,
What lady would not love a shepherd swain?

His flocks are folded, he comes home at night,
As merry as a king in his delight,
> And merrier too;
For kings bethink them what the state require,
Where shepherds careless carol by the fire.
> Ah then, ah then,
If country loves such sweet desires gain,
What lady would not love a shepherd swain?

He kisseth first, then sits as blithe to eat
His cream and curds, as doth the king his meat,
　　　And blither too;
For kings have often fears when they do sup,
Where shepherds dread no poison in their cup.
　　　Ah then, ah then,
If country loves such sweet desires gain,
What lady would not love a shepherd swain?

To bed he goes, as wanton then I ween,
As is a king in dalliance with a queen,
　　　More wanton too;
For kings have many griefs affects to move,
Where shepherds have no greater grief than love.
　　　Ah then, ah then,
If country loves such sweet desires gain,
What lady would not love a shepherd swain?

Upon his couch of straw he sleeps as sound,
As doth the king upon his bed of down,
　　　More sounder too;
For cares cause kings full oft their sleep to spill.
Where weary shepherds lie and snort their fill.
　　　Ah then, ah then,
If country loves such sweet desires gain,
What lady would not love a shepherd swain?

Thus with his wife he spends the year as blithe,
As doth the king at every tide or sithe,
　　　And blither too;

For kings have war and broils to take in hand,
Where shepherds laugh, and love upon the land.
    Ah then, ah then,
If country loves such sweet desires gain,
What lady would not love a shepherd swain?

UNKNOWN

GRIEF'S SHIP

These lines I send by waves of woe,
    And bale becomes my boat;
Which sighs of sorrows still shall keep
    On floods of fear afloat.

My sighs shall serve me still for wind,
    My lading is my smart;
And true report my pilot is,
    My haven is thy heart.

My keel is fram'd of crabbed care,
    My ribs are all of ruth;
My planks are nothing else but plaints,
    With treenails join'd with truth.

My main-mast made of nought but moan,
    My tackling trickling tears,
And topyard like a troubled mind
    A flag of folly bears.

My cable is a constant heart,
    My anchor luckless love,

Which reason's capstans from the ground
　　Of grief cannot remove.

My decks are all of deep disgrace,
　　My compass discontent;
And peril is my northern pole,
　　And death my orient.

My sailors are my sorrowing thoughts,
　　The boatswain bitter sense;
The master, misery; his mate
　　Is doleful diligence.

The Phoenix Nest.

GEORGE CHAPMAN
(1559—1634)

VIRTUE THE SAFEST GUIDE

... Fortune, not reason, rules the state of things;
Reward goes backwards, honour on his head;
Who is not poor, is monstrous; only need
Gives form and worth to every human seed.
As cedars beaten with continual storms,
So great men flourish; and do imitate
Unskilful statuaries, who suppose
(In forming a Colossus) if they make him
Straddle enough, strut, and look big and gape,
Their work is goodly; so men merely great
(In their affected gravity of voice,
Sourness of countenance, manners, cruelty,
Authority, wealth, and all the spawn of fortune)

Think they bear all the kingdom's worth before them;
Yet differ not from those Colossic statues,
Which with heroic forms without o'erspread,
Within are naught but mortar, flint, and lead.
Man is a torch borne in the wind; a dream
But of a shadow, summ'd with all his substance;
And as great seamen using all their wealth
And skills in Neptune's deep invisible paths,
In tall ships richly built and ribb'd with brass,
To put a girdle round about the world,
When they have done it (coming near their haven)
Are fain to give a warning piece, and call
A poor strayed fisherman, that never past
His country's sight, to waft and guide them in:
So when we wander furthest through the waves
Of glassy glory and the gulfs of state,
Topp'd with all titles, spreading all our reaches,
As if each private arm would sphere the earth,
We must to virtue for her guide resort,
Or we shall shipwreck in our safest port...

Bussy D'Ambois, Act I, Sc. i.

LAST WORDS OF BYRON

...Such is the endless exile of dead men.
Summer succeeds the spring; autumn the summer;
The frosts of Winter, the fall'n leaves of autumn:
All these, and all fruits in them yearly fade,
And every year return: but cursed man
Shall never more renew his vanish'd face.
Fall on your knees, then, statists, ere ye fall,
That you may rise again; knees bent too late

Stick you in earth like statues; see in me
How you are pour'd down from your clearest heavens;
Fall lower yet, mix'd with th'unmoved centre,
That your own shadows may no longer mock ye.
Strike, strike, O strike; fly, fly, commanding soul,
And on thy wings for this thy body's breath
Bear the eternal victory of death.

Byron's Tragedy, Act V, Sc. i

ROBERT SOUTHWELL
(1561?—1598)

THE BURNING BABE

As I in hoary winter's night stood shivering in the snow,
Surprised I was with sudden heat which made my heart to glow;
And lifting up a fearful eye to view what fire was near,
A pretty Babe all burning bright did in the air appear;
Who, scorched with excessive heat, such floods of tears did shed,
As though his floods should quench his flames which with his
    tears were fed.
'Alas!' quoth he, 'but newly born in fiery heats I fry,
Yet none approach to warm their hearts or feel my fire but I
My faultless breast the furnace is, the fuel wounding thorns;
Love is the fire, and sighs the smoke, the ashes shame and scorns
The fuel justice layeth on, and mercy blows the coals;
The metal in this furnace wrought are men's defiled souls:
For which, as now on fire I am to work them to their good
So will I melt into a bath to wash them in my blood.'
With this he vanished out of sight and swiftly shrunk away
And straight I called unto mind that it was Christmas day.

SAMUEL DANIEL
(1563?—1619)

SONNET

Care-charmer Sleep, son of the sable Night,
  Brother to Death, in silent darkness born,
Relieve my languish, and restore the light,
  With dark forgetting of my cares return.
And let the day be time enough to mourn
  The shipwreck of my ill-adventured youth;
Let waking eyes suffice to wail their scorn,
  Without the torment of the night's untruth.
Cease, dreams, the images of day-desires,
  To model forth the passions of the morrow;
Never let rising sun approve you liars,
  To add more grief to aggravate my sorrow.
    Still let me sleep, embracing clouds in vain;
    And never wake to feel the day's disdain.

MICHAEL DRAYTON
(1563—1631)

TO THE VIRGINIAN VOYAGE

  You brave heroic minds
    Worthy your country's name,
    That honour still pursue;
    Go and subdue!
  Whilst loitering hinds
    Lurk here at home with shame.

Britons, you stay too long:
  Quickly aboard bestow you,
    And with a merry gale
    Swell your stretch'd sail
With vows as strong
  As the winds that blow you.

Your course securely steer,
  West and by south forth keep!
    Rocks, lee-shores, nor shoals
    When Eolus scowls
You need not fear;
  So absolute the deep.

And cheerfully at sea
  Success you still entice
    To get the pearl and gold,
    And ours to hold
Virginia,
  Earth's only paradise.

Where nature hath in store
  Fowl, venison, and fish,
    And the fruitfull'st soil
    Without your toil
Three harvests more,
  All greater than your wish.

And the ambitious vine
  Crowns with his purple mass
    The cedar reaching high
    To kiss the sky,

The cypress, pine,
  And useful sassafras.

To whom the Golden Age
  Still nature's laws doth give,
    No other cares attend,
    But them to defend
From winter's rage,
  That long there doth not live.

When as the luscious smell
  Of that delicious land
    Above the seas that flows
    The clear wind throws,
Your hearts to swell
  Approaching the dear strand;

In kenning of the shore
  (Thanks to God first given)
    O you the happiest men,
    Be frolic then!
Let cannons roar,
  Frighting the wide heaven.

And in regions far,
  Such heroes bring ye forth
    As those from whom we came;
    And plant our name
Under that star
  Not known unto our North.

And as there plenty grows
    Of laurel everywhere—
        Apollo's sacred tree—
        You it may see
A poet's brows
    To crown, that may sing there.

Thy *Voyages* attend,
    Industrious Hakluyt,
        Whose reading shall inflame
        Men to seek fame,
And much commend
    To after times thy wit.

SONNET

Since there's no help, come let us kiss and part.
    Nay, I have done; you get no more of me,
And I am glad, yea, glad with all my heart,
    That thus so cleanly I myself can free;
Shake hands for ever, cancel all our vows,
    And when we meet at any time again,
Be it not seen in either of our brows
    That we one jot of former love retain.
Now at the last gasp of Love's latest breath,
    When, his pulse failing, Passion speechless lies,
When Faith is kneeling by his bed of death,
    And Innocence is closing up his eyes,
        Now if thou wouldst, when all have given him over
        From death to life thou mightst him yet recover.

CHRISTOPHER MARLOWE
(1564—1593)

AMBITION

... The thirst of reign and sweetness of a crown,
That caused the eldest son of heavenly Ops
To thrust his doting father from his chair
And place himself in the imperial heaven,
Moved me to manage arms against thy state.
What better precedent than mighty Jove?
Nature that fram'd us of four elements,
Warring within our breasts for regiment,
Doth teach us all to have aspiring minds.
Our souls, whose faculties can comprehend
The wondrous architecture of the world,
And measure every wandering planet's course,
Still climbing after knowledge infinite,
And always moving as the restless spheres,
Will us to wear ourselves and never rest
Until we reach the ripest fruit of all,
That perfect bliss and sole felicity,
The sweet fruition of an earthly crown...

Tamburlaine the Great, Part I, Act II, Sc. vi.

TAMBURLAINE ON POETRY

... What is beauty, saith my sufferings, then?
If all the pens that ever poets held
Had fed the feeling of their masters' thoughts,
And every sweetness that inspir'd their hearts,

Their minds, and muses on admired themes;
If all the heavenly quintessence they still
From their immortal flowers of poesy,
Wherein, as in a mirror, we perceive
The highest reaches of a human wit;
If these had made one poem's period,
And all combin'd in beauty's worthiness,
Yet should there hover in their restless heads
One thought, one grace, one wonder, at the least,
Which into words no virtue can digest...

Tamburlaine the Great, Part I, Act V, Sc. ii.

BARABAS IN HIS COUNTING-HOUSE

... Fie, what a trouble 'tis to count this trash!
Well fare the Arabians, who so richly pay
The things they traffic for with wedge of gold,
Whereof a man may easily in a day
Tell that which may maintain him all his life.
The needy groom, that never finger'd groat,
Would make a miracle of thus much coin;
But he whose steel-barr'd coffers are cramm'd full
And all his life-time hath been tired,
Wearying his fingers' ends with telling it,
Would in his age be loath to labour so,
And for a pound to sweat himself to death.
Give me the merchants of the Indian mines,
That trade in metal of the purest mould;
The wealthy Moor, that in the eastern rocks
Without control can pick his riches up,
And in his house heap pearl like pebble-stones,
Receive them free, and sell them by the weight;

Bags of fiery opals, sapphires, amethysts,
Jacinths, hard topaz, grass-green emeralds,
Beauteous rubies, sparkling diamonds,
And seld-seen; costly stones of so great price,
As one of them, indifferently rated,
And of a caract of this quantity,
May serve, in peril of calamity,
To ransom great kings from captivity.
This is the ware wherein consists my wealth;
And thus, methinks, should men of judgment frame
Their means of traffic from the vulgar trade,
And, as their wealth increaseth, so inclose
Infinite riches in a little room. . . .

The Jew of Malta, Act I, Sc. i.

HELEN OF TROY

. . . Was this the face that launch'd a thousand ships,
And burnt the topless towers of Ilium? —
Sweet Helen, make me immortal with a kiss —
Her lips suck forth my soul: see, where it flies!
Come, Helen, come, give me my soul again.
Here will I dwell, for heaven is in those lips,
And all is dross that is not Helena.
I will be Paris, and for love of thee
Instead of Troy, shall Wertenberg be sack'd;
And I will combat with weak Menelaus,
And wear thy colours on my pluméd crest:
Yea, I will wound Achilles in the heel,
And then return to Helen for a kiss.
O, thou art fairer than the evening air
Clad in the beauty of a thousand stars;

Brighter art thou than flaming Jupiter
When he appear'd to hapless Semele;
More lovely than the monarch of the sky
In wanton Arethusa's azure arms;
And none but thou shalt be my paramour!

The Tragical History of Dr. Faustus.

FIRST SIGHT

... It lies not in our power to love or hate,
For will in us is overruled by fate.
When two are stripped, long ere the course begin
We wish that one should lose, the other win;
And one especially do we affect
Of two gold ingots, like in each respect.
The reason no man knows, let it suffice,
What we behold is censured by our eyes.
Where both deliberate, the love is slight;
Who ever loved, that loved not at first sight? ...

Hero and Leander.

WILLIAM SHAKESPEARE
(1564—1616)

SONNETS

(i)

Shall I compare thee to a summer's day?
Thou art more lovely and more temperate:
Rough winds do shake the darling buds of May,
And summer's lease hath all too short a date:

Sometime too hot the eye of heaven shines,
　And often is his gold complexion dimmed;
And every fair from fair sometime declines,
　By chance, or nature's changing course untrimmed;
But thy eternal summer shall not fade,
　Nor lose possession of that fair thou owest,
Nor shall death brag thou wander'st in his shade,
　When in eternal lines to time thou growest;
　　So long as men can breathe, or eyes can see,
　　So long lives this, and this gives life to thee.

(ii)

Devouring Time, blunt thou the lion's paws,
　And make the earth devour her own sweet brood;
Pluck the keen teeth from the fierce tiger's jaws,
　And burn the long-lived phoenix in her blood;
Make glad and sorry seasons as thou fleets,
　And do whate'er thou wilt, swift-footed Time,
To the wide world and all her fading sweets;
　But I forbid thee one most heinous crime:
O! carve not with thy hours my Love's fair brow,
　Nor draw no lines there with thine antique pen;
Him in thy course untainted do allow
　For beauty's pattern to succeeding men.
　　Yet, do thy worst, old Time: despite thy wrong,
　　My Love shall in my verse ever live young.

(iii)

When in disgrace with fortune and men's eyes
　I all alone beweep my outcast state,
And trouble deaf heaven with my bootless cries,
　And look upon myself, and curse my fate,

Wishing me like to one more rich in hope,
　　Featured like him, like him with friends possessed,
Desiring this man's art, and that man's scope,
　　With what I most enjoy contented least;
Yet in these thoughts myself almost despising,
　　Haply I think on thee, and then my state,
Like to the lark at break of day arising
　　From sullen earth, sings hymns at heaven's gate;
　　　For thy sweet love remembered such wealth brings
　　　That then I scorn to change my state with kings.

(iv)

Full many a glorious morning have I seen
　　Flatter the mountain-tops with sovereign eye,
Kissing with golden face the meadows green,
　　Gilding pale streams with heavenly alchemy;
Anon permit the basest clouds to ride
　　With ugly rack on his celestial face,
And from the forlorn world his visage hide,
　　Stealing unseen to west with this disgrace:
Even so my sun one early morn did shine,
　　With all-triumphant splendour on my brow;
But, out! alack! he was but one hour mine,
　　The region cloud hath masked him from me now.
　　　Yet him for this my love no whit disdaineth;
　　　Suns of the world may stain when heaven's
　　　　　　　　　　　　　sun staineth.

(v)

Then hate me when thou wilt; if ever, now;
　　Now, while the world is bent my deeds to cross,

Join with the spite of fortune, make me bow,
   And do not drop in for an after-loss:
Ah! do not, when my heart hath 'scaped this sorrow,
   Come in the rearward of a conquered woe;
Give not a windy night a rainy morrow,
   To linger out a purposed overthrow.
If thou wilt leave me, do not leave me last,
   When other petty griefs have done their spite,
But in the onset come; so shall I taste
   At first the very worst of fortune's might.
     And other strains of woe, which now seem woe,
     Compared with loss of thee will not seem so.

(vi)

Like as the waves make towards the pebbled shore,
   So do our minutes hasten to their end;
Each changing place with that which goes before,
   In sequent toil all forwards do contend.
Nativity, once in the main of light,
   Crawls to maturity, wherewith being crowned,
Crooked eclipses 'gainst his glory fight,
   And Time that gave doth now his gift confound.
Time doth transfix the flourish set on youth
   And delves the parallels in beauty's brow,
   Feeds on the rarities of nature's truth,
   And nothing stands but for his scythe to mow.
     And yet to times in hope my verse shall stand,
     Praising thy worth, despite his cruel hand.

J. 2. N.
28.9.50

(vii)

When I have seen by Time's fell hand defaced
   The rich proud cost of outworn buried age;

When sometime lofty towers I see down razed,
And brass eternal slave to mortal rage;
When I have seen the hungry ocean gain
Advantage on the kingdom of the shore,
And the firm soil win of the watery main,
Increasing store with loss, and loss with store;
When I have seen such interchange of state,
Or state itself confounded to decay,
Ruin hath taught me thus to ruminate,
That Time will come and take my Love away.
This thought is as a death, which cannot choose
But weep to have that which it fears to lose.

(viii)

That time of year thou mayst in me behold
When yellow leaves, or none, or few, do hang
Upon those boughs which shake against the cold,
Bare ruined choirs, where late the sweet birds sang.
In me thou see'st the twilight of such day
As after sunset fadeth in the west;
Which by and by black night doth take away,
Death's second self, that seals up all in rest.
In me thou see'st the glowing of such fire,
That on the ashes of his youth doth lie,
As the death-bed whereon it must expire,
Consumed with that which it was nourished by.
This thou perceivest, which makes thy love
more strong,
To love that well which thou must leave ere long.

(ix)

Let me not to the marriage of true minds
   Admit impediments. Love is not love
Which alters when it alteration finds,
   Or bends with the remover to remove.
O, no! it is an ever-fixed mark,
   That looks on tempests and is never shaken;
It is the star to every wandering bark,
   Whose worth's unknown, although his height be taken.
Love's not Time's fool, though rosy lips and cheeks
   Within his bending sickle's compass come;
Love alters not with his brief hours and weeks,
   But bears it out even to the edge of doom.
     If this be error, and upon me proved,
     I never writ, nor no man ever loved.

(x)

The expense of spirit in a waste of shame
   Is lust in action; and till action, lust
Is perjured, murderous, bloody, full of blame,
   Savage, extreme, rude, cruel, not to trust;
Enjoyed, no sooner but despised straight;
   Past reason hunted; and no sooner had,
Past reason hated, as a swallowed bait,
   On purpose laid to make the taker mad:
Mad in pursuit, and in possession so;
   Had, having, and in quest to have, extreme;
A bliss in proof, and proved, a very woe;
   Before, a joy proposed; behind, a dream.
     All this the world well knows; yet none knows well
     To shun the heaven that leads men to this hell.

(xi)

They that have power to hurt and will do none,
That do not do the thing they most do show,
Who, moving others, are themselves as stone,
Unmovèd, cold, and to temptation slow—
They rightly do inherit Heaven's graces,
And husband Nature's riches from expense;
They are the lords and owners of their faces,
Others, but stewards of their excellence.
The Summer's flower is to the Summer sweet,
Though to itself it only live and die;
But if that flower with base infection meet,
The basest weed outbraves his dignity:
  For sweetest things turn sourest by their deeds;
  Lilies that fester smell far worse than weeds.

(xii)

Not marble, nor the gilded monuments
  Of princes, shall outlive this powerful rhyme;
But you shall shine more bright in these contents
  Than unswept stone, besmeared with sluttish time.
When wasteful war shall statues overturn
  And broils root out the work of masonry,
Nor Mars his sword nor war's quick fire shall burn
  The living record of your memory.
'Gainst death and all oblivious enmity
  Shall you pace forth; your praise shall still find room
Even in the eyes of all posterity
  That wear this world out to the ending doom.
    So, till the judgment that yourself arise,
    You live in this, and dwell in lovers' eyes.

(xiii)

Since brass, nor stone, nor earth, nor boundless sea,
But sad mortality o'ersways their power,
How with this rage shall beauty hold a plea,
Whose action is no stronger than a flower?
O how shall summer's honey breath hold out
Against the wreckful siege of battering days,
When rocks impregnable are not so stout
Nor gates of steel so strong, but time decays?
O fearful meditation! where, alack!
Shall Time's best jewel from Time's chest lie hid?
Or what strong hand can hold his swift foot back,
Or who his spoil of beauty can forbid?
    O none! Unless this miracle have might,
    That in black ink my love may still shine bright.

(xiv)

My love is strengthened, though more weak in seeming;
    I love not less, though less the show appear:
That love is merchandized whose rich esteeming
    The owner's tongue doth publish everywhere.
Our love was new, and then but in the spring,
    When I was wont to greet it with my lays,
As Philomel in summer's front doth sing,
    And stops her pipe in growth of riper days:
Not that the summer is less pleasant now
    Than when her mournful hymns did hush the night,
But that wild music burthens every bough,
    And sweets grown common lose their dear delight.
      Therefore, like her, I sometime hold my tongue,
      Because I would not dull you with my song.

FESTE'S SONGS

(i)

O mistress mine, where are you roaming?
O! stay and hear; your true love's coming,
That can sing both high and low.
Trip no further, pretty sweeting;
Journeys end in lovers meeting,
Every wise man's son doth know.

What is love? 'Tis not hereafter;
Present mirth hath present laughter;
What's to come is still unsure.
In delay there lies no plenty;
Then come kiss me, sweet and twenty;
Youth's a stuff will not endure.

(ii)

Come away, come away, death,
And in sad cypress let me be laid.
Fly away, fly away, breath;
I am slain by a fair cruel maid.
My shroud of white, stuck all with yew,
O! prepare it.
My part of death, no one so true
Did share it.

Not a flower, not a flower sweet,
On my black coffin let there be strown;
Not a friend, not a friend greet
My poor corpse, where my bones shall be thrown

A thousand thousand sighs to save,
　　Lay me, O! where
Sad true lover never find my grave,
　　To weep there.

Twelfth Night.

FIDELE'S DIRGE

Fear no more the heat o' the sun,
　　Nor the furious winter's rages;
Thou thy worldly task hast done,
　　Home art gone, and ta'en thy wages.
Golden lads and girls all must,
As chimney-sweepers, come to dust.

Fear no more the frown o' the great,
　　Thou art past the tyrant's stroke;
Care no more to clothe and eat,
　　To thee the reed is as the oak.
The sceptre, learning, physic, must
All follow this, and come to dust.

Fear no more the lightning-flash,
　　Nor the all-dreaded thunder-stone;
Fear not slander, censure rash;
　　Thou hast finished joy and moan.
All lovers young, all lovers must
Consign to thee, and come to dust.

No exorciser harm thee!
Nor no witchcraft charm thee!
Ghost unlaid forbear thee!

Nothing ill come near thee!
Quiet consummation have,
And renowned be thy grave!

Cymbeline.

ARIEL'S SONG

Full fathom five thy father lies;
Of his bones are coral made;
Those are pearls that were his eyes:
Nothing of him that doth fade,
But doth suffer a sea-change
Into something rich and strange:
Sea nymphs hourly ring his knell.
Ding-dong!
Hark! now I hear them,
Ding-dong, bell!

The Tempest.

LOVE AND THE POET

... From women's eyes this doctrine I derive:
They are the ground, the books, the academes,
From whence doth spring the true Promethean fire.
Why, universal plodding poisons up
The nimble spirits in the arteries,
As motion and long-during action tires
The sinewy vigour of the traveller.
Now, for not looking on a woman's face,
You have in that forsworn the use of eyes,
And study too, the causer of your vow;
For where is any author in the world
Teaches such beauty as a woman's eye?
Learning is but an adjunct to ourself,

And where we are our learning likewise is:
Then when ourselves we see in ladies' eyes,
Do we not likewise see our learning there?
O! we have made a vow to study, lords,
And in that vow we have forsworn our books:
For when would you, my liege, or you, or you,
In leaden contemplation have found out
Such fiery numbers as the prompting eyes
Of beauty's tutors have enrich'd you with?
Other slow arts entirely keep the brain,
And therefore, finding barren practisers,
Scarce show a harvest of their heavy toil;
But love, first learned in a lady's eyes,
Lives not alone immured in the brain,
But, with the motion of all elements,
Courses as swift as thought in every power,
And gives to every power a double power,
Above their functions and their offices.
It adds a precious seeing to the eye;
A lover's eyes will gaze an eagle blind;
A lover's ear will hear the lowest sound,
When the suspicious head of theft is stopp'd:
Love's feeling is more soft and sensible
Than are the tender horns of cockled snails:
Love's tongue proves dainty Bacchus gross in taste.
For valour, is not Love a Hercules,
Still climbing trees in the Hesperides?
Subtle as Sphinx; as sweet and musical
As bright Apollo's lute, strung with his hair;
And when Love speaks, the voice of all the gods
Makes heaven drowsy with the harmony.

Never durst poet touch a pen to write
Until his ink were temper'd with Love's sighs;
O! then his lines would ravish savage ears,
And plant in tyrants mild humility...

Love's Labour's Lost, Act IV, Sc. iii.

INSPIRATION

...Lovers and madmen have such seething brains,
Such shaping fantasies, that apprehend
More than cool reason ever comprehends.
The lunatic, the lover, and the poet,
Are of imagination all compact:
One sees more devils than vast hell can hold,
That is, the madman; the lover, all as frantic,
Sees Helen's beauty in a brow of Egypt:
The poet's eye, in a fine frenzy rolling,
Doth glance from heaven to earth, from earth to heaven
And, as imagination bodies forth
The forms of things unknown, the poet's pen
Turns them to shapes, and gives to airy nothing
A local habitation and a name...

A Midsummer Night's Dream, Act V, Sc.

FEAR OF DEATH

(i)

...Be absolute for death; either death or life
Shall thereby be the sweeter. Reason thus with life:
If I do lose thee, I do lose a thing
That none but fools would keep: a breath thou art,
Servile to all the skyey influences,
That dost this habitation, where thou keep'st,

Hourly affict. Merely, thou art death's fool;
For him thou labour'st by thy flight to shun,
And yet run'st toward him still. Thou art not noble:
For all th' accommodations that thou bear'st
Are nurs'd by baseness. Thou art by no means valiant;
For thou dost fear the soft and tender fork
Of a poor worm. Thy best of rest is sleep,
And that thou oft provok'st; yet grossly fear'st
Thy death, which is no more. Thou art not thyself;
For thou exist'st on many a thousand grains
That issue out of dust. Happy thou art not;
For what thou hast not, still thou striv'st to get,
And what thou hast, forget'st. Thou art not certain;
For thy complexion shifts to strange effects,
After the moon. If thou art rich, thou'rt poor;
For, like an ass whose back with ingots bows,
Thou bear'st thy heavy riches but a journey,
And death unloads thee. Friend hast thou none;
For thine own bowels, which do call thee sire,
The mere effusion of thy proper loins,
Do curse the gout, serpigo, and the rheum,
For ending thee no sooner. Thou hast nor youth nor age;
But, as it were, an after-dinner's sleep,
Dreaming on both; for all thy blessed youth
Becomes as aged, and doth beg the alms
Of palsied eld; and when thou art old and rich,
Thou hast neither heat, affection, limb, nor beauty,
To make thy riches pleasant. What's yet in this
That bears the name of life? Yet in this life
Lie hid moe thousand deaths: yet death we fear,
That makes these odds all even...

Measure for Measure, Act III, Sc. i.

(ii)

Isabella. What says my brother?

Claudio.   Death is a fearful thing.

Isabella. And shamed life a hateful.

Claudio. Ay, but to die, and go we know not where;
To lie in cold obstruction and to rot;
This sensible warm motion to become
A kneaded clod; and the delighted spirit
To bathe in fiery floods, or to reside
In thrilling region of thick-ribbed ice;
To be imprison'd in the viewless winds,
And blown with restless violence round about
The pendant world; or to be worse than worst
Of those that lawless and incertain thoughts
Imagine howling: 'tis too horrible!
The weariest and most loathed worldly life
That age, ache, penury and imprisonment
Can lay on nature is a paradise
To what we fear of death...

Measure for Measure, Act III, Sc. i.

TIME

... Time hath, my lord, a wallet at his back,
Wherein he puts alms for oblivion,
A great-siz'd monster of ingratitudes:
Those scraps are good deeds past; which are devour'd
As fast as they are made, forgot as soon
As done: perseverance, dear my lord,
Keeps honour bright: to have done, is to hang
Quite out of fashion, like a rusty mail
In monumental mockery. Take the instant way;

For honour travels in a strait so narrow
Where one but goes abreast: keep, then, the path;
For emulation hath a thousand sons
That one by one pursue: if you give way,
Or hedge aside from the direct forthright,
Like to an enter'd tide they all rush by
And leave you hindmost;
Or, like a gallant horse fall'n in first rank,
Lie there for pavement to the abject rear,
O'errun and trampled on: then what they do in present
Though less than yours in past, must o'ertop yours;
For time is like a fashionable host,
That slightly shakes his parting guest by the hand,
And with his arms outstretch'd, as he would fly,
Grasps in the comer: welcome ever smiles,
And farewell goes out sighing. O! let not virtue seek
Remuneration for the thing it was;
For beauty, wit,
High birth, vigour of bone, desert in service,
Love, friendship, charity, are subjects all
To envious and calumniating time.
One touch of nature makes the whole world kin,
That all with one consent praise new-born gawds,
Though they are made and moulded of things past,
And give to dust that is a little gilt
More laud than gilt o'er-dusted.
The present eye praises the present object:
Then marvel not, thou great and complete man,
That all the Greeks begin to worship Ajax;
Since things in motion sooner catch the eye
Than what not stirs...

Troilus and Cressida, Act III, Sc. iii.

MACBETH ON HIS WIFE'S DEATH

Seyton.   The queen, my lord, is dead.
Macbeth.   She should have died hereafter;
            There would have been a time for such a word.
            To-morrow, and to-morrow, and to-morrow,
            Creeps in this petty pace from day to day.
            To the last syllable of recorded time;
            And all our yesterdays have lighted fools
            The way to dusty death. Out, out, brief candle!
            Life's but a walking shadow, a poor player
            That struts and frets his hour upon the stage,
            And then is heard no more; it is a tale
            Told by an idiot, full of sound and fury,
            Signifying nothing . . .

                                    Macbeth, Act V, Sc. v.

CLEOPATRA

Enobarbus. The barge she sat in, like a burnish'd throne,
             Burn'd on the water; the poop was beaten gold,
             Purple the sails, and so perfumed, that
             The winds were love-sick with them; the oars were
                                                    silver,
             Which to the tune of flutes kept stroke, and made
             The water which they beat to follow faster,
             As amorous of their strokes. For her own person,
             It beggar'd all description; she did lie
             In her pavilion,—cloth-of-gold of tissue,—
             O'er-picturing that Venus where we see
             The fancy outwork nature; on each side her
             Stood pretty dimpled boys, like smiling Cupids,

With divers-colour'd fans, whose wind did seem
To glow the delicate cheeks which they did cool,
And what they undid did.

Agrippa.   O! rare for Antony.

Enobarbus. Her gentlewomen, like the Nereides,
So many mermaids, tended her i' the eyes,
And made their bends adornings; at the helm
A seeming mermaid steers; the silken tackle
Swell with the touches of those flower-soft hands,
That yarely frame the office. From the barge
A strange invisible perfume hits the sense
Of the adjacent wharfs. The city cast
Her people out upon her; and Antony,
Enthron'd i' the market-place, did sit alone,
Whistling to the air; which, but for vacancy,
Had gone to gaze on Cleopatra too,
And made a gap in nature...

Antony and Cleopatra, Act II, Sc. ii.

CALIBAN ON THE ISLAND

...Be not afeard: the isle is full of noises,
Sounds, and sweet airs, that give delight, and hurt not.
Sometimes a thousand twangling instruments
Will hum about mine ears; and sometime voices,
That, if I then had wak'd after long sleep,
Will make me sleep again: and then, in dreaming,
The clouds methought would open and show riches
Ready to drop upon me; that, when I wak'd
I cried to dream again...

The Tempest, Act III, Sc. ii.

THOMAS NASHE
(1567—1601?)

SPRING

Spring, the sweet spring, is the year's pleasant king;
Then blooms each thing, then maids dance in a ring,
Cold doth not sting, the pretty birds do sing:
    Cuckoo, jug-jug, pu-we, to-witta-woo!

The palm and may make country houses gay,
Lambs frisk and play, the shepherds pipe all day,
And we hear aye birds tune this merry lay:
    Cuckoo, jug-jug, pu-we, to-witta-woo!

The fields breathe sweet, the daisies kiss our feet,
Young lovers meet, old wives a-sunning sit;
In every street these tunes our ears do greet:
    Cuckoo, jug-jug, pu-we, to-witta-woo!
      Spring, the sweet spring!

IN TIME OF PESTILENCE

Adieu, farewell earth's bliss,
This world uncertain is;
Fond are life's lustful joys,
Death proves them all but toys,
None from his darts can fly.
I am sick, I must die.
     Lord, have mercy on us!

Rich men, trust not in wealth,
Gold cannot buy you health;

Physic himself must fade,
All things to end are made.
The plague full swift goes by.
I am sick, I must die.
       Lord, have mercy on us!

Beauty is but a flower
Which wrinkles will devour;
Brightness falls from the air,
Queens have died young and fair
Dust hath closed Helen's eye.
I am sick, I must die.
       Lord, have mercy on us!

Strength stoops unto the grave,
Worms feed on Hector brave,
Swords may not fight with fate,
Earth still holds ope her gate.
Come! come! the bells do cry.
I am sick, I must die.
       Lord, have mercy on us!

Wit with his wantonness
Tasteth death's bitterness;
Hell's executioner
Hath no ears for to hear
What vain art can reply.
I am sick, I must die.
       Lord, have mercy on us!

Haste, therefore, each degree
To welcome destiny.

Heaven is our heritage,
Earth but a player's stage;
Mount we unto the sky.
I am sick, I must die.
        Lord, have mercy on us!

THOMAS CAMPION
(1567—1620)

SONGS FROM LUTE BOOKS
(i)

Follow your saint, follow with accents sweet;
Haste you, sad notes, fall at her flying feet.
There, wrapped in cloud of sorrow, pity move,
And tell the ravisher of my soul I perish for her love.
But if she scorns my never-ceasing pain,
Then burst with sighing in her sight, and ne'er return again.

All that I sung still to her praise did tend.
Still she was first, still she my songs did end.
Yet she my love and music both doth fly,
The music that her echo is, and beauty's sympathy.
Then let my notes pursue her scornful flight;
It shall suffice that they were breathed, and died for her delight.

(ii)

When thou must home to shades of underground,
    And there arrived, a new admired guest,
The beauteous spirits do engirt thee round,
    White Iope, blithe Helen and the rest,
To hear the stories of thy finished love
From that smooth tongue, whose music hell can move:

Then wilt thou speak of banqueting delights,
  Of masks and revels which sweet youth did make,
Of tourneys and great challenges of knights,
  And all these triumphs, for thy beauty's sake.
When thou hast told these honours done to thee,
Then tell, O! tell, how thou didst murder me.

(iii)

Come, you pretty false-eyed wanton,
  Leave your crafty smiling.
Think you to escape me now
  With slippery words beguiling?
No, you mocked me th' other day,
When you got loose, you fled away.
But since I have caught you now,
  I'll clip your wings for flying;
Smothering kisses fast I'll heap,
  And keep you so from crying.

Sooner may you count the stars,
  And number hail down-pouring,
Tell the osiers of the Thames,
  Or Goodwin Sands devouring,
Than the thick-showered kisses here,
Which now thy tired lips must bear.
Such a harvest never was,
  So rich and full of pleasure;
But 'tis spent as soon as reaped,
  So trustless is love's treasure.

Would it were dumb midnight now,
  When all the world lies sleeping.

Would this place some desert were,
  Which no man hath in keeping.
My desires should then be safe,
  And when you cried, then would I laugh.
But if aught might breed offence,
  Love only should be blamed.
I would live your servant still,
  And you my saint unnamed.

(iv)

Sleep, angry beauty, sleep and fear not me
  For who a sleeping lion dares provoke?
It shall suffice me here to sit and see
  Those lips shut up that never kindly spoke:
What sight can more content a lover's mind
Than beauty seeming harmless, if not kind?

My words have charm'd her, for secure she sleeps,
  Though guilty much of wrong done to my love;
And in her slumber, see! she close-eyed weeps:
  Dreams often more than waking passions move.
Plead, Sleep, my cause, and make her soft like thee,
That she in peace may wake and pity me.

(v)

Never weather-beaten sail more willing bent to shore,
  Never tired pilgrim's limbs affected slumber more,
Than my weary spright now longs to fly out of my troubled
                                        breast.
  O! come quickly, sweetest Lord, and take my soul to rest.

Ever blooming are the joys of Heaven's high Paradise.
  Cold age deafs not there our ears, nor vapour dims our eyes;
Glory there the sun outshines, whose beams the blessed only see.
  O! come quickly, glorious Lord, and raise my spright to thee.

UNKNOWN

SONGS SET BY JOHN DOWLAND

(i)

Dear, if you change, I'll never choose again;
  Sweet, if you shrink, I'll never think of love;
Fair, if you fail, I'll judge all beauty vain;
  Wise, if too weak, mo wits I'll never prove.
Dear, Sweet, Fair, Wise, change, shrink, nor be not weak;
And, on my faith, my faith shall never break.

Earth with her flowers shall sooner heaven adorn;
  Heaven her brights stars through earth's dim globe shall move;
Fire heat shall lose, and frosts of flames be born;
  Air, made to shine, as black as hell shall prove.
Earth, Heaven, Fire, Air, the world transformed shall view,
Ere I prove false to faith, or strange to you.

(ii)

I saw my lady weep,
  And Sorrow proud to be advanced so
In those fair eyes where all perfections keep.
  Her face was full of woe;
But such a woe, believe me, as wins more hearts,
Than Mirth can do with her enticing parts.

Sorrow was there made fair,
And Passion wise, tears a delightful thing;
Silence beyond all speech a wisdom rare.
She made her sighs to sing,
And, all things with so sweet a sadness move,
As made my heart at once both grieve and love.

O fairer than aught else
The world can show, leave off in time to grieve
Enough, enough your joyful looks excels;
Tears kills the heart, believe.
O! strive not to be excellent in woe,
Which only breeds your beauty's overthrow.

(iii)

Weep you no more, sad fountains;
What need you flow so fast?
Look how the snowy mountains
Heaven's sun doth gently waste.
But my sun's heavenly eyes
View not your weeping,
That now lies sleeping
Softly, now softly lies
Sleeping.

Sleep is a reconciling,
A rest that peace begets.
Doth not the sun rise smiling
When fair at even he sets?
Rest you then, rest, sad eyes,

Melt not in weeping,
While she lies sleeping
Softly, now softly lies
Sleeping.

MADRIGAL

Thule, the period of Cosmography,
   Doth vaunt of Hecla, whose sulphurious fire
Doth melt the frozen clime and thaw the sky;
   Trinacrian Ætna's flames ascend not higher.
These things seem wondrous, yet more wondrous I,
Whose heart with fear doth freeze, with love doth fry.

The Andalusian merchant, that returns
   Laden with cochineal and china dishes,
Reports in Spain how strangely Fogo burns
   Amidst an ocean full of flying fishes.
These things seem wondrous, yet more wondrous I,
Whose heart with fear doth freeze, with love doth fry.

MADRIGAL

My Love in her attire doth show her wit,
   It doth so well become her:
For every season she hath dressings fit,
   For winter, spring, and summer.
No beauty she doth miss,
   When all her robes are on:
But Beauty's self she is,
   When all her robes are gone.

JERUSALEM

Jerusalem, my happy home,
 When shall I come to thee?
When shall my sorrows have an end,
 Thy joys when shall I see?

O happy harbour of the saints,
 O sweet and pleasant soil,
In thee no sorrow may be found,
 No grief, no care, no toil.

There lust and lucre cannot dwell,
 There envy bears no sway;
There is no hunger, heat, nor cold,
 But pleasure every way.

Thy walls are made of precious stones,
 Thy bulwarks diamonds square;
Thy gates are of right orient pearl,
 Exceeding rich and rare.

Thy turrets and thy pinnacles
 With carbuncles do shine;
Thy very streets are paved with gold,
 Surpassing clear and fine.

Ah, my sweet home Jerusalem,
 Would God I were in thee!
Would God my woes were at an end,
 Thy joys that I might see!

Thy gardens and thy gallant walks
 Continually are green;

There grows such sweet and pleasant flowers
    As nowhere else are seen.

Quite through the streets, with silver sound,
    The flood of life doth flow;
Upon whose banks on every side
    The wood of life doth grow.

There trees for evermore bear fruit,
    And evermore do spring;
There evermore the angels sit,
    And evermore do sing.

Our Lady sings *Magnificat*
    With tune surpassing sweet;
And all the virgins bear their part,
    Sitting about her feet.

Jerusalem, my happy home,
    Would God I were in thee!
Would God my woes were at an end,
    Thy joys that I might see!

SIR HENRY WOTTON
(1568—1639)

ON HIS MISTRESS, THE QUEEN OF BOHEMIA

You meaner beauties of the night,
    That poorly satisfy our eyes
More by your number than your light,
    You common people of the skies;
    What are you when the moon shall rise?

You curious chanters of the wood,
    That warble forth Dame Nature's lays,
Thinking your passions understood
    By your weak accents; what's your praise
    When Philomel her voice shall raise?

You violets that first appear,
    By your pure purple mantles known
Like the proud virgins of the year,
    As if the spring were all your own;
    What are you when the rose is blown?

So, when my mistress shall be seen
    In form and beauty of her mind,
By virtue first, then choice, a Queen,
    Tell me, if she were not design'd
    Th' eclipse and glory of her kind.

SIR JOHN DAVIES
(1569—1626)

AFFLICTION

If aught can teach us aught, Affliction's looks,
    Making us look into ourselves so near,
Teach us to know ourselves beyond all books,
    Or all the learned schools that ever were.

This mistress lately plucked me by the ear,
    And many a golden lesson hath me taught;
Hath made my senses quick, and reason clear,
    Reformed my will, and rectified my thought.

So do the winds and thunders cleanse the air;
  So working seas settle and purge the wine;
So lopped and pruned trees do flourish fair;
  So doth the fire the drossy gold refine.

Neither Minerva nor the learned Muse,
  Nor rules of art, nor precepts of the wise,
Could in my brain those beams of skill infuse,
  As but the glance of this dame's angry eyes.

She within lists my ranging mind hath brought,
  That now beyond myself I list not go;
Myself am centre of my circling thought,
  Only myself I study, learn, and know.

I know my body's of so frail a kind
  As force without, fevers within, can kill;
I know the heavenly nature of my mind,
  But 'tis corrupted both in wit and will;

I know my soul hath power to know all things,
  Yet is she blind and ignorant in all;
I know I am one of nature's little kings,
  Yet to the least and vilest things am thrall.

I know my life's a pain and but a span,
  I know my sense is mocked with everything,
And to conclude, I know myself a man,
  Which is a proud, and yet a wretched thing.

Nosce Teipsum.

THOMAS DEKKER
(c. 1570—c. 1632)

COUNTRY GLEE

Haymakers, rakers, reapers and mowers,
  Wait on your Summer Queen;
Dress up with musk-rose her eglantine bowers,
  Daffodils strew the green.
     Sing, dance and play,
     'Tis holiday;
  The sun does bravely shine
    On our ears of corn.
     Rich as a pearl
     Comes every girl;
  This is mine, this is mine, this is mine;
    Let us die, ere away they be borne.

Bow to the Sun, to our Queen, and that fair one
  Come to behold our sports.
Each bonny lass here is counted a rare one,
  As those in princes' courts.
     These and we
     With country glee
  Will teach the woods to resound,
    And the hills with Echo's hollow.
     Skipping lambs
     Their bleating dams
'Mongst kids shall trip it round;
    For joy thus our wenches we follow.

Wind, jolly huntsmen, your neat bugles shrilly,
   Hounds make a lusty cry;
Spring up, you falconers, the partridges freely,
   Then let your brave hawks fly.
      Horses amain,
        Over ridge, over plain;
The dogs have the stag in chase.
  'Tis a sport to content a king.
     So ho ho! through the skies
     How the proud bird flies,
And sousing kills with a grace!
    Now the deer falls. Hark, how they ring!

UNKNOWN

TOM O' BEDLAM

From the hag and hungry goblin
That into rags would rend ye,
And the spirit that stands by the naked man
In the Book of Moons defend ye!
That of your five sound senses
You never be forsaken,
Nor wander from yourselves with Tom
Abroad to beg your bacon.
    While I do sing 'Any food, any feeding,
    Feeding, drink or clothing.'
    Come dame or maid, be not afraid,
    Poor Tom will injure nothing.

Of thirty bare years have I
Twice twenty been enragéd,

And of forty been three times fifteen
In durance soundly cagéd
On the lordly lofts of Bedlam,
With stubble soft and dainty,
Brave bracelets strong, sweet whips ding-dong,
And wholesome hunger plenty.
    And now I sing &c.

With a thought I took for maudlin
And a cruse of cockle porridge,
With a thing thus tall, sky bless you all,
I befell into this dotage.
I slept not since the conquest,
Till then I never waked,
Till the roguish boy of love where I lay
Me found and stripp'd me naked.
    And now I sing &c.

When I short have shorn my sour face
And swigg'd my horny barrel,
In an oaken inn I pound my skin
As a suit of gilt apparel.
The moon's my constant mistress,
And the lowly owl my marrow,
The flaming drake and the nightcrow make
Me music to my sorrow.
    While I do sing &c.

The palsy plagues my pulses
When I prig your pigs or pullen,
Your culvers take, or matchless make
Your chanticleer or sullen.

When I want provant with Humphrey
I sup, and when benighted
I repose in Paul's with waking souls,
Yet never am affrighted.
  But I do sing &c.

I know more than Apollo,
For oft when he lies sleeping
I see the stars at bloody wars
In the wounded welkin weeping;
The moon embrace her shepherd
And the queen of love her warrior,
While the first doth horn the star of morn
And the next the heavenly farrier.
  While I do sing &c.

The gipsy snap and Pedro
Are none of Tom's comradoes.
The punk I scorn and the cut-purse sworn
And the roaring boys' bravado.
The meek, the white, the gentle,
Me handle, touch and spare not,
But those that cross Tom Rhinosceros
Do what the panther dare not.
  Although I sing &c.

With a host of furious fancies
Whereof I am commander,
With a burning spear and a horse of air
To the wilderness I wander.

By a knight of ghosts and shadows
I summon'd am to tourney,
Ten leagues beyond the wide world's end.
Methinks it is no journey.
    Yet will I sing &c.

JOHN DONNE
(1573—1631)

THE GOOD-MORROW

I wonder, by my troth, what thou and I
Did, till we loved? were we not weaned till then?
But sucked on country pleasures, childishly?
Or snorted we in the Seven Sleepers' den?
'Twas so; but this, all pleasures fancies be;
If ever any beauty I did see,
Which I desired, and got, 'twas but a dream of thee.

And now good-morrow to our waking souls,
Which watch not one another out of fear;
For love all love of other sights controls,
And makes one little room an everywhere.
Let sea-discoverers to new worlds have gone;
Let maps to other, worlds on worlds have shown;
Let us possess one world; each hath one, and is one.

My face in thine eye, thine in mine appears,
And true plain hearts do in the faces rest;
Where can we find two better hemispheres
Without sharp north, without declining west?

Whatever dies, was not mixed equally;
If our two loves be one, or thou and I
Love so alike that none can slacken, none can die.

SONG

Sweetest love, I do not go
  For weariness of thee,
Nor in hope the world can show
  A fitter love for me;
    But since that I
Must die at last, 'tis best,
To use myself in jest
  Thus by feigned deaths to die.

Yesternight the sun went hence,
  And yet is here to-day;
He hath no desire nor sense,
  Nor half so short a way;
    Then fear not me,
But believe that I shall make
Speedier journeys, since I take
  More wings and spurs than he.

Oh, how feeble is man's power,
  That if good fortune fall,
Cannot add another hour,
  Nor a lost hour recall!
    But come bad chance,
And we join to it our strength,
And we teach it art and length,
  Itself o'er us to advance.

When thou sigh'st, thou sigh'st not wind,
   But sigh'st my soul away;
When thou weep'st, unkindly kind,
   My life's blood doth decay.
     It cannot be
That thou lov'st me, as thou say'st,
If in thine my life thou waste;
   Thou art the best of me.

Let not thy divining heart
   Forethink me any ill,
Destiny may take thy part,
   And may thy fears fulfil;
     But think that we
Are but turned aside to sleep;
They who one another keep
   Alive, ne'er parted be.

THE ANNIVERSARY

All Kings, and all their favourites,
   All glory of honours, beauties, wits,
The sun itself, which makes times, as they pass,
Is elder by a year now, than it was
When thou and I first one another saw:
All other things to their destruction draw,
   Only our love hath no decay;
This, no tomorrow hath, nor yesterday;
Running, it never runs from us away,
But truly keeps his first, last, everlasting day.

Two graves must hide thine and my corse;
 If one might, death were no divorce.
Alas, as well as other princes, we,
(Who prince enough in one another be)
Must leave at last in death, these eyes and ears
Oft fed with true oaths and with sweet salt tears;
 But souls where nothing dwells but love
(All other thoughts being inmates) then shall prove
This, or a love increased there above,
When bodies to their graves, souls from their graves
                                        remove.

And then we shall be throughly blest,
 But we no more than all the rest;
Here upon earth, we're kings, and none but we
Can be such kings, nor of such subjects be.
Who is so safe as we? where none can do
Treason to us, except one of us two.
 True and false fears let us refrain,
Let us love nobly, and live, and add again
Years and years unto years, till we attain
To write threescore: this is the second of our reign.

A VALEDICTION: FORBIDDING MOURNING

As virtuous men pass mildly away,
 And whisper to their souls, to go,
Whilst some of their sad friends do say
 'The breath goes now,' and some say 'no':

So let us melt, and make no noise,
 No tear-floods nor sigh-tempests move;

'Twere profanation of our joys
  To tell the laity our love.

Moving of th'earth brings harms and fears.
  Men reckon what it did and meant;
But trepidation of the spheres,
  Though greater far, is innocent.

Dull sublunary lovers' love
  (Whose soul is sense) cannot admit
Absence, because it doth remove
  Those things which elemented it.

But we by a love so much refin'd
  That ourselves know not what it is,
Inter-assured of the mind,
  Care less, eyes, lips and hands to miss.

Our two souls therefore, which are one,
  Though I must go, endure not yet
A breach, but an expansion,
  Like gold to airy thinness beat.

If they be two, they are two so
  As stiff twin compasses are two;
Thy soul, the fixed foot, makes no show
  To move, but doth if th'other do.

And though it in the centre sit,
  Yet when the other far doth roam
It leans, and harkens after it,
  And grows erect as that comes home.

Such wilt thou be to me, who must
　　Like th'other foot obliquely run;
Thy firmness makes my circle just,
　　And makes me end where I begun.

THE DREAM

Dear love, for nothing less than thee
Would I have broke this happy dream,
　　　It was a theme
For reason, much too strong for fantasy.
Therefore thou waked'st me wisely; yet
My dream thou brok'st not, but continued'st it.
Thou art so true that thoughts of thee suffice
To make dreams truths and fables histories;
Enter these arms, for since thou thought'st it best
Not to dream all my dream, let's act the rest.

As lightning, or a taper's light,
Thine eyes, and not thy noise, waked me;
　　　Yet I thought thee—
For thou lov'st truth—an angel, at first sight;
But when I saw thou saw'st my heart,
And knew'st my thoughts beyond an angel's art,
When thou knew'st what I dreamt, when
　　　　　　thou knew'st when
Excess of joy would wake me, and cam'st then,
I must confess it could not choose but be
Profane to think thee anything but thee.

Coming and staying show'd thee thee,
But rising makes me doubt that now
　　　Thou art not thou.

That Love is weak where Fear's as strong as he;
'Tis not all spirit pure and brave
If mixture it of Fear, Shame, Honour have
Perchance as torches, which must ready be,
Men light and put out, so thou deal'st with me.
Thou cam'st to kindle, go'st to come: then I
Will dream that hope again, but else would die.

THE ECSTASY

Where, like a pillow on a bed,
  A pregnant bank swell'd up, to rest
The violet's reclining head,
  Sat we two, one another's best.
Our hands were firmly cèmented
  By a fast balm which thence did spring;
Our eye-beams twisted, and did thread
  Our eyes upon one double string.
So to engraft our hands, as yet
  Was all the means to make us one;
And pictures in our eyes to get
  Was all our propagation.
As 'twixt two equal armies Fate
  Suspends uncertain victory,
Our souls—which to advance their state
  Were gone out—hung 'twixt her and me.
And whilst our souls negotiate there,
  We like sepulchral statues lay;
All day the same our postures were,
  And we said nothing, all the day.
If any, so by love refined,
  That he soul's language understood,

And by good love were grown all mind,
  Within convenient distance stood,
He (though he knew not which soul spake,
  Because both meant, both spake the same)
Might thence a new concoction take,
  And part far purer than he came.
This Ecstasy doth unperplex
  (We said) and tell us what we love,
We see by this, it was not sex,
  We see, we saw not what did move:
But as all several souls contain
  Mixture of things, they know not what,
Love, these mixed souls doth mix again,
  And makes both one, each this and that.
A single violet transplant,
  The strength, the colour, and the size
(All which before was poor and scant)
  Redoubles still, and multiplies.
When love, with one another so
  Interinanimates two souls,
That abler soul, which thence doth flow,
  Defects of loneliness controls.
We then, who are this new soul, know,
  Of what we are composed and made,
For th' Atomies of which we grow,
  Are souls, whom no change can invade.
But O alas, so long, so far
  Our bodies why do we forbear?
They are ours, though they are not we, we are
  The intelligences, they the sphere.
We owe them thanks, because they thus,
  Did us, to us, at first convey,

Yielded their forces, sense, to us,
　　Nor are dross to us, but allay.
On man heaven's influence works not so
　　But that it first imprints the air,
So soul into the soul may flow,
　　Though it to body first repair.
As our blood labours to beget
　　Spirits, as like souls as it can,
Because such fingers need to knit
　　That subtle knot, which makes us man:
So must pure lovers' souls descend
　　T'affections, and to faculties,
Which sense may reach and apprehend,
　　Else a great Prince in prison lies.
To our bodies turn we then, that so
　　Weak men on love revealed may look;
Love's mysteries in souls do grow,
　　But yet the body is his book.
And if some lover, such as we,
　　Have heard this dialogue of one,
Let him still mark us, he shall see
　　Small change, when we are to bodies gone.

FROM 'THE SECOND ANNIVERSARY'

... Think then, my soul, that death is but a groom,
Which brings a taper to the outward room,
Whence thou spiest first a little glimmering light,
And after brings it nearer to thy sight;
For such approaches doth heaven make in death.
Think thyself labouring now with broken breath,

And think those broken and soft notes to be
Division, and thy happiest harmony.
Think thee laid on thy death-bed, loose and slack,
And think that but unbinding of a pack,
To take one precious thing, thy soul, from thence.
Think thyself parch'd with fever's violence;
Anger thine ague more, by calling it
Thy physic; chide the slackness of the fit.
Think that thou hear'st thy knell, and think no more,
But that, as bells call'd thee to church before,
So this to the triumphant church calls thee.
Think Satan's sergeants round about thee be,
And think that but for legacies they thrust;
Give one thy pride, to another give thy lust;
Give them those sins which they gave thee before,
And trust th'immaculate blood to wash thy score,
Think thy friends weeping round, and think that they
Weep but because they go not yet thy way.
Think that they close thine eyes, and think in this,
That they confess much in the world amiss,
Who dare not trust a dead man's eye with that
Which they from God and angels cover not.
Think that they shroud thee up, and think from thence
They reinvest thee in white innocence.
Think that thy body rots, and—if so low,
Thy soul exalted so, thy thoughts can go—
Think thee a prince, who of themselves create
Worms, which insensibly devour their state.
Think that they bury thee, and think that rite
Lays thee to sleep but a Saint Lucy's night. . . .

HYMN TO GOD, MY GOD, IN MY SICKNESS

Since I am coming to that holy room,
　　Where, with thy choir of saints for evermore,
I shall be made thy music; as I come
　　I tune the instrument here at the door,
　　And what I must do then, think here before.

Whilst my physicians by their love are grown
　　Cosmographers, and I their map, who lie
Flat on this bed, that by them may be shown
　　That this is my south-west discovery
　　Per fretum febris, by these straits to die,

I joy, that in these straits, I see my west;
　　For, though their currents yield return to none,
What shall my west hurt me? As west and east
　　In all flat maps (and I am one) are one,
　　So death doth touch the resurrection.

Is the pacific sea my home? Or are
　　The eastern riches? Is Jerusalem?
Anyan, and Magellan, and Gibraltar,
　　All straits, and none but straits, are ways to them,
　　Whether where Japhet dwelt, or Cham, or Sem

We think that Paradise and Calvary,
　　Christ's Cross, and Adam's tree, stood in one place;
Look, Lord, and find both Adams met in me;
　　As the first Adam's sweat surrounds my face,
　　May the last Adam's blood my soul embrace.

So, in his purple wrapp'd, receive me, Lord,
　　By these his thorns give me his other crown;

And as to others' souls I preach'd thy word,
  Be this my text, my sermon to mine own,
  Therefore that he may raise the Lord throws down.

SONNETS

(i)

At the round earth's imagin'd corners, blow
Your trumpets, Angels, and arise, arise
From death, you numberless infinities
Of souls, and to your scatter'd bodies go,
All whom the flood did, and fire shall o'erthrow,
All whom war, dearth, age, agues, tyrannies,
Despair, law, chance, hath slain, and you whose eyes,
Shall behold God, and never taste death's woe.
But let them sleep, Lord, and me mourn a space,
For, if above all these, my sins abound,
'Tis late to ask abundance of thy grace,
When we are there; here on this lowly ground,
Teach me how to repent; for that's as good
As if thou hadst seal'd my pardon, with thy blood.

(ii)

Batter my heart, three-person'd God; for, you
As yet but knock, breathe, shine, and seek to mend;
That I may rise, and stand, o'erthrow me, and bend
Your force, to break, blow, burn and make me new.
I, like an usurped town, to another due,
Labour to admit you, but O, to no end.
Reason, your viceroy in me, me should defend,
But is captiv'd, and proves weak or untrue.
Yet dearly I love you, and would be loved fain,

But am betroth'd unto your enemy:
Divorce me, untie, or break that knot again,
Take me to you, imprison me, for I
Except you enthrall me, never shall be free,
Nor ever chaste, except you ravish me.

BEN JONSON
(1573—1637)

SONG

Still to be neat, still to be drest,
As you were going to a feast;
Still to be powder'd, still perfumed:
Lady, it is to be presumed,
Though art's hid causes are not found,
All is not sweet, all is not sound.

Give me a look, give me a face
That makes simplicity a grace;
Robes loosely flowing, hair as free:
Such sweet neglect more taketh me
Than all th' adulteries of art;
They strike mine eyes, but not my heart.

EPITAPH ON SALATHIEL PAVY

A CHILD OF QUEEN ELIZABETH'S CHAPEL

Weep with me, all you that read
　　This little story;
And know, for whom a tear you shed
　　Death's self is sorry.

'Twas a child that so did thrive
   In grace and feature,
As Heaven and Nature seem'd to strive
   Which own'd the creature.
Years he number'd scarce thirteen
   When Fates turn'd cruel,
Yet three fill'd zodiacs had he been
   The Stage's jewel;
And did act (what now we moan)
   Old men so duly,
As sooth the Parcae thought him one,
   He play'd so truly.
So, by error, to his fate
   They all consented;
But, viewing him since, alas, too late!
   They have repented;
And have sought, to give new birth,
   In baths to steep him;
But, being so much too good for earth,
   Heaven vows to keep him.

THE TRIUMPH

See the Chariot at hand here of Love,
   Wherein my Lady rideth!
Each that draws is a swan or a dove,
   And well the car Love guideth.
As she goes, all hearts do duty
         Unto her beauty;
And enamour'd do wish, so they might
         But enjoy such a sight.

That they still were to run by her side,
Thorough swords, thorough seas, whither she would
ride.

Do but look on her eyes, they do light
    All that Love's world compriseth!
Do but look on her hair, it is bright
    As Love's star when it riseth!
Do but mark, her forehead's smoother
                Than words that soothe her;
And from her arch'd brows such a grace
                Sheds itself through the face,
As alone there triumphs to the life
All the gain, all the good, of the elements' strife.

Have you seen but a bright lily grow
    Before rude hands have touch'd it?
Have you mark'd but the fall of the snow
    Before the soil hath smutch'd it?
Have you felt the wool of beaver,
                Or swan's down ever?
Or have smelt o' the bud o' the brier,
                Or the nard in the fire?
Or have tasted the bag of the bee?
O so white, O so soft, O so sweet is she!

ODE TO HIMSELF

Come, leave the loathed stage,
    And the more loathsome age,
Where pride and impudence, in faction knit,
    Usurp the chair of wit!

Indicting and arraigning every day
    Something they call a play.
  Let their fastidious vain
  Commission of the brain
Run on, and rage, sweat, censure and condemn:
They were not made for thee, less thou for them.

    Say, that thou pour'st them wheat,
    And they will acorns eat:
'Twere simple fury, still, thyself to waste
    On such as have no taste!
To offer them a surfeit of pure bread,
    Whose appetites are dead!
  No, give them grains their fill,
  Husks, draff to drink and swill.
If they love lees, and leave the lusty wine,
Envy them not, their palate's with the swine.

    No doubt some mouldy tale
    Like *Pericles*, and stale
As the shrieve's crusts, and nasty as his fish —
    Scraps out of every dish
Thrown forth, and rak'd into the common tub,
    May keep up the Play-club.
    There, sweepings do as well
    As the best order'd meal,
For who the relish of these guests will fit
Needs set them but the alms-basket of wit.

    And much good do't you then:
    Brave plush and velvet men

Can feed on orts; and safe in your stage-clothes
  Dare quit, upon your oaths,
The stagers and the stage-wrights too, your peers,
  Of larding your large ears
  With their foul comic socks,
  Wrought upon twenty blocks:
Which, if they are torn and turn'd and patch'd enough,
The gamesters share your gilt, and you their stuff.

  Leave things so prostitute,
  And take the Alcaic lute;
Or thine own Horace's or Anacreon's lyre;
  Warm thee by Pindar's fire:
And though their nerves be shrunk and blood be cold,
  Ere years have made thee old,
  Strike that disdainful heat
  Throughout, to their defeat:
As curious fools, and envious of thy strain,
May, blushing, swear no palsy's in thy brain.
  But when they hear thee sing
  The glories of thy king,
His zeal to God, and his just awe o'er men:
  They may, blood-shaken, then
Feel such a flesh-quake to possess their powers
  As they shall cry, Like ours
  In sound of peace or wars,
  No harp e'er hit the stars,
In tuning forth the acts of his sweet reign,
And raising Charles his chariot 'bove his Wain.

AEGLAMOUR SEEKS HIS SHEPHERDESS

...Here was she wont to go! and here! and here!
Just where those daisies, pinks, and violets grow:
The world may find the spring by following her,
For other print her airy steps ne'er left.
Her treading would not bend a blade of grass,
Or shake the downy blow-ball from his stalk!
But like the soft west wind she shot along,
And where she went, the flowers took thickest root,
As she had sow'd them with her odorous foot...

The Sad Shepherd, Act I, Sc. i.

THE PARASITE

...I fear, I shall begin to grow in love
With my dear self, and my most prosperous parts,
They do so spring and burgeon; I can feel
A whimsy in my blood: I know not how,
Success hath made me wanton. I could skip
Out of my skin, now, like a subtle snake,
I am so limber. O! Your parasite
Is a most precious thing, dropt from above,
Not bred 'mongst clods and clodpoles, here on earth.
I muse, the mystery was not made a science,
It is so liberally profest! Almost
All the wise world is little else, in nature,
But parasites or sub-parasites. — And yet,
I mean not those that have your bare town-art,
To know who's fit to feed them; have no house,
No family, no care, and therefore mould

Tales for men's ears, to bait that sense; or get
Kitchen-invention, and some stale receipts
To please the belly, and the groin; not those,
With their court dog-tricks, that can fawn and fleer,
Make their revenue out of legs and faces,
Echo my lord, and lick away a moth:
But your fine elegant rascal, that can rise,
And stoop, almost together, like an arrow;
Shoot through the air as nimbly as a star;
Turn short as doth a swallow; and be here,
And there, and here, and yonder, all at once;
Present to any humour, all occasion;
And change a visor, swifter than a thought!
This is the creature had the art born with him;
Toils not to learn it, but doth practise it
Out of most excellent nature: and such sparks
Are the true parasites, others but their zanies...

Volpone, Act III, Sc. i.

CYRIL TOURNEUR
(1575?—1626)

TO HIS MISTRESS' SKULL

...And now methinks I could e'en chide myself
For doting on her beauty, tho' her death
Shall be reveng'd after no common action.
Does the silk-worm expend her yellow labours
For thee? For thee does she undo herself?
Are lordships sold to maintain ladyships,
For the poor benefit of a bewildering minute?

Why does yon fellow falsify highways,
And put his life between the judge's lips;
To refine such a thing, keeps horse and men
To beat their valours for her?
Surely we are all mad people, and they
Whom we think are, are not; we mistake those;
'Tis we are mad in sense, they but in clothes...

The Revenger's Tragedy, Act III, Sc. i.

JOHN MARSTON
(1575—1634)

PROLOGUE

The rawish dank of clumsy winter ramps
The fluent summer's vein; and drizzling sleet
Chilleth the wan bleak cheek of the numb'd earth,
Whilst snarling gusts nibble the juiceless leaves
From the nak'd shudd'ring branch; and pulls the skin
From off the soft and delicate aspects.
O now, methinks, a sullen tragic scene
Would suit the time with pleasing congruence.
May we be happy in our weak devoir,
And all part pleased in most wish'd content!
But sweat of Hercules can ne'er beget
So blest an issue. Therefore we proclaim,
If any spirit breathes within this round,
Uncapable of weighty passion,
(As from his birth, being hugged in the arms
And nuzzled 'twixt the breasts of happiness)
Who winks, and shuts his apprehension up

From common sense of what men were, and are,
Who would not know what men must be; let such
Hurry amain from our black-visag'd shows;
We shall affright their eyes. But if a breast
Nail'd to the earth with grief; if any heart
Pierc'd through with anguish pant within this ring;
If there be any blood, whose heat is choked
And stifled with true sense of misery;
If aught of these strains fills this consort up,
They arrive most welcome. O that our power
Could lackey or keep wing with our desires;
That with unused peise of style and sense
We might weight massy in judicious scale!
Yet here's the prop that doth support our hopes;
   When our scenes falter, or invention halts,
   Your favour will give crutches to our faults.

Antonio's Revenge.

JOHN FLETCHER
(1579—1625)

ORPHEUS

Orpheus with his lute made trees
And the mountain tops that freeze
Bow themselves when he did sing.
To his music, plants and flowers
Ever sprung; as sun and showers
There had made a lasting spring.
Everything that heard him play,
Even the billows of the sea,
Hung their heads, and then lay by.

In sweet music is such art,
Killing care, and grief of heart,
Fall asleep, or hearing die.

Henry VIII, Act III, Sc. i.

TOBIAS HUME
(?—1645)

SONG

Fain would I change that note
To which fond Love hath charm'd me
Long, long to sing by rote,
Fancying that that harm'd me:
Yet when this thought doth come,
'Love is the perfect sum
   Of all delight,'
I have no other choice
Either for pen or voice
   To sing or write.

O Love! they wrong thee much
That say thy sweet is bitter,
When thy rich fruit is such
As nothing can be sweeter.
Fair house of joy and bliss,
Where truest pleasure is,
   I do adore thee:
I know thee what thou art,
I serve thee with my heart,
   And fall before thee.

JOHN WEBSTER
(1580?—1630?)

CORNELIA'S SONG

Call for the robin-redbreast and the wren,
Since o'er shady groves they hover,
And with leaves and flowers do cover
The friendless bodies of unburied men.
Call unto his funeral dole
The ant, the field-mouse, and the mole,
To rear him hillocks that shall keep him warm,
And (when gay tombs are robb'd) sustain no harm;
But keep the wolf far thence, that's foe to men,
For with his nails he'll dig them up again.

The White Devil.

THE SHROUDING OF THE DUCHESS OF MALFI

Hark! Now everything is still,
The screech-owl and the whistler shrill,
Call upon our dame aloud,
And bid her quickly don her shroud!

Much you had of land and rent;
Your length in clay's now competent:
A long war disturb'd your mind;
Here your perfect peace is sign'd.

Of what is't fools make such vain keeping?
Sin their conception, their birth weeping,
Their life a general mist of error,
Their death a hideous storm of terror.
Strew your hair with powders sweet,
Don clean linen, bathe your feet,
And—the foul fiend more to check—
A crucifix let bless your neck:
'Tis now full tide 'tween night and day;
End your groan and come away.

The Duchess of Malfi.

ALL IS VANITY

All the flowers of the spring
Meet to perfume our burying;
These have but their growing prime,
And man does flourish but his time:
Survey our progress from our birth—
We are set, we grow, we turn to earth.
Courts adieu, and all delights,
All bewitching appetites!
Sweetest breath and clearest eye
Like perfumes go out and die;
And consequently this is done
As shadows wait upon the sun.
Vain the ambition of kings
Who seek by trophies and dead things
To leave a living name behind,
And weave but nets to catch the wind

The Devil's Law-case.

PHINEAS FLETCHER
(1580—1650)

AN HYMN

Drop, drop, slow tears,
　　And bathe those beauteous feet
Which brought from Heaven
　　The news and Prince of Peace:
Cease not, wet eyes,
　　His mercy to entreat;
To cry for vengeance
　　Sin doth never cease.
In your deep floods
　　Drown all my faults and fears;
Nor let His eye
　　See sin, but through my tears.

AURELIAN TOWNSHEND
(1583?—1643)

ROCK CONSTANCY

Though regions far divided
　　And tedious tracts of time,
By my misfortunes guided,
　　Make absence thought a crime;
Though we were set asunder
　　As far as East from West
Love still would work this wonder,
　　Thou shouldst be in my breast.

How slow, alas, are paces,
  Compared to thoughts that fly
In moment back to places,
  Whole ages scarce descry.
The body must have pauses;
  The mind requires no rest;
Love needs no second causes
  To guide thee to my breast.

Accept in that poor dwelling,
  But welcome, nothing great,
With pride no turrets swelling,
  But lowly as the seat;
Where, though not much delighted,
  In peace thou mayst be blest,
Unfeasted yet unfrighted
  By rivals, in my breast.

But this is not the diet
  That doth for glory strive;
Poor beauties seek in quiet
  To keep one heart alive.
The price of his ambition
  That looks for such a guest
Is, hopeless of fruition,
  To beat an empty breast.

See then my last lamenting.
  Upon a cliff I'll sit,
Rock Constancy presenting,
  Till I grow part of it;
My tears a quicksand feeding,
  Whereon no foot can rest,

My sighs a tempest breeding
  About my stony breast.

Those arms, wherein wide open
  Love's fleet was wont to put,
Shall laid across betoken
  That haven's mouth is shut.
Mine eyes no light shall cherish
  For ships at sea distrest,
But darkling let them perish
  Or split against my breast.

Yet if I can discover
  When thine before it rides,
To show I was thy lover
  I'll smooth my rugged sides,
And so much better measure
  Afford thee than the rest,
Thou shalt have no displeasure
  By knocking at my breast.

A DIALOGUE BETWIXT TIME AND A PILGRIM

Pilgrim. Aged man, that mows these fields!
Time.   Pilgrim, speak, what is thy will?
Pilgrim. Whose soil is this that such sweet pasture yields?
           Or who art thou, whose foot stands never still?
           Or where am I? *Time.* In love.
Pilgrim.   His Lordship lies above.
Time.   Yes, and below, and round about,
             Wherein all sorts of flowers are growing,
           Which, as the early spring puts out,
             Time falls as fast a-mowing.

Pilgrim. If thou art Time, these flowers have lives,
          And then I fear
       Under some lily she I love
       May now be growing there.

Time.   And in some thistle or some spire of grass
       My scythe thy stalk before hers come may pass.

Pilgrim. Wilt thou provide it may? *Time.* No. *Pilg.* Allege the
                                                  cause.

Time.   Because Time cannot alter but obey Fate's laws.

Chorus. Then happy those whom Fate, that is the stronger,
       Together twists their threads, and yet draws hers the
                                                  longer.

LORD HERBERT OF CHERBURY
(1583—1648)

AN ODE UPON A QUESTION MOVED, WHETHER LOVE SHOULD CONTINUE FOR EVER?

Having interr'd her infant-birth,
   The watery ground that late did mourn
   Was strew'd with flowers for the return
Of the wish'd bridegroom of the earth.

The well accorded birds did sing
   Their hymns unto the pleasant time,
   And in a sweet consorted chime
Did welcome in the cheerful spring.

To which, soft whistles of the wind
   And warbling murmurs of a brook
   And varied notes of leaves that shook
As harmonies of parts did bind.

While doubling joy unto each other,
    All in so rare consent was shown,
    No happiness that came alone,
Nor pleasure that was not another.

When, with a love none can express,
    That mutually happy pair
    Melander and Celinda fair
The season with their loves did bless.

Walking thus towards a pleasant grove,
    Which did, it seem'd, in new delight
    The pleasures of the time unite
To give a triumph to their love,

They stay'd at last, and on the grass
    Reposed so, as o'er his breast
    She bow'd her gracious head to rest,
Such a weight as no burden was.

While over either's compass'd waist
    Their folded arms were so compos'd
    As if, in straitest bonds inclos'd,
They suffer'd for joys they did taste.

Long their fix'd eyes to heaven bent,
    Unchanged, they did never move,
    As if so great and pure a love
No glass but it could represent.

When with a sweet, though troubled look,
    She first brake silence, saying, 'Dear friend,
    O that our love might take no end,
Or never had beginning took!

I speak not this with a false heart —'
   (Wherewith his hand she gently strain'd) —
   'Or that would change a love maintain'd
With so much faith on either part.

Nay, I protest, though Death with his
   Worst counsel should divide us here,
   His terrors could not make me fear
To come where your lov'd presence is.

Only if love's fire with the breath
   Of life be kindled, I doubt
   With our last air 'twill be breath'd out,
And quenched with the cold of death.

That if affection be a line
   That is clos'd up in our last hour,
   O how 'twould grieve me, any power
Could force so dear a love as mine!'

She scarce had done, when his shut eyes
   An inward joy did represent,
   To hear Celinda thus intent
To a love he so much did prize.

Then with a look, it seem'd, denied
   All earthly pow'r but hers, yet so
   As if to her breath he did owe
This borrow'd life, he thus replied:

'O you, wherein, they say, souls rest
   Till they descend pure heavenly fires,
   Shall lustful and corrupt desires
With your immortal seed be blest?

And shall our love, so far beyond
    That low and dying appetite,
    And which so chaste desires unite,
Not hold in an eternal bond?

Is it because we should decline
    And wholly from our thoughts exclude
    Objects that may the sense delude,
And study only the divine?

No, sure, for if none can ascend
    Ev'n to the visible degree
    Of things created, how should we
The invisible comprehend?

Or rather, since that Pow'r express'd
    His greatness in his works alone,
    Being here best in his creatures known,
Why is he not lov'd in them best?

But is't not true, which you pretend,
    That since our love and knowledge here
    Only as parts of life appear
So they with it should take their end.

O no, Belov'd, I am most sure
    Those virtuous habits we acquire
    As being with the soul entire
Must with it evermore endure.

For if where sins and vice reside
    We find so foul a guilt remain,
    As never dying in his stain
Still punish'd in the soul doth bide,

Much more that true and real joy
   Which in a virtuous love is found
   Must be more solid in its ground
Than fate or death can e'er destroy.

Else should our souls in vain elect,
   And vainer yet were heaven's laws,
   When to an everlasting cause
They gave a perishing effect.

Not here on earth, then, nor above,
   Our good affection can impair,
   For where God doth admit the fair
Think you that he excludeth love?

These eyes again, then, eyes shall see,
   And hands again these hands enfold,
   And all chaste pleasures can be told
Shall with us everlasting be.

For if no use of sense remain
   When bodies once this life forsake,
   Or could they no delight partake,
Why should they ever rise again?

And if every imperfect mind
   Make love the end of knowledge here,
   How perfect will our love be, where
All imperfection is refin'd?

Let then no doubt, Celinda, touch,
   Much less your fairest mind invade;
   Were not our souls immortal made,
Our equal loves can make them such.

So when one wing can make no way,
  Two joined can themselves dilate,
  So can two persons propagate
When singly either would decay.

So when from hence we shall be gone,
  And be no more, nor you, nor I,
  As one another's mystery
Each shall be both, yet both be one.'

This said, in her uplifted face
  Her eyes, which did that beauty crown,
  Were like two stars, that having fall'n down
Look up again to find their place:

While such a moveless silent peace
  Did seize on their becalmèd sense,
  One would have thought some influence
Their ravish'd spirits did possess.

UNKNOWN
(W. BASSE? c. 1602)

A MEMENTO FOR MORTALITY
(On the Tombs in Westminster Abbey)

Mortality, behold and fear;
What a change of flesh is here!
Think how many royal bones
Sleep within this heap of stones;

Hence remov'd from beds of ease,
Dainty fare, and what might please,
Fretted roofs, and costly shows,
To a roof that flats the nose:
Which proclaims all flesh is grass,
How the world's fair glories pass:
That there is no trust in health,
In youth, in age, in greatness, wealth:
For if such could have repriev'd,
Those had been immortal lived.
Know from this the world's a snare,
How that greatness is but care,
How all pleasures are but pain,
And how short they do remain:
For here they lie had realms and lands,
That now want strength to stir their hands;
Where from their pulpits seal'd with dust
They preach *In greatness is no trust.*
Here's an acre sown indeed
With the richest royal seed
That the earth did e'er suck in
Since the first man died for sin.
Here the bones of birth have cried
Though Gods they were, as men have died.
Here are sands, ignoble things,
Dropped from the ruined sides of kings;
With whom the poor man's earth being shown
The difference is not easily known.
Here's a world of pomp and state,
Forgotten, dead, disconsolate.
Think then, this scythe that mows down kings
Exempts no meaner mortal things.

Then bid the wanton lady tread
Amid these mazes of the dead.
And these truly understood
More shall cool and quench the blood
Than her many sports a day
And her nightly wanton play.
Bid her paint till day of doom,
To this favour she must come.
Bid the merchant gather wealth,
The usurer exact by stealth,
The proud man beat it from his thought,
Yet to this shape all must be brought.

WILLIAM DRUMMOND
(1585—1649)

THE WORLD A HUNT

The World a hunting is,
The prey, poor Man, the Nimrod fierce is Death;
His speedy greyhounds are
Lust, Sickness, Envy, Care,
Strife that ne'er falls amiss,
With all those ills which haunt us while we breathe
Now if, by chance, we fly
Of these the eager chase,
Old Age with stealing pace
Casts up his nets, and there we panting die.

GEORGE WITHER
(1588—1667)

WHAT CARE I?

Shall I, wasting in despair,
Die because a woman's fair?
Or make pale my cheeks with care
'Cause another's rosy are?
Be she fairer than the day,
Or the flow'ry meads in May,
  If she think not well of me,
  What care I how fair she be?

Shall my silly heart be pined
'Cause I see a woman kind?
Or a well disposèd nature
Joinèd with a lovely feature?
Be she meeker, kinder, than
Turtle-dove or pelican,
  If she be not so to me,
  What care I how kind she be?

Shall a woman's virtues move
Me to perish for her love?
Or her well-deservings known
Make me quite forget my own?
Be she with that goodness blest
Which may merit name of Best,
  If she be not such to me,
  What care I how good she be?

'Cause her fortune seems too high,
Shall I play the fool and die?
She that bears a noble mind,
If not outward helps she find,
Thinks what with them he would do
That without them dares her woo;
   And unless that mind I see,
   What care I how great she be?

Great, or good, or kind, or fair,
I will ne'er the more despair;
If she love me, this believe,
I will die ere she shall grieve;
If she slight me when I woo,
I can scorn and let her go;
   For if she be not for me,
   What care I for whom she be?

ROBERT HERRICK
(1591—1674)

TO DAFFODILS

Fair daffodils, we weep to see
   You haste away so soon;
As yet the early-rising sun
    Has not attain'd his noon.
     Stay, stay
    Until the hasting day
     Has run
    But to the evensong;

And, having pray'd together, we
    Will go with you along.

We have short time to stay, as you,
  We have as short a spring;
As quick a growth to meet decay,
    As you, or anything.
        We die
     As your hours do, and dry
        Away
    Like to the summer's rain;
Or as the pearls of morning's dew,
    Ne'er o be found again.

UPON JULIA'S CLOTHES

Whenas in silks my Julia goes,
Then, then, methinks, how sweetly flows
The liquefaction of her clothes!

Next, when I cast mine eyes and see
That brave vibration each way free,
—O how that glittering taketh me!

THE NIGHT-PIECE: TO JULIA

Her eyes the glow-worm lend thee,
The shooting stars attend thee;
    And the elves also,
     Whose little eyes glow
Like the sparks of fire, befriend thee.

No Will-o'-the-wisp mislight thee,
Nor snake or slow-worm bite thee;
  But on, on thy way
  Not making a stay,
Since ghost there's none to affright thee.

Let not the dark thee cumber:
What though the moon does slumber?
  The stars of the night
  Will lend thee their light
Like tapers clear without number,

Then, Julia, let me woo thee,
Thus, thus to come unto me;
  And when I shall meet
  Thy silv'ry feet,
My soul I'll pour into thee.

TO MUSIC, TO BECALM HIS FEVER

Charm me asleep, and melt me so
 With thy delicious numbers,
That, being ravish'd, hence I go
 Away in easy slumbers.
  Ease my sick head,
  And make my bed,
Thou power that canst sever
  From me this ill,
  And quickly still,
  Though thou not kill
  My fever.

Thou sweetly canst convert the same
 From a consuming fire

Into a gentle licking flame,
And make it thus expire.
Then make me weep
My pains asleep;
And give me such reposes
That I, poor I,
May think thereby
I live and die
'Mongst roses.

Fall on me like the silent dew,
Or like those maiden showers
Which, by the peep of day, do strew
A baptism o'er the flowers.
Melt, melt my pains
With thy soft strains;
That, having ease me given,
With full delight
I leave this light,
And take my flight
For Heaven.

HIS POETRY HIS PILLAR

Only a little more
I have to write,
Then I'll give o'er,
And bid the world good-night.

'Tis but a flying minute
That I must stay,
Or linger in it;
And then I must away.

O time that cutt'st down all!
    And scarce leav'st here
    Memorial
Of any men that were.

How many lie forgot
    In vaults beneath?
    And piecemeal rot
Without a fame in death?

Behold this living stone
    I rear for me,
    Ne'er to be thrown
Down, envious Time, by thee.

Pillars let some set up,
    If so they please;
    Here is my hope,
And my Pyramides.

WILLIAM BROWNE
(1592—1643?)

SONG OF THE SIRENS

Steer hither, steer, your wingéd pines,
    All beaten mariners,
Here lie Love's undiscovered mines
    A prey to passengers;
    Perfumes far sweeter than the best
Which make the Phoenix urn and nest.
    Fear not your ships,

Nor any to oppose you save our lips,
   But come on shore,
Where no joy dies till love hath gotten more.

For swelling waves, our panting breasts,
   Where never storms arise,
Exchange; and be awhile our guests;
   For stars gaze on our eyes.
The compass love shall hourly sing,
And as he goes about the ring,
   We will not miss
To tell each point he nameth with a kiss.

                   The Inner Temple Masque.

EPITAPH ON THE COUNTESS DOWAGER OF PEMBROKE

Underneath this sable hearse
Lies the subject of all verse:
Sidney's sister, Pembroke's mother:
Death, ere thou hast slain another
Fair and learn'd and good as she,
Time shall throw a dart at thee.

FRANCIS QUARLES
(1592—1644)

THE UNSETTLED SOUL

Like to the arctic needle, that doth guide
   The wand'ring shade by his magnetic pow'r,
And leaves his silken gnomon to decide
   The question of the controverted hour,

First frantics up and down from side to side,
　　And restless beats his crystal'd iv'ry case,
　　With vain impatience jets from place to place,
And seeks the bosom of his frozen bride;
　　At length he slacks his motion, and doth rest
His trembling point at his bright pole's beloved breast

E'en so my soul, being hurried here and there,
　　By ev'ry object that presents delight,
Fain would be settled, but she knows not where;
　　She likes at morning what she loathes at night:
She bows to honour; then she lends an ear
　　　　To that sweet swan-like voice of dying pleasure,
　　　　Then tumbles in the scatter'd heaps of treasure;
Now flatter'd with false hope; now foil'd with fear:
　　　　Thus finding all the world's delight to be
But empty toys, good God, she points alone to thee.

But hath the virtued steel a power to move?
　　Or can the untouch'd needle point aright?
Or can my wand'ring thoughts forbear to rove,
　　Unguided by the virtue of thy sprite?
O hath my leaden soul the art t'improve
　　　　Her wasted talent, and, unrais'd, aspire
　　　　In this sad moulting time of her desire?
Not first belov'd, have I the power to love;
　　　　I cannot stir, but as thou please to move me,
Nor can my heart return thee love, until thou love me.

The still commandress of the silent night
　　Borrows her beams from her bright brother's eye;

His fair aspect fills her sharp horns with light,
  If he withdraw, her flames are quench'd and die:
E'en so the beams of thy enlight'ning sprite,
    Infus'd and shot into my dark desire,
    Inflame my thoughts, and fill my soul with fire,
That I am ravish'd with a new delight;
    But if thou shroud thy face, my glory fades,
And I remain a nothing, all compos'd of shades.

Eternal God! O thou that only art
  The sacred fountain of eternal light,
And blessed loadstone of my better part,
  O thou, my heart's desire, my soul's delight!
Reflect upon my soul, and touch my heart,
    And then my heart shall prize no good above thee;
    And then my soul shall know thee; knowing, love thee;
And then my trembling thoughts shall never start
  Fro thy commands, or swerve the least degree,
Or once presume to move, but as they move in thee.

HENRY KING
(1592—1669)

AN ACKNOWLEDGMENT
(of a Locket received)

  My best of friends! what needs a chain to tie
  One by your merit bound a votary?
  Think you I have some plot upon my peace,
  I would this bondage change for a release?
  Since 'twas my fate your prisoner to be,
  Heav'n knows, I nothing fear but liberty.

Yet you do well, that study to prevent,
After so rich a stock of favour spent
On one so worthless, lest my memory
Should let so dear an obligation die
Without record. This made my precious friend
Her token, as an antidote, to send,
Against forgetful poisons; that as they
Who Vespers late, and early Mattins say
Upon their beads, so on this linked score
In golden numbers I might reckon o'er
Your virtues and my debt, which does surmount
The trivial laws of popular account:
For that, within this emblematic knot,
Your beauteous mind, and my own fate is wrote.

The sparkling constellation which combines
The lock, is your dear self, whose worth outshines
Most of your sex; so solid and so clear
You like a perfect diamond appear;
Casting from your example, fuller light
Than those dim sparks which glaze the brow of night
And gladding all your friends, as doth the ray
Of that east-star which wakes the cheerful day.

But the black map of death and discontent
Behind that adamantine firmament,
That luckless figure, which, like Calvary,
Stands strew'd and copied out in skulls, is I:
Whose life your absence clouds, and makes my time
Move blindfold in the dark ecliptic line.

Then wonder not, if my removed sun
So low within the western tropic run;
My eyes no day in this horizon see,
Since where you are not, all is night to me.

Lastly, the anchor which enfasten'd lies
Upon a pair of deaths, sadly applies
That monument of rest, which harbour must
Our shipwrecked fortunes in a road of dust.

So then, how late soe'er my joyless life
Be tired out in this affection's strife:
Though my tempestuous fancy, like the sky,
Travail with storms, and through my watery eye
Sorrow's high-going waves spring many a leak;
Though sighs blow loud, till my heart's cordage break;
Though faith, and all my wishes, prove untrue,
Yet death shall fix and anchor me with you.
'Tis some poor comfort, that this mortal scope
Will period, though never crown, my hope.

THE SURRENDER

My once dear love! hapless that I no more
Must call thee so; the rich affection's store
That fed our hopes, lies now exhaust and spent,
Like sums of treasure unto bankrupts lent.

We, that did nothing study but the way
To love each other, with which thoughts the day

Rose with delight to us and, with them, set,
Must learn the hateful art, how to forget.

We, that did nothing wish that Heav'n could give,
Beyond ourselves, nor did desire to live
Beyond that wish, all these now cancel must,
As if not writ in faith, but words and dust.

Yet witness those clear loves which lovers make,
Witness the chaste desires that never brake
Into unruly heats; witness that breast
Which in thy bosom anchor'd his whole rest,
'Tis no default in us; I dare acquite
Thy maiden faith, thy purpose, fair and white
As thy pure self. Cross planets did envy
Us to each other, and Heaven did untie
Faster than vows could bind. O that the stars,
When lovers meet, should stand opposed in wars!

Since then some higher destinies command,
Let us not strive nor labour to withstand
What is past help. The longest date of grief
Can never yield a hope of our relief;
And though we waste ourselves in moist laments,
Tears may drown us, but not our discontents.

Fold back our arms, take home our fruitless loves,
That must new fortunes try, like turtle doves
Dislodged from their haunts. We must in tears
Unwind a love knit up in many years.
In this last kiss I here surrender thee
Back to thyself, — so thou again art free.

Thou in another, sad as that, resend
The truest heart that lover e'er did lend.

Now turn from each. So fare our sever'd hearts
As the divorc'd soul from her body parts.

THE EXEQUY

Accept, thou shrine of my dead saint,
Instead of dirges, this complaint;
And for sweet flowers to crown thy hearse
Receive a strew of weeping verse
From thy griev'd friend, whom thou mightst see
Quite melted into tears for thee.

Dear loss! since thy untimely fate,
My talk hath been to meditate
On thee, on thee; thou art the book,
The library whereon I look
Though almost blind. For thee, loved clay,
I languish out, not live the day,
Using no other exercise
But what I practise with my eyes:
By which wet glasses I find out
How lazily time creeps about
To one that mourns: this, only this,
My exercise and business is:
So I compute the weary hours
With sighs dissolved into showers.

Nor wonder if my time go thus
Backward and most preposterous;

Thou hast benighted me, thy set
This eve of blackness did beget,
Who wast my day, (though overcast
Before thou hadst thy noon-tide past)
And I remember must in tears,
Thou scarce hadst seen so many years
As day tells hours. By thy clear sun
My love and fortune first did run;
But thou wilt never more appear
Folded within my hemisphere,
Since both thy light and motion
Like a fled star is fall'n and gone,
And 'twixt me and my soul's dear wish
The earth now interposed is,
Which such a strange eclipse doth make
As ne'er was read in almanac.

I could allow thee for a time
To darken me and my sad clime,
Were it a month, a year, or ten,
I would thy exile live till then;
And all that space my mirth adjourn,
So thou wouldst promise to return;
And putting off thy ashy shroud
At length disperse this sorrow's cloud.

But woe is me! the longest date
Too narrow is to calculate
These empty hopes; never shall I
Be so much blest as to descry
A glimpse of thee, till that day come
Which shall the earth to cinders doom,

And a fierce fever must calcine
The body of this world like thine,
(My little world!); that fit of fire
Once off, our bodies shall aspire
To our souls' bliss: then we shall rise,
And view our selves with clearer eyes
In that calm region, where no night
Can hide us from each other's sight.

Meantime, thou hast her, earth; much good
May my harm do thee. Since it stood
With Heaven's will I might not call
Her longer mine, I give thee all
My short-lived right and interest
In her, whom living I loved best:
With a most free and bounteous grief,
I give thee what I could not keep.
Be kind to her, and prithee look
Thou write into thy doomsday book
Each parcel of this rarity
Which in thy casket shrin'd doth lie.
See that thou make thy reck'ning straight,
And yield her back again by weight;
For thou must audit on thy trust
Each grain and atom of this dust,
As thou wilt answer Him that lent,
Not gave thee, my dear monument.

So close the ground, and 'bout her shade
Black curtains draw; my bride is laid.

Sleep on, my love, in thy cold bed
Never to be disquieted!

My last good-night! Thou wilt not wake
Till I thy fate shall overtake:
Till age, or grief, or sickness must
Marry my body to that dust
It so much loves; and fill the room
My heart keeps empty in thy tomb.
Stay for me there; I will not fail
To meet thee in that hollow vale.
And think not much of my delay;
I am already on the way,
And follow thee with all the speed
Desire can make, or sorrows breed.
Each minute is a short degree,
And ev'ry hour a step towards thee.
At night when I betake to rest,
Next morn I rise nearer my west
Of life, almost by eight hours' sail,
Than when sleep breath'd his drowsy gale.

Thus from the sun my bottom steers,
And my day's compass downward bears:
Nor labour I to stem the tide
Through which to thee I swiftly glide.

'Tis true, with shame and grief I yield,
Thou like the van first took'st the field,
And gotten hast the victory
In thus adventuring to die
Before me, whose more years might crave
A just precedence in the grave.
But hark! my pulse, like a soft drum,
Beats my approach, tells thee I come;

And slow howe'er my marches be,
I shall at last sit down by thee.

The thought of this bids me go on,
And wait my dissolution
With hope and comfort. Dear, (forgive
The crime), I am content to live
Divided, with but half a heart,
Till we shall meet and never part.

GEORGE HERBERT

(1593—1633)

AFFLICTION

When first thou didst entice to thee my heart,
        I thought the service brave:
So many joys I writ down for my part,
        Besides what I might have
Out of my stock of natural delights,
Augmented with thy gracious benefits.

I looked on thy furniture so fine,
        And made it fine to me:
Thy glorious household-stuff did me entwine,
        And 'tice me unto thee;
Such stars I counted mine: both heav'n and earth
Paid me my wages in a world of mirth.

What, pleasures could I want, whose King I served,
        Where joys my fellows were?

Thus argu'd into hopes, my thoughts reserved
        No place for grief or fear.
Therefore my sudden soul caught at the place,
And made her youth and fierceness seek thy face.

At first thou gav'st me milk and sweetnesses;
        I had my wish and way:
My days were strew'd with flow'rs and happiness;
        There was no month but May.
But with my years sorrow did twist and grow,
And made a party unawares for woe.

My flesh began unto my soul in pain,
        Sicknesses cleave my bones;
Consuming agues dwell in ev'ry vein,
        And tune my breath to groans.
Sorrow was all my soul; I scarce believed,
Till grief did tell me roundly, that I lived.

When I got health, thou took'st away my life
        And more; for my friends die:
My mirth and edge was lost; a blunted knife
        Was of more use than I.
Thus thin and lean without a fence or friend,
I was blown through with ev'ry storm and wind.

Whereas my birth and spirit rather took
        The way that takes the town,
Thou didst betray me to a lingering book,
        And wrap me in a gown.

I was entangled in the world of strife,
Before I had the power to change my life.

Yet, for I threaten'd oft the siege to raise,
    Not simp'ring all mine age,
Thou often didst with academic praise
    Melt and dissolve my rage.
I took thy sweeten'd pill, till I came near;
I could not go away, nor persevere.

Yet lest perchance I should too happy be
    In my unhappiness,
Turning my purge to food, thou throwest me
    Into more sicknesses.
Thus doth thy power cross-bias me, not making
Thine own gift good, yet me from my ways taking.

Now I am here, what thou wilt do with me
    None of my books will show:
I read, and sigh, and wish I were a tree;
    For sure then I should grow
To fruit or shade: at least some bird would trust
Her household to me, and I should be just.

Yet, though thou troublest me, I must be meek;
    In weakness must be stout.
Well, I will change the service, and go seek
    Some other master out.
Ah my dear God! though I am clean forgot,
Let me not love thee, if I love thee not.

JORDAN

Who says that fictions only and false hair
Become a verse? Is there no truth in beauty
Is all good structure in a winding stair?
May no lines pass, except they do their duty
     Not to a true, but painted chair?

Is it no verse, except enchanted groves
And sudden arbours shadow coarse-spun lines?
Must purling streams refresh a lover's loves?
Must all be veil'd, while he that reads, divines
     Catching the sense at two removes?

Shepherds are honest people; let them sing:
Riddle who list, for me, and pull for prime:
I envy no man's nightingale or spring;
Nor let them punish me with loss of rhyme,
     Who plainly say, *My God, my King.*

VIRTUE

Sweet day, so cool, so calm, so bright!
The bridal of the earth and sky—
The dew shall weep thy fall to-night;
     For thou must die.

Sweet rose, whose hue angry and brave
Bids the rash gazer wipe his eye,
Thy root is ever in its grave,
     And thou must die.

Sweet spring, full of sweet days and roses,
A box where sweets compacted lie,
My music shows ye have your closes,
    And all must die.

Only a sweet and virtuous soul,
Like season'd timber, never gives;
But though the whole world turn to coal,
    Then chiefly lives.

THE COLLAR

I struck the board, and cried, No more.
  I will abroad.
What? shall I ever sigh and pine?
My lines and life are free; free as the road,
  Loose as the wind, as large as store.
   Shall I be still in suit?
  Have I no harvest but a thorn
  To let me blood, and not restore
What I have lost with cordial fruit?
     Sure there was wine
    Before my sighs did dry it: there was corn
     Before my tears did drown it.
   Is the year only lost to me?
    Have I no bays to crown it?
  No flowers, no garlands gay? all blasted?
    All wasted?
    Not so, my heart: but there is fruit,
    And thou hast hands.
    Recover all thy sigh-blown age

On double pleasures: leave thy cold dispute
Of what is fit, and not; forsake thy cage,
        Thy rope of sands,
Which petty thoughts have made, and made to thee
    Good cable, to enforce and draw,
            And be thy law,
    While thou didst wink and wouldst not see.
            Away: take heed:
            I will abroad.
Call in thy death's head there: tie up thy fears.
            He that forbears
        To suit and serve his need
            Deserves his load.
But as I rav'd and grew more fierce and wild
            At every word,
    Methought I heard one calling, *Child*:
            And I replied, *My Lord*.

THE PULLEY

When God at first made Man,
Having a glass of blessings standing by—
Let us (said He) pour on him all we can;
Let the world's riches, which dispersèd lie,
            Contract into a span.

            So strength first made a way,
Then beauty flow'd, then wisdom, honour, pleasure
When almost all was out, God made a stay,
Perceiving that, alone of all His treasure,
            Rest in the bottom lay.

For if I should (said He)
Bestow this jewel also on My creature,
He would adore My gifts instead of Me,
And rest in Nature, not the God of Nature:
So both should losers be.

Yet let him keep the rest.
But keep them with repining restlessness;
Let him be rich and weary, that at least,
If goodness lead him not, yet weariness
May toss him to My breast.

LOVE

Love bade me welcome; yet my soul drew back,
   Guilty of dust and sin.
But quick-eyed Love, observing me grow slack
   From my first entrance in,
Drew nearer to me, sweetly questioning
   If I lack'd anything.

'A guest,' I answer'd, 'worthy to be here:'
   Love said, 'You shall be he.'
'I, the unkind, ungrateful? Ah, my dear,
   I cannot look on Thee.'
Love took my hand and smiling did reply,
   'Who made the eyes but I?'

'Truth, Lord; but I have marr'd them: let my shame
   Go where it doth deserve.'

'And know you not,' says Love, 'Who bore the blame?'
'My dear, then I will serve.'
'You must sit down,' says Love, 'and taste my meat.'
So I did sit and eat.

UNKNOWN

THE GUEST

Yet if His Majesty, our sovereign lord,
Should of his own accord
Friendly himself invite,
And say 'I'll be your guest to-morrow night',
How should we stir ourselves, call and command
All hands to work! 'Let no man idle stand!

'Set me fine Spanish tables in the hall;
See they be fitted all;
Let there be room to eat
And order taken that there want no meat.
See every sconce and candlestick made bright,
That without tapers they may give a light.

'Look to the presence: are the carpets spread,
The dazie o'r the head,
The cushions in the chairs,
And all the candles lighted on the stairs?
Perfume the chambers, and in any case
Let each man give attendance in his place!

Thus, if a king were coming, would we do;
And 'twere good reason too;

For 'tis a duteous thing
To show all honour to an earthly king,
And after all our travail and our cost,
So he be pleased, to think no labour lost.

But at the coming of the King of Heaven
All's set at six and seven;
We wallow in our sin,
Christ cannot find a chamber in the inn.
We entertain Him always like a stranger,
And, as at first, still lodge Him in the manger.

THOMAS CAREW
(1595?—1639?)

INGRATEFUL BEAUTY THREATENED

Know, Celia, since thou art so proud,
　'Twas I that gave thee thy renown.
Thou hadst in the forgotten crowd
　Of common beauties lived unknown,
Had not my verse extoll'd thy name,
And with it imp'd the wings of Fame.

That killing power is none of thine;
　I gave it to thy voice and eyes;
Thy sweets, thy graces, all are mine;
　Thou art my star, shin'st in my skies;
Then dart not from thy borrow'd sphere
Lightning on him that fix'd thee there.

Tempt me with such affrights no more,
   Lest what I made I uncreate;
Let fools thy mystic form adore,
   I know thee in thy mortal state.
Wise poets, that wrapt Truth in tales,
Knew her themselves through all her veils.

SONG

Ask me no more where Jove bestows,
When June is past, the fading rose;
For in your beauty's orient deep
These flowers, as in their causes, sleep.

Ask me no more whither do stray
The golden atoms of the day;
For in pure love heaven did prepare
Those powders to enrich your hair.

Ask me no more whither doth haste
The nightingale when May is past;
For in your sweet dividing throat
She winters and keeps warm her note.

Ask me no more where those stars 'light
That downwards fall in dead of night;
For in your eyes they sit, and there
Fixèd become as in their sphere.

Ask me no more if east or west
The Phœnix builds her spicy nest;
For unto you at last she flies,
And in your fragrant bosom dies.

A DEPOSITION FROM LOVE

I was foretold your rebel sex
   Nor love nor pity knew;
And with what scorn you use to vex
   Poor hearts that humbly sue;
Yet I believ'd, to crown our pain,
   Could we the fortress win,
The happy lover sure should gain
   A paradise within:
I thought love's plagues, like dragons, sate
Only to fright us at the gate.

But I did enter and enjoy
   What happy lovers prove;
For I could kiss, and sport, and toy,
   And taste those sweets of love;
Which had they but a lasting state,
   Or if in Celia's breast
The force of love might not abate,
   Jove were too mean a guest.
But now her breach of faith far more
Afflicts, than did her scorn before.

Hard fate! to have been once possest
   As victor of a heart,
Achieved with labour and unrest,
   And then forc'd to depart.
If the stout foe will not resign
   When I besiege a town,

I lose but what was never mine;
    But he that is cast down
From enjoy'd beauty, feels a woe
Only deposed kings can know.

THE INSCRIPTION ON THE TOMB OF THE
LADY MARY WENTWORTH

And here the precious dust is laid;
Whose purely-tempered clay was made
So fine, that it the guest betray'd.

Else the soul grew so fast within,
It broke the outward shell of sin,
And so was hatch'd a cherubin.

In height, it soar'd to God above;
In depth, it did to knowledge move,
And spread in breadth to general love.

Good to the poor, to kindred dear,
To servants kind, to friendship clear,
To nothing but herself severe.

So though a virgin, yet a bride
To every grace, she justified
A chaste polygamy, and died.

Learn from hence, reader, what small trust
We owe this world, where virtue must
Frail as our flesh crumble to dust.

TO A LADY THAT DESIRED I WOULD LOVE HER

Now you have freely given me leave to love,
    What will you do?
  Shall I your mirth, or passion move,
    When I begin to woo?
Will you torment, or scorn, or love me too?

Each petty beauty can disdain, and I,
    'Spite of your hate,
  Without your leave can see, and die;
    Dispense a nobler fate,
'Tis easy to destroy, you may create.

Then give me leave to love, and love me too,
    Not with design
  To raise, as Love's curst rebels do,
    When puling poets whine,
Fame to their beauty, from their blubber'd eyen.

Grief is a puddle, and reflects not clear
    Your beauty's rays;
  Joys are pure streams; your eyes appear
    Sullen in sadder lays,
In cheerful numbers they shine bright with praise.

Which shall not mention, to express you fair,
    Wounds, flames and darts,
  Storms in your brow, nets in your hair,
    Suborning all your parts,
Or to betray or torture captive hearts.

I'll make your eyes like morning suns appear,
     As mild and fair;
   Your brow as crystal smooth and clear,
     And your dishevell'd hair
Shall flow like a calm region of the air.

Rich Nature's store, which is the poet's treasure,
     I'll spend, to dress
   Your beauties, if your mine of pleasure
     In equal thankfulness
You but unlock, so we each other bless.

JAMES SHIRLEY
(1596—1666)

DEATH THE LEVELLER

The glories of our blood and state
   Are shadows, not substantial things;
There is no armour against Fate;
   Death lays his icy hand on kings:
     Sceptre and Crown
     Must tumble down,
And in the dust be equal made
With the poor crookèd scythe and spade.

Some men with swords may reap the field,
   And plant fresh laurels where they kill:
But their strong nerves at last must yield;
   They tame but one another still:
     Early or late
     They stoop to fate,

And must give up their murmuring breath
When they, pale captives, creep to death.

The garlands wither on your brow;
   Then boast no more your mighty deeds!
Upon Death's purple altar now
   See where the victor-victim bleeds.
      Your heads must come
      To the cold tomb:
Only the actions of the just
Smell sweet and blossom in their dust.

WILLIAM HABINGTON
(1605—1654)

NOX NOCTI INDICAT SCIENTIAM

When I survey the bright
      Celestial sphere;
So rich with jewels hung, that Night
   Doth like an Ethiop bride appear:

My soul her wings doth spread
      And heavenward flies,
Th' Almighty's mysteries to read
   In the large volumes of the skies.

For the bright firmament
      Shoots forth no flame
So silent, but is eloquent
   In speaking the Creator's name.

No unregarded star
          Contracts its light
Into so small a character,
     Removed far from our human sight

But if we steadfast look
          We shall discern
In it, as in some holy book,
     How man may heavenly knowledge learn.

It tells the conqueror
          That far-stretch'd power,
Which his proud dangers traffic for,
     Is but the triumph of an hour:

That from the farthest North,
          Some nation may,
Yet undiscover'd, issue forth
     And o'er his new-got conquest sway:

Some nation yet shut in
          With hills of ice
May be let out to scourge his sin,
     Till they shall equal him in vice.

And then they likewise shall
          Their ruin have;
For as yourselves your empires fall,
     And every kingdom hath a grave.

Thus those celestial fires,
          Though seeming mute,
The fallacy of our desires
     And all the pride of life confute:—

For they have watch'd since first
            The World had birth:
And found sin in itself accurst,
    And nothing permanent on Earth.

EDMUND WALLER
(1606—1687)

SONG

Go, lovely Rose—
Tell her that wastes her time and me,
        That now she knows,
When I resemble her to thee,
How sweet and fair she seems to be.

'Tell her that's young,
And shuns to have her graces spied,
        That hadst thou sprung
In deserts where no men abide,
Thou must have uncommended died.

Small is the worth
Of beauty from the light retired:
        Bid her come forth,
Suffer herself to be desired,
And not blush so to be admired.

Then die—that she
The common fate of all things rare
        May read in thee;
How small a part of time they share
That are so wondrous sweet and fair!

JOHN MILTON
(1608—1674)

ECHO

Sweet Echo, sweetest Nymph that liv'st unseen
     Within thy airy shell
  By slow Meander's margent green,
  And in the violet embroider'd vale
    Where the love-lorn Nightingale
Nightly to thee her sad song mourneth well,
Canst thou not tell me of a gentle pair
    That likest thy Narcissus are?
      O if thou have
    Hid them in some flow'ry Cave,
     Tell me but where
Sweet Queen of Parley, Daughter of the Sphere!
So may'st thou be translated to the skies,
And give resounding grace to all Heav'ns harmonies!

Comus, A Mas

COMUS TEMPTS THE LADY

...O foolishness of men! that lend their ears
To those budge doctors of the Stoic fur,
And fetch their precepts from the Cynic tub,
Praising the lean and sallow Abstinence.
Wherefore did Nature pour her beauties forth
With such a full and unwithdrawing hand,
Covering the earth with odours, fruits, and flocks,

Thronging the seas with spawn innumerable,
But all to please and sate the curious taste?
And set to work millions of spinning worms,
That in their green shops weave the smooth-hair'd silk
To deck her sons, and that no corner might
Be vacant of her plenty, in her own loins
She hutch'd th'all-worshipp'd ore, and precious gems
To store her children with; if all the world
Should in a fit of temperance feed on pulse,
Drink the clear stream, and nothing wear but frieze,
Th'all-giver would be unthank'd, would be unprais'd
Not half his riches known, and yet despis'd,
And we should serve him as a grudging master,
As a penurious niggard of his wealth,
And live like Nature's bastards, not her sons;
Who would be quite surcharged with her own weight,
And strangled with her waste fertility;
Th'earth cumber'd, and the wing'd air dark'd with plumes,
The herds would over-multitude their lords,
The sea o'erfraught would swell, and th'unsought diamonds
Would so emblaze the forehead of the deep,
And so bestud with stars, that they below
Would grow inured to light, and come at last
To gaze upon the sun with shameless brows.
List, Lady, be not coy, and be not cozen'd
With that same vaunted name, Virginity;
Beauty is nature's coin, must not be hoarded,
But must be current, and the good thereof
Consists in mutual and partaken bliss,
Unsavoury in th'enjoyment of itself.
If you let slip time, like a neglected rose
It withers on the stalk with languish'd head.

Beauty is nature's brag, and must be shown
In courts, at feasts, and high solemnities,
Where most may wonder at the workmanship;
It is for homely features to keep home,
They had their name thence; coarse complexions
And cheeks of sorry grain will serve to ply
The sampler, and to tease the housewife's wool.
What need a vermeil-tinctured lip for that,
Love-darting eyes, or tresses like the morn?
There was another meaning in these gifts;
Think what, and be advis'd; you are but young yet ..

Comus, A Mask

LYCIDAS

A LAMENT FOR A FRIEND DROWNED IN HIS PASSAGE FROM CHESTER ON THE IRISH SEAS, 1637

Yet once more, O ye laurels, and once more
Ye myrtles brown, with ivy never sear,
I come to pluck your berries harsh and crude,
And with forced fingers rude,
Shatter your leaves before the mellowing year.
Bitter constraint, and sad occasion dear,
Compels me to disturb your season due:
For Lycidas is dead, dead ere his prime
Young Lycidas, and hath not left his peer:
Who would not sing for Lycidas? he knew
Himself to sing, and build the lofty rhyme.
He must not float upon his wat'ry bier
Unwept, and welter to the parching wind,
Without the meed of some melodious tear.

Begin, then, Sisters of the sacred well,
That from beneath the seat of Jove doth spring,
Begin, and somewhat loudly sweep the string.
Hence with denial vain, and coy excuse,
So may some gentle Muse
With lucky words favour my destin'd urn,
And as he passes turn,
And bid fair peace be to my sable shroud.
For we were nursed upon the self-same hill,
Fed the same flock, by fountain, shade, and rill

Together both, ere the high lawns appear'd
Under the opening eye-lids of the morn,
We drove afield, and both together heard
What time the gray-fly winds her sultry horn,
Batt'ning our flocks with the fresh dews of night,
Oft till the star rose, at ev'ning, bright
Towards Heav'n's descent had slop'd his westering wheel.
Meanwhile the rural ditties were not mute,
Temper'd to th'oaten flute;
Rough Satyrs danc'd, and Fauns with cloven heel,
From the glad sound would not be absent long,
And old Damætas lov'd to hear our song.

But O the heavy change, now thou art gone,
Now thou art gone, and never must return!
Thee shepherd, thee the woods, and desert caves,
With wild thyme and the gadding vine o'ergrown,
And all their echoes mourn.
The willows, and the hazel copses green,
Shall now no more be seen,
Fanning their joyous leaves to thy soft lays.
As killing as the canker to the rose,
Or taint-worm to the weanling herds that graze,

Or frost to flowers, that their gay wardrobe wear,
When first the whitethorn blows;
Such, Lycidas, thy loss to shepherds' ear.

Where were ye, Nymphs, when the remorseless deep.
Clos'd o'er the head of your lov'd Lycidas?
For neither were ye playing on the steep,
Where your old Bards, the famous Druids lie,
Nor on the shaggy top of Mona high,
Nor yet where Deva spreads her wizard stream:
Ay me, I fondly dream!
Had ye been there—for what could that have done?
What could the Muse herself that Orpheus bore,
The Muse herself, for her enchanting son
Whom universal nature did lament,
When by the rout that made the hideous roar,
His gory visage down the stream was sent,
Down the swift Hebrus to the Lesbian shore.

Alas! what boots it with uncessant care
To tend the homely slighted shepherd's trade,
And strictly meditate the thankless Muse?
Were it not better done as others use,
To sport with Amaryllis in the shade,
Or with the tangles of Neæra's hair?
Fame is the spur that the clear spirit doth raise
(That last infirmity of noble mind)
To scorn delights, and live laborious days;
But the fair guerdon when we hope to find,
And think to burst out into sudden blaze,
Comes the blind Fury with th'abhorrèd shears,
And slits the thin spun life. But not the praise,
Phœbus repli'd, and touch'd my trembling ears;

Fame is no plant that grows on mortal soil,
Nor in the glistering foil
Set off to th'world, nor in broad rumour lies,
But lives and spreads aloft by those pure eyes,
And perfect witness of all judging Jove;
As he pronounces lastly on each deed,
Of so much fame in Heav'n expect thy meed.

O fountain Arethuse, and thou honour'd flood,
Smooth-sliding Mincius, crown'd with vocal reeds,
That strain I heard was of a higher mood:
But now my oat proceeds,
And listens to the herald of the sea
That came in Neptune's plea,
He ask'd the waves, and ask'd the felon winds,
What hard mishap hath doom'd this gentle swain?
And question'd every gust of rugged wings
That blows from off each beakèd promontory,
They knew not of his story,
And sage Hippotades their answer brings,
That not a blast was from his dungeon stray'd,
The air was calm, and on the level brine,
Sleek Panope with all her sisters play'd.
It was that fatal and perfidious bark
Built in th'eclipse, and rigg'd with curses dark,
That sunk so low that sacred head of thine.

Next Camus, reverend sire, went footing slow,
His mantle hairy, and his bonnet sedge,
Inwrought with figures dim, and on the edge
Like to that sanguine flower inscrib'd with woe.
'Ah! Who hath reft' (quoth he) 'my dearest pledge?'
Last came, and last did go,
The Pilot of the Galilean lake,

Two massy keys he bore of metals twain,
(The golden opes, the iron shuts amain)
He shook his mitred locks, and stern bespake,
'How well could I have spar'd for thee, young swain,
Enow of such as for their bellies sake,
Creep and intrude, and climb into the fold!
Of other care they little reck'ning make,
Than how to scramble at the shearers' feast,
And shove away the worthy bidden guest.
Blind mouths! that scarce themselves know how to hold
A sheep-hook, or have learn'd ought else the least
That to the faithful herdman's art belongs!
What recks it them? What need they? They are sped;
And when they list, their lean and flashy songs
Grate on their scrannel pipes of wretched straw,
The hungry sheep look up, and are not fed,
But swol'n with wind, and the rank mist they draw,
Rot inwardly, and foul contagion spread:
Besides what the grim wolf with privy paw
Daily devours apace, and nothing said,
But that two-handed engine at the door,
Stands ready to smite once, and smite no more.

Return, Alpheus, the dread voice is past,
That shrunk thy streams; Return, Sicilian Muse,
And call the vales, and bid them hither cast
Their bells, and flowerets of a thousand hues.
Ye valleys low where the mild whispers use,
Of shades and wanton winds, and gushing brooks,
On whose fresh lap the swart star sparely looks,
Throw hither all your quaint enamel'd eyes,
That on the green turf suck the honied showers,
And purple all the ground with vernal flowers.

Bring the rathe primrose that forsaken dies.
The tufted crow-toe, and pale jessamine,
The white pink, and the pansie freakt with jet,
The glowing violet.
The musk-rose, and the well attir'd woodbine.
With cowslips wan that hang the pensive head,
And every flower that sad embroidery wears:
Bid amaranthus all his beauty shed,
And daffadillies fill their cups with tears,
To strew the laureat hearse where Lycid lies.
For so to interpose a little ease,
Let our frail thoughts dally with false surmise.
Ay me! Whilst thee the shores, and sounding seas
Wash far away, where'er thy bones are hurl'd,
Whether beyond the stormy Hebrides,
Where thou perhaps under the whelming tide
Visit'st the bottom of the monstrous world;
Or whether thou to our moist vows deny'd,
Sleep'st by the fable of Bellerus old,
Where the great vision of the guarded mount
Looks toward Namancos and Bayona's hold;
Look homeward, Angel, now, and melt with ruth.
And, O ye dolphins, waft the hapless youth.

Weep no more, woeful shepherds, weep no more,
For Lycidas your sorrow is not dead,
Sunk though he be beneath the wat'ry floor,
So sinks the day-star in the ocean bed,
And yet anon repairs his drooping head,
And tricks his beams, and with new sprangled ore,
Flames in the forehead of the morning sky:
So Lycidas sunk low, but mounted high,

Through the dear might of him that walk'd the waves
Where, other groves and other streams along,
With nectar pure his oozy locks he laves,
And hears the unexpressive nuptial song,
In the blest Kingdoms meek of joy and love.
There entertain him all the Saints above,
In solemn troops, and sweet societies
That sing, and singing in their glory move,
And wipe the tears for ever from his eyes.
Now, Lycidas, the shepherds weep no more;
Henceforth thou art the genius of the shore,
In thy large recompense, and shalt be good
To all that wander in that perilous flood.

   Thus sang the uncouth swain to th'oaks and rills,
While the still morn went out with sandals gray,
He touch'd the tender stops of various quills,
With eager thought warbling his Doric lay:
And now the sun had stretch'd out all the hills.
And now was dropt into the western bay;
At last he rose, and twitch'd his mantle blue:
Tomorrow to fresh woods, and pastures new.

ON HIS BLINDNESS

When I consider how my light is spent,
  E're half my days, in this dark world and wide,
  And that one talent which is death to hide,
  Lodg'd with me useless, though my soul more bent
To serve therewith my Maker, and present
  My true account, lest he returning chide,
  Doth God exact day-labour, light denied,
  I fondly ask; But patience to prevent

That murmur, soon replies, God doth not need
   Either man's work or his own gifts; who best
   Bear his mild yoke, they serve him best; his state
Is kingly. Thousands at his bidding speed
   And post o'er land and ocean without rest:
They also serve who only stand and wait.

ON THE LATE MASSACRE IN PIEDMONT

Avenge, O Lord! Thy slaughter'd saints, whose bones
Lie scatter'd on the Alpine mountains cold;
Even them who kept Thy truth so pure of old
When all our fathers worshipt stocks and stones
Forget not: In Thy book record their groans
Who were thy sheep, and in their ancient fold
Slain by the bloody Piemontese, that roll'd
Mother with infant down the rocks. Their moans
The vales redoubled to the hills, and they
To Heaven. Their martyr'd blood and ashes sow
O'er all the Italian fields, where still doth sway
The triple Tyrant, that from these may grow
A hundred-fold, who, having learnt Thy way,
Early may fly the Babylonian woe.

SATAN AND THE FALLEN ANGELS

...He scarce had ceas'd when the superior Fiend
Was moving toward the shore; his ponderous shield
Ethereal temper, massy, large and round,
Behind him cast; the broad circumference
Hung on his shoulders like the moon, whose orb
Through optic glass the Tuscan artist views

At ev'ning from the top of Fesole,
Or in Valdarno, to descry new lands,
Rivers or mountains in her spotty globe.
His spear, to equal which the tallest pine
Hewn on Norwegian hills, to be the mast
Of some great Admiral, were but a wand,
He walk'd with to support uneasy steps
Over the burning marle, not like those steps
On Heaven's azure, and the torrid clime
Smote on him sore besides, vaulted with fire;
Nathless he so endur'd, till on the beach
Of that inflamed sea he stood, and call'd
His legions, Angel forms, who lay entranc'd
Thick as autumnal leaves that strew the brooks
In Vallombrosa, where th'Etrurian shades
High overarch'd embower; or scatter'd sedge
Afloat, when with fierce winds Orion arm'd
Hath vex'd the Red Sea coast, whose waves o'erthrew
Busiris and his Memphian chivalry,
While with perfidious hatred they pursu'd
The sojourners of Goshen, who beheld
From the safe shore their floating carcasses
And broken chariot wheels; so thick bestrown,
Abject and lost lay these, covering the flood,
Under amazement of their hideous change....

Paradise Lost, Book I.

A UNIVERSE OF DEATH

... Thus roving on
In confus'd march forlorn, th'adventurous bands
With shuddering horror pale, and eyes aghast,

View'd first their lamentable lot, and found
No rest; through many a dark and dreary vale
They pass'd, and many a region dolorous,
O'er many a frozen, many a fiery Alp,
Rocks, caves, lakes, fens, bogs, dens, and shades of death,
A universe of death, which God by curse
Created evil, for evil only good,
Where all life dies, death lives, and nature breeds,
Perverse, all monstrous, all prodigious things,
Abominable, inutterable, and worse
Than fables yet have feign'd or fear conceiv'd,
Gorgons and Hydras and Chimaeras dire. . . .

Paradise Lost, Book II.

INVOCATION TO LIGHT

Hail, holy Light! offspring of Heav'n first-born,
Or of th'Eternal Coeternal beam,
May I express thee unblam'd? Since God is light,
And never but in unapproached light
Dwelt from eternity, dwelt then in thee,
Bright effluence of bright essence increate.
Or hear'st thou rather, pure ethereal stream,
Whose fountain who shall tell?, before the sun,
Before the heavens thou wert, and at the voice
Of God, as with a mantle didst invest
The rising world of waters dark and deep,
Won from the void and formless infinite.
Thee I revisit now with bolder wing,
Escap'd the Stygian pool, though long detain'd
In that obscure sojourn, while in my flight

Through utter and through middle darkness borne
With other notes than to th'Orphean lyre
I sung of Chaos and Eternal Night,
Taught by the heav'nly Muse to venture down
The dark descent, and up to reascend,
Though hard and rare. Thee I revisit safe,
And feel thy sovereign vital lamp; but thou
Revisit'st not these eyes, that roll in vain
To find thy piercing ray, and find no dawn;
So thick a drop serene hath quench'd their orbs,
Or dim suffusion veil'd. Yet not the more
Cease I to wander where the Muses haunt
Clear spring, or shady grove, or sunny hill,
Smit with the love of sacred song; but chief
Thee, Sion, and the flowery brooks beneath
That wash thy hallow'd feet, and warbling flow,
Nightly I visit; nor sometimes forget
Those other two, equall'd with me in fate,
So were I equall'd with them in renown,
Blind Thamyris and blind Mæonides,
And Tiresias and Phineus, prophets old.
Then feed on thoughts, that voluntary move
Harmonious numbers; as the wakeful bird
Sings darkling, and in shadiest covert hid
Tunes her nocturnal note. Thus with the year
Seasons return, but not to me returns
Day, or the sweet approach of ev'n or morn,
Or sight of vernal bloom, or summer's rose,
Or flocks, or herds, or human face divine;
But cloud instead, and ever-during dark
Surrounds me, from the cheerful ways of men

Cut off, and for the book of knowledge fair
Presented with a universal blank
Of Nature's works to me expung'd and raz'd,
And wisdom at one entrance quite shut out.
So much the rather, thou celestial Light,
Shine inward, and the mind through all her powers
Irradiate; there plant eyes, all mist from thence
Purge and disperse, that I may see and tell
Of things invisible to mortal sight. . . .

Paradise Lost, Book III.

SATAN REFLECTS

. . . O thou that with surpassing glory crown'd
Look'st from thy sole dominion like the God
Of this new world; at whose sight all the stars
Hide their diminish'd heads; to thee I call,
But with no friendly voice, and add thy name,
O Sun, to tell thee how I hate thy beams,
That bring to my remembrance from what state
I fell, how glorious once above thy sphere;
Till pride and worse ambition threw me down,
Warring in Heav'n against Heav'n's matchless King.
Ah, wherefore! He deserv'd no such return
From me, whom he created what I was
In that bright eminence, and with his good
Upbraided none; nor was his service hard.
What could be less than to afford him praise,
The easiest recompense, and pay him thanks,
How due! Yet all his good prov'd ill in me,
And wrought but malice; lifted up so high
I 'sdained subjection, and thought one step higher

Would set me highest, and in a moment quit
The debt immense of endless gratitude,
So burdensome, still paying, still to owe;
Forgetful what from him I still receiv'd,
And understood not that a grateful mind
By owing owes not, but still pays, at once
Indebted and discharg'd; what burden then?
O had his powerful destiny ordain'd
Me some inferior angel, I had stood
Then happy; no unbounded hope had rais'd
Ambition. Yet why not? Some other power
As great might have aspir'd, and me, though mean,
Drawn to his part; but other powers as great
Fell not, but stand unshaken, from within
Or from without, to all temptations arm'd.
Hadst thou the same free will and power to stand?
Thou hadst. Whom hast thou then or what to accuse,
But Heavn's free Love dealt equally to all?
Be then his Love accurst, since love or hate,
To me alike, it deals eternal woe.
Nay, curs'd be thou; since against his thy will
Chose freely what it now so justly rules.
Me miserable! Which way shall I fly
Infinite wrath and infinite despair?
Which way I fly is Hell; myself am Hell;
And in the lowest deep a lower deep
Still threat'ning to devour me opens wide,
To which the Hell I suffer seems a Heaven....

Paradise Lost, Book IV.

SIR JOHN SUCKLING
(1609—1642)

SONG

Of thee, kind boy, I ask no red and white
  To make up my delight,
  No odd becoming graces,
Black eyes, or little know-not-whats, in faces;
Make me but mad enough, give me good store
Of love, for her I court,
    I ask no more;
'Tis love in love that makes the sport.

There's no such thing as that we beauty call,
  It is mere cozenage all;
  For though some time ago
Liked certain colours mingled so and so,
That doth not tie me now from choosing new;
If I a fancy take
    To black and blue,
That fancy doth it beauty make.

'Tis not the meat, but 'tis the appetite
  Makes eating a delight;
  And if I like one dish
More than another, that a pheasant is.
What in our watches, that in us is found;
So to the height and nick
    We up be wound,
No matter by what hand or trick.

SONG

Out upon it, I have loved
   Three whole days together!
And am like to love three more,
   If it prove fair weather.

Time shall moult away his wings
   Ere he shall discover
In the whole wide world again
   Such a constant lover.

But the spite on 't is, no praise
   Is due at all to me:
Love with me had made no stays,
   Had it any been but she.

Had it any been but she,
   And that very face,
There had been at least ere this
   A dozen dozen in her place.

JAMES GRAHAM
(1612—1650)

MY DEAR AND ONLY LOVE

My dear and only Love, I pray
   That little world of thee
Be govern'd by no other sway
   Than purest monarchy;

For if confusion have a part
  (Which virtuous souls abhor),
And hold a synod in thine heart,
  I'll never love thee more.

Like Alexander I will reign,
  And I will reign alone;
My thoughts did evermore disdain
  A rival on my throne.
He either fears his fate too much,
  Or his deserts are small,
That dares not put it to the touch,
  To gain or lose it all.

And in the empire of thine heart,
  Where I should solely be,
If others do pretend a part
  Or dare to vie with me,
Or if committees thou erect,
  And go on such a score,
I'll laugh and sing at thy neglect,
  And never love thee more.

But if thou wilt prove faithful then,
  And constant of thy word,
I'll make thee glorious by my pen
  And famous by my sword;
I'll serve thee in such noble ways
  Was never heard before;
I'll crown and deck thee all with bays,
  And love thee more and more.

SAMUEL BUTLER
(1612—1680)

THE PRESBYTERIAN KNIGHT

...He was in Logic a great critic,
Profoundly skilled in analytic.
He could distinguish, and divide
A hair 'twixt south and south-west side:
On either which he would dispute,
Confute, change hands, and still confute.
He'd undertake to prove by force
Of argument, a man's no horse.
He'd prove a buzzard is no fowl,
And that a lord may be an owl;
A calf an alderman, a goose a justice,
And rooks committee-men and trustees.
He'd run in debt by disputation,
And pay with ratiocination.
All this by syllogism, true
In mood and figure, he would do.

For Rhetoric, he could not ope
His mouth, but out there flew a trope:
And when he happened to break off
I'th' middle of his speech, or cough,
He'd hard words, ready to show why,
And tell what rules he did it by.
Else, when with greatest art he spoke,
You'd think he talked like other folk.

For all a rhetorician's rules
Teach nothing but to name his tools.
His ordinary rate of speech
In loftiness of sound was rich,
A Babylonish dialect,
Which learned pedants much affect.
It was a parti-coloured dress
Of patch'd and piebald languages:
'Twas English cut on Greek and Latin,
Like fustian heretofore on satin.
It had an odd promiscuous tone
As if he'd talked three parts in one,
Which made some think, when he did gabble,
They'd heard three labourers of Babel,
Or Cerberus himself pronounce
A leash of languages at once.
This he as volubly would vent
As if his stock would ne'er be spent;
And truly to support that charge
He had supplies as vast and large. . . .

. . . In Mathematics he was greater
Than Tycho Brahe or Erra Pater;
For he by geometric scale
Could take the size of pots of ale,
Resolve by signs and tangents straight
If bread or butter wanted weight;
And wisely tell what hour o' the day
The clock does strike, by algebra. . . .

. . . Besides he was a shrewd Philosopher,
And had read every text and gloss over;

Whate'er the crabbed'st author hath
He understood by implicit faith,
Whatever sceptic could inquire for;
For every Why he had a Wherefore:
Knew more than forty of them do,
As far as words and terms could go.
All which he understood by rote,
And as occasion serv'd, would quote;
No matter whether right or wrong,
They might be either said or sung.
His notions fitted things so well
That which was which he could not tell;
But oftentimes mistook the one
For th'other, as great clerks have done.
He could reduce all things to acts,
And knew their natures by abstracts,
Where entity and quiddity,
The ghosts of defunct bodies, fly;
Where truth in person does appear,
Like words congeal'd in northern air.
He knew what's what, and that's as high
As metaphysic wit can fly. . . .

. . . For his Religion, it was fit
To match his learning and his wit.
'Twas Presbyterian true blue,
For he was of that stubborn crew
Of errant saints, whom all men grant
To be the true Church Militant:
Such as do build their faith upon
The holy text of pike and gun;

Decide all controversies by
Infallible artillery;
And prove their doctrine orthodox
By apostolic blows and knocks;
Call fire and sword and desolation
A godly-thorough reformation,
Which always must be carried on,
And still be doing, never done.
As if religion were intended
For nothing else but to be mended.
A sect, whose chief devotion lies
In odd perverse antipathies,
In falling out with that or this,
And finding somewhat still amiss;
More peevish, cross and splenetic
Than dog distract, or monkey sick.
That with more care keep holy-day
The wrong, than others the right way;
Compound for sins they are inclined to
By damning those they have no mind to;
Still so perverse and opposite,
As if they worshipped God for spite;
The self-same thing they will abhor
One way, and long another for.
Free-will they one way disavow,
Another, nothing else allow.
All piety consists therein
In them, in other men all sin.
Rather than fail, they will defy
That which they love most tenderly;
Quarrel with minced pies, and disparage
Their best and dearest friend, plum-porridge;

Fat pig and goose itself oppose,
And blaspheme custard through the nose.
The apostles of this fierce religion,
Like Mahomet's, were ass and widgeon;
To whom our Knight, by fast instinct
Of wit and temper was so link'd,
As if hypocrisy and nonsense
Had got th'advowson of his conscience. . . .

Hudibras, First Part, Canto III.

RICHARD CRASHAW
(1613?—1649)

A HYMN TO THE NAME AND HONOUR OF THE ADMIRABLE SAINT TERESA

Love, thou art absolute sole lord
Of life and death. To prove the word,
We'll now appeal to none of all
Those thy old soldiers, great and tall,
Ripe men of martyrdom, that could reach down
With strong arms their triumphant crown;
Such as could with lusty breath
Speak loud into the face of death
Their great Lord's glorious name; to none
Of those whose spacious bosoms spread a throne
For Love at large to fill. Spare blood and sweat;
And see him take a private seat,
Making his mansion in the mild
And milky soul of a soft child.

Scarce has she learn'd to lisp the name
Of martyr, yet she thinks it shame
Life should so long play with that breath
Which spent can buy so brave a death.
She never undertook to know
What death with love should have to do;
Nor has she e'er yet understood
Why, to show love, she should shed blood;
Yet though she cannot tell you why,
She can love and she can die.

Scarce has she blood enough to make
A guilty sword blush for her sake;
Yet has she a heart dares hope to prove
How much less strong is death than love.

Be love but there, let poor six years
Be pos'd with the maturest fears
Man trembles at, you straight shall find
Love knows no nonage, nor the mind.
'Tis love, not years or limbs that can
Make the martyr, or the man.

Love touch'd her heart; and lo, it beats
High, and burns with such brave heats,
Such thirsts to die, as dares drink up
A thousand cold deaths in one cup.
Good reason. For she breathes all fire.
Her weak breast heaves with strong desire
Of what she may with fruitless wishes
Seek for amongst her mother's kisses.

Since 'tis not to be had at home
She'll travel to a martyrdom.
No home for hers confesses she
But where she may a martyr be.

She'll to the Moors, and trade with them
For this unvalued diadem.
She'll offer them her dearest breath,
With Christ's name in't, in change for death.
She'll bargain with them, and will give
Them God; teach them how to live
In him; or, if they this deny,
For him she'll teach them how to die.
So shall she leave among them sown
Her Lord's blood; or at least her own.

   Farewell then, all the world, adieu!
Teresa is no more for you.
Farewell, all pleasures, sports and joys,
Never till now esteemed toys!
Farewell, whatever dear may be
Mother's arms or Father's knee;
Farewell house and farewell home!
She's for the Moors and Martyrdom.

   Sweet, not so fast! Lo, thy fair Spouse,
Whom thou seek'st with so swift vows,
Calls thee back, and bids thee come
T'embrace a milder martyrdom.

   Blest powers forbid, thy tender life
Should bleed upon a barb'rous knife,
Or some base hand have power to raze
Thy breast's chaste cabinet, and uncase
A soul kept there so sweet. O no!
Wise heav'n will never have it so.
Thou art Love's victim, and must die
A death more mystical and high.
Into Love's arms thou shalt let fall
A still-surviving funeral.

His is the dart must make the death
Whose stroke shall taste thy hallow'd breath;
A dart thrice dipt in that rich flame
Which writes thy Spouse's radiant name
Upon the roof of heav'n; where ay
It shines, and with a sovereign ray
Beats bright upon the burning faces
Of souls which in that name's sweet graces
Find everlasting smiles. So rare,
So spiritual, pure and fair
Must be th'immortal instrument
Upon whose choice point shall be sent
A life so lov'd. And that there be
Fit executioners for thee,
The fair'st and first-born sons of fire,
Blest Seraphim, shall leave their choir
And turn Love's soldiers, upon thee
To exercise their archery.

   O how oft shalt thou complain
Of a sweet and subtle pain,
Of intolerable joys!
Of a death, in which who dies
Loves his death and dies again,
And would for ever so be slain,
And lives and dies; and knows not why
To live, but that he thus may never leave to die.

   How kindly will thy gentle heart
Kiss the sweetly-killing dart!
And close in his embraces keep
Those delicious wounds, that weep
Balsam to heal themselves with. Thus,
When these thy deaths, so numerous,

Shall all at last die into one,
And melt thy soul's sweet mansion;
Like a soft lump of incense, hasted
By too hot a fire, and wasted
Into perfuming clouds, so fast
Shalt thou exhale to heaven at last
In a resolving sigh, and then —
O what? Ask not the tongues of men.
Angels cannot tell; suffice
Thyself shall feel thy own full joys
And hold them fast for ever. There,
So soon as thou shalt first appear,
The moon of maiden stars, thy white
Mistress, attended by such bright
Souls as thy shining self, shall come
And in her first ranks make thee room;
Where 'mongst her snowy family
Immortal welcomes wait for thee.

O what delight, when reveal'd Life shall stand
And teach thy lips heav'n with his hand;
On which thou now may'st to thy wishes
Heap up thy consecrated kisses.
What joys shall seize thy soul, when she
Bending her blessed eyes on thee
(Those second smiles of heav'n) shall dart
Her mild rays through thy melting heart!

Angels, thy old friends, there shall greet thee,
Glad at their own home now to meet thee.

All thy good works, which went before
And waited for thee at the door,
Shall own thee there; and all in one
Weave a constellation

Of crowns, with which the King thy Spouse
Shall build up thy triumphant brows.

    All thy old woes shall now smile on thee
And thy pains sit bright upon thee;
All thy sorrows here shall shine,
All thy sufferings be divine.
Tears shall take comfort, and turn gems,
And wrongs repent to diadems.
Even thy deaths shall live, and new
Dress the soul that erst they slew.
Thy wounds shall blush to such bright scars
As keep account of the Lamb's wars.

    Those rare works where thou shalt leave writ
Love's noble history, with wit
Taught thee by none but him, while here
They feed our souls, shall clothe thine there.
Each heavenly word, by whose hid flame
Our hard hearts shall strike fire, the same
Shall flourish on thy brows, and be
Both fire to us and flame to thee;
Whose light shall live bright in thy face
By glory, in our hearts by grace.

    Thou shalt look round about, and see
Thousands of crown'd souls throng to be
Themselves thy crown, sons of thy vows,
The virgin-births with which thy sovereign Spouse
Made fruitful thy fair soul; go now,
And with them all about thee, bow
To him. 'Put on,' he'll say, 'put on
(My rosy love) that thy rich zone,
Sparkling with the sacred flames
Of thousand souls, whose happy names

Heav'n keeps upon thy score. Thy bright
Life brought them first to kiss the light
That kindled them to stars.' And so
Thou with the Lamb, thy Lord, shalt go;
And wheresoe'er he sets his white
Steps, walk with him those ways of light
Which who in death would live to see,
Must learn in life to die like thee.

SIR JOHN DENHAM
(1615—1669)

THE THAMES FROM COOPER'S HILL

My eye descending from the hill surveys
Where Thames amongst the wanton valleys strays.
Thames, the most lov'd of all the Ocean's sons,
By his old sire to his embraces runs,
Hasting to pay his tribute to the sea,
Like mortal life to meet eternity.
Though with those streams he no resemblance hold,
Whose foam is amber, and their gravel gold,
His genuine, and less guilty, wealth t'explore,
Search not his bottom, but survey his shore;
O'er which he kindly spreads his spacious wing,
And hatches plenty for th'ensuing spring.
Nor then destroys it with too fond a stay,
Like mothers who their infants overlay.
Nor with a sudden and impetuous wave,
Like profuse kings, resumes the wealth he gave.

No unexpected inundations spoil
The mower's hopes, nor mock the ploughman's toil:
But god-like his unwearied bounty flows,
First loves to do, then loves the good he does.
Nor are his blessings to his banks confin'd,
But free and common, as the sea or wind;
When he to boast, or to disperse his stores
Full of the tributes of his grateful shores,
Visits the world, and in his flying towers
Brings home to us, and makes both Indies ours;
Finds wealth where 'tis, bestows it where it wants,
Cities in deserts, woods in cities plants.
So that to us no thing, no place, is strange,
While his fair bosom is the world's exchange.
O could I flow like thee, and make thy stream
My great example, as it is my theme!
Though deep, yet clear, though gentle, yet not dull,
Strong without rage, without o'erflowing full.

Cooper's Hill.

RICHARD LOVELACE
(1618—1658)

TO LUCASTA, GOING TO THE WARS

Tell me not, Sweet, I am unkind,
    That from the nunnery
Of thy chaste breast and quiet mind
    To war and arms I fly.

True, a new mistress now I chase,
    The first foe in the field;

And with a stronger faith embrace
A sword, a horse, a shield.

Yet this inconstancy is such
As thou too shalt adore;
I could not love thee, Dear, so much,
Loved I not Honour more.

ABRAHAM COWLEY
(1618—1667)

ON THE DEATH OF MR WILLIAM HERVEY

It was a dismal and a fearful night,
Scarce could the morn drive on th'unwilling light,
When sleep, death's image, left my troubled breast,
By something liker death possest.
My eyes with tears did uncommanded flow,
And on my soul hung the dull weight
Of some intolerable fate.
What bell was that? Ah me! Too much I know.

My sweet companion and my gentle peer,
Why hast thou left me thus unkindly here,
Thy end for ever, and my life, to moan?
O, thou hast left me all alone!
Thy soul and body, when death's agony
Besieg'd around thy noble heart,
Did not with more reluctance part
Than I, my dearest friend, do part from thee.

My dearest friend, would I had died for thee!
Life and this world henceforth will tedious be.
Nor shall I know hereafter what to do
    If once my griefs prove tedious too.
Silent and sad I walk about all day,
    As sullen ghosts stalk speechless by
    Where their hid treasures lie;
Alas, my treasure's gone, why do I stay?

He was my friend, the truest friend on earth;
A strong and mighty influence joined our birth.
No did we envy the most sounding name
    By friendship given of old to fame.
None but his brethren he, and sisters knew,
    Whom the kind youth preferred to me;
    And ev'n in that we did agree,
For much above myself I lov'd them too.

Say, for you saw us, ye immortal lights,
How oft unwearied have we spent the nights!
Till the Ledean stars so fam'd for love
    Wondered at us from above.
We spent them not in toys, in lusts, or wine;
    But search of deep philosophy,
    Wit, eloquence and poetry,
Arts which I lov'd, for they, my friend, were thine.

Ye fields of Cambridge, our dear Cambridge, say,
Have ye not seen us walking every day?
Was there a tree about which did not know
    The love between us two?

Henceforth, ye gentle trees, for ever fade;
　　Or your sad branches thicker join,
　　And into darksome shades combine,
Dark as the grave wherein my friend is laid. ...

... Large was his soul; as large a soul as e'er
Submitted to inform a body here.
High as the place 'twas shortly in heav'n to have,
　　But low and humble as his grave.
So high that all the virtues there did come
　　As to their chiefest seat
　　Conspicuous and great;
So low that for me too it made a room.

He scorn'd this busy world below, and all
That we mistaken mortals pleasure call;
Was fill'd with innocent gallantry and truth,
　　Triumphant o'er the sins of youth.
He, like the stars to which he now is gone,
　　That shine with beams like flame
　　Yet burn not with the same,
Had all the light of youth, of the fire none.

Knowledge he only sought, and so soon caught,
As if for him Knowledge had rather sought.
Nor did more learning ever crowded lie
　　In such a short mortality.
When e'er the skilful youth discoursed or writ,
　　Still did the notions throng
　　About his eloquent tongue,
Nor could his ink flow faster than his wit. ...

... With as much zeal, devotion, piety,
He always lived, as other saints do die.
Still with his soul severe account he kept,
Weeping all debts out ere he slept.
Then down in peace and innocence he lay,
Like the sun's laborious light,
Which still in water sets at night,
Unsullied with his journey of the day. ...

... But happy thou, ta'en from this frantic age,
Where ignorance and hypocrisy do rage!
A fitter time for heav'n no soul e'er chose,
The place now only free from those.
There 'mong the blest thou dost for ever shine,
And wheresoe'er thou cast'st thy view
Upon that white and radiant crew,
Seest not a soul clothed with more light than thine.

And if the glorious saints cease not to know
Their wretched friends who fight with life below,
Thy flame to me does still the same abide,
Only more pure and rarified.
There, whilst immortal hymns thou dost rehearse,
Thou dost with holy pity see
Our dull and earthly poesy,
Where grief and misery can be joined with verse.

BEAUTY

Beauty, thou wild fantastic ape,
Who dost in ev'ry country change thy shape!
Here black, there brown, here tawny, and there white;
Thou flatt'rer which compli'st with every sight!

Thou Babel which confound'st the eye
With unintelligible variety!
   Who hast no certain What, nor Where,
But vari'st still, and dost thy self declare
Inconstant, as thy she-possessors are.

   Beauty, love's scene and masquerade,
So gay by well-placed lights, and distance made!
False coin, with which th' impostor cheats us still;
The stamp and colour good, but metal ill!
   Which light, or base we find, when we
Weigh by enjoyment, and examine thee!
   For though thy being be but show,
'Tis chiefly night which men to thee allow:
And choose t' enjoy thee, when thou least art thou.

   Beauty, thou active, passive ill!
Which diest thy self as fast as thou dost kill!
Thou tulip, who thy stock in paint dost waste,
Neither for physic good, nor smell, nor taste.
   Beauty, whose flames but meteors are,
Short-lived and low, though thou wouldst seem a star
   Who dar'st not thine own home descry,
Pretending to dwell richly in the eye,
When thou, alas, dost in the fancy lie.

   Beauty, whose conquests still are made
O'er hearts by cowards kept, or else betray'd!
Weak victor! who thyself destroy'd must be
When sickness storms or time besieges thee!
   Thou unwholesome thaw to frozen age!
Thou strong wine, which youth's fevers dost enrage,

Thou tyrant, which leav'st no man free!
Thou subtle thief, from whom nought safe can be!
Thou murderer which hast kill'd, and devil which
                                    wouldst damn me!

ANDREW MARVELL
(1621—1678)

TO HIS COY MISTRESS

Had we but world enough, and time,
This coyness, Lady, were no crime.
We would sit down and think—which way
To walk and pass our long love's day.
Thou by the Indian Ganges' side
Shouldst rubies find: I by the tide
Of Humber would complain. I would
Love you ten years before the Flood,
And you should, if you please, refuse
Till the conversion of the Jews.
My vegetable love should grow
Vaster than empires, and more slow;
An hundred years should go to praise
Thine eyes and on thy forehead gaze;
Two hundred to adore each breast;
But thirty thousand to the rest;
An age at least to every part,
And the last age should show your heart;
For, Lady, you deserve this state,
Nor would I love at lower rate.
    But at my back I always hear
Time's wingèd chariot hurrying near;

And yonder all before us lie
Deserts of vast eternity.
Thy beauty shall no more be found,
Nor, in thy marble vault, shall sound
My echoing song: then worms shall try
That long preserved virginity,
And your quaint honour turn to dust,
And into ashes all my lust:
The grave's a fine and private place,
But none, I think, do there embrace.

Now therefore, while the youthful hue
Sits on thy skin like morning dew,
And while thy willing soul transpires
At every pore with instant fires,
Now let us sport us while we may,
And now, like amorous birds of prey,
Rather at once our time devour
Than languish in his slow-chapt power.
Let us roll all our strength and all
Our sweetness up into one ball,
And tear our pleasures with rough strife
Thorough the iron gates of life:
Thus, though we cannot make our sun
Stand still, yet we will make him run.

THE DEFINITION OF LOVE

My Love is of a birth as rare
As 'tis for object strange and high:
It was begotten by Despair
Upon Impossibility.

Magnanimous Despair alone
Could show me so divine a thing,
Where feeble Hope could ne'er have flown
But vainly flapt its tinsel wing.

And yet I quickly might arrive
Where my extended Soul is fixt,
But Fate does iron wedges drive,
And always crowds it self betwixt.

For Fate with jealous eye does see
Two perfect Loves; nor lets them close:
Their union would her ruin be,
And her tyrannic pow'r depose.

And therefore her decrees of steel
Us as the distant poles have plac'd,
(Though Love's whole world on us doth wheel)
Not by themselves to be embrac'd.

Unless the giddy Heaven fall,
And Earth some new convulsion tear;
And, us to join, the World should all
Be cramp'd into a planisphere.

As lines so loves oblique may well
Themselves in every angle greet:
But ours so truly parallel,
Though infinite can never meet.

Therefore the Love which us doth bind
But Fate so enviously debars,
Is the conjunction of the mind,
And opposition of the stars.

THE GARDEN

How vainly men themselves amaze
To win the palm, the oak, or bays,
And their uncessant labours see
Crown'd from some single herb or tree,
Whose short and narrow-vergèd shade
Does prudently their toils upbraid;
While all the flowers and trees do close
To weave the garlands of repose!

Fair Quiet, have I found thee here,
And Innocence thy sister dear?
Mistaken long, I sought you then
In busy companies of men:
Your sacred plants, if here below,
Only among the plants will grow:
Society is all but rude
To this delicious solitude.

No white nor red was ever seen
So amorous as this lovely green.
Fond lovers, cruel as their flame,
Cut in these trees their mistress' name:
Little, alas! they know or heed
How far these beauties hers exceed!
Fair trees! wheres'e'er your barks I wound,
No name shall but your own be found.

When we have run our passions' heat,
Love hither makes his best retreat:

The gods, that mortal beauty chase,
Still in a tree did end their race;
Apollo hunted Daphne so
Only that she might laurel grow;
And Pan did after Syrinx speed
Not as a nymph, but for a reed.

What wondrous life is this I lead!
Ripe apples drop about my head;
The luscious clusters of the vine
Upon my mouth do crush their wine;
The nectarine and curious peach
Into my hands themselves do reach;
Stumbling on melons, as I pass,
Ensnared with flowers, I fall on grass.

Meanwhile the mind from pleasure less
Withdraws into its happiness;
The mind, that Ocean where each kind
Does straight its own resemblance find;
Yet it creates, transcending these,
Far other worlds, and other seas;
Annihilating all that's made
To a green thought in a green shade.

Here at the fountain's sliding foot,
Or at some fruit-tree's mossy root,
Casting the body's vest aside,
My soul into the boughs does glide;
There, like a bird, it sits and sings,
Then whets and combs its silver wings,

And, till prepared for longer flight,
Waves in its plumes the various light.

Such was that happy Garden-state
While man there walk'd without a mate
After a place so pure and sweet,
What other help could yet be meet!
But 'twas beyond a mortal's share
To wander solitary there:
Two paradises 'twere in one,
To live in Paradise alone.

How well the skilful gard'ner drew
Of flowers and herbs this dial new!
Where, from above, the milder sun
Does through a fragrant zodiac run:
And, as it works, th' industrious bee
Computes its time as well as we.
How could such sweet and wholesome hours
Be reckon'd, but with herbs and flowers!

HORATIAN ODE UPON CROMWELL'S RETURN FROM IRELAND

The forward youth that would appear,
Must now forsake his Muses dear,
        Nor in the shadows sing
        His numbers languishing.
'Tis time to leave the books in dust,
And oil the unusèd armour's rust,
        Removing from the wall
        The corslet of the hall.

So restless Cromwell could not cease
In the inglorious arts of peace,
    But through adventurous war
    Urgèd his active star:
And like the three-fork'd lightning, first
Breaking the clouds where it was nurst,
    Did thorough his own side
    His fiery way divide:
For 'tis all one to courage high,
The emulous, or enemy;
    And with such, to enclose
    Is more than to oppose.
Then burning through the air he went
And palaces and temples rent;
    And Caesar's head at last
    Did through his laurels blast.
'Tis madness to resist or blame
The face of angry heaven's flame;
    And if we would speak true,
    Much to the Man is due
Who, from his private gardens, where
He lived reservèd and austere,
    (As if his highest plot
    To plant the bergamot)
Could by industrious valour climb
To ruin the great work of time,
    And cast the Kingdoms old
    Into another mould.
Though Justice against Fate complain,
And plead the ancient Rights in vain—
    But those do hold or break
    As men are strong or weak.

Nature, that hateth emptiness,
Allows of penetration less,
    And therefore must make room
    Where greater spirits come.
What field of all the civil war
Where his were not the deepest scar?
    And Hampton shows what part
    He had of wiser art,
Where, twining subtle fears with hope,
He wove a net of such a scope
    That Charles himself might chase
    To Carisbrook's narrow case,
That thence the Royal actor borne
The tragic scaffold might adorn:
    While round the armèd bands
    Did clap their bloody hands:
He nothing common did or mean
Upon that memorable scene,
    But with his keener eye
    The axe's edge did try;
Nor call'd the Gods, with vulgar spite,
To vindicate his helpless right;
    But bow'd his comely head
    Down, as upon a bed.
—This was that memorable hour
Which first assured the forcèd power:
    So when they did design
    The Capitol's first line,
A Bleeding Head, where they begun,
Did fright the architects to run;
    And yet in that the State
    Foresaw its happy fate!

And now the Irish are ashamed
To see themselves in one year tamed:
    So much one man can do
    That does both act and know.
They can affirm his praises best,
And have, though overcome, confest
    How good he is, how just
    And fit for highest trust;
Nor yet grown stiffer with command,
But still in the Republic's hand—
    How fit he is to sway
    That can so well obey!
He to the Commons' feet presents
A Kingdom for his first year's rents,
    And (what he may) forbears
    His fame, to make it theirs:
And has his sword and spoils ungirt
To lay them at the Public's skirt.
    So when the falcon high
    Falls heavy from the sky
She, having kill'd, no more does search
But on the next green bough to perch,
    Where, when he first does lure,
    The falconer has her sure.
—What may not then our Isle presume
While victory his crest does plume?
    What may not others fear
    If thus he crowns each year?
As Caesar he, ere long, to Gaul,
To Italy an Hannibal,
    And to all States not free
    Shall climacteric be.

The Pict no shelter now shall find
Within his parti-colour'd mind,
    But from this valour, sad
    Shrink underneath the plaid—
Happy, if in the tufted brake
The English hunter him mistake,
    Nor lay his hounds in near
    The Caledonian deer.
But Thou, the War's and Fortune's son,
March indefatigably on;
    And for the last effect
    Still keep the sword erect:
Besides the force it has to fright
The spirits of the shady night,
    The same arts that did gain
    A power, must it maintain.

A DIALOGUE BETWEEN THE SOUL AND BODY

Soul

O who shall, from this dungeon, raise
A soul enslav'd so many ways?
With bolts of bones, that fetter'd stands
In feet; and manacled in hands.
Here blinded with an eye; and there
Deaf with the drumming of an ear.
A soul hung up, as 'twere, in chains
Of nerves, and arteries, and veins.
Tortur'd, besides each other part,
In a vain head, and double heart.

Body

O who shall me deliver whole,
From bonds of this tyrannic soul?
Which, stretched upright, impales me so,
That mine own precipice I go;
And warms and moves this needless frame:
(A fever could but do the same.)
And, wanting where its spite to try,
Has made me live to let me die.
A body that could never rest,
Since this ill spirit it possessed.

Soul

What magic could me thus confine
Within another's grief to pine?
Where whatsoever it complain,
I feel, that cannot feel, the pain.
And all my care itself employs,
That to preserve, which me destroys:
Constrain'd not only to endure
Diseases, but, what's worse, the cure:
And ready oft the port to gain
Am shipwrecked into health again.

Body

But physic yet could never reach
The maladies thou me dost teach;
Whom first the cramp of hope does tear:
And then the palsy shakes of fear.
The pestilence of love does heat:
Or hatred's hidden ulcer eat.

Joy's cheerful madness does perplex:
Or sorrow's other madness vex.
Which knowledge forces me to know;
And memory will not forgo.
What but a soul could have the wit
To build me up for sin so fit?
So architects do square and hew
Green trees that in the forest grew.

THE CORONET

When for the thorns with which I long, too long,
With many a piercing wound,
  My Saviour's head have crown'd,
I seek with garlands to redress that wrong:
  Through every garden, every mead,
I gather flow'rs (my fruits are only flow'rs)
  Dismantling all the fragrant towers
That once adorn'd my shepherdess's head.
And now when I have summ'd up all my store,
  Thinking (so I myself deceive)
  So rich a chaplet thence to weave
As never yet the king of glory wore:
  Alas, I find the serpent old
  That, twining in his speckled breast,
  About the flow'rs disguised does fold,
  With wreaths of fame and interest.
Ah, foolish Man, that would'st debase with them,
And mortal glory, Heaven's diadem!
But thou who only could'st the serpent tame,
Either his slipp'ry knots at once untie,
And disentangle all his winding snare:

Or shatter too with him my curious frame
And let these wither, so that he may die,
Though set with skill and chosen out with care,
That they, while Thou on both their spoils dost tread,
May crown thy feet, that could not crown thy head.

BERMUDAS

Where the remote Bermudas ride
In the ocean's bosom unespied,
From a small boat that row'd along
The listening woods received this song:

'What should we do but sing His praise
That led us through the watery maze
Unto an isle so long unknown,
And yet far kinder than our own?
Where He the huge sea-monsters wracks,
That lift the deep upon their backs,
He lands us on a grassy stage,
Safe from the storms' and prelates' rage:
He gave us this eternal Spring
Which here enamels everything,
And sends the fowls to us in care
On daily visits through the air:
He hangs in shades the orange bright
Like golden lamps in a green night,
And does in the pomegranates close
Jewels more rich than Ormus shows:
He makes the figs our mouths to meet
And throws the melons at our feet;
But apples plants of such a price,
No tree could ever bear them twice.

With cedars chosen by His hand
From Lebanon He stores the land;
And makes the hollow seas that roar
Proclaim the ambergris on shore.
He cast (of which we rather boast)
The Gospel's pearl upon our coast;
And in these rocks for us did frame
A temple where to sound His name.
O, let our voice His praise exalt
Till it arrive at Heaven's vault,
Which thence (perhaps) rebounding may
Echo beyond the Mexique bay!'

Thus sung they in the English boat
A holy and a cheerful note:
And all the way, to guide their chime,
With falling oars they kept the time.

HENRY VAUGHAN
(1621—1695)

THE RETREAT

Happy those early days, when I
Shin'd in my Angel-infancy!
Before I understood this place
Appointed for my second race,
Or taught my soul to fancy aught
But a white celestial thought:
When yet I had not walk'd above
A mile or two from my first Love,

And looking back—at that short space—
Could see a glimpse of His bright face:
When on some gilded cloud, or flow'r,
My gazing soul would dwell an hour,
And in those weaker glories spy
Some shadows of eternity:
Before I taught my tongue to wound
My conscience with a sinful sound,
Or had the black art to dispense
A several sin to ev'ry sense,
But felt through all this fleshly dress
Bright shoots of everlastingness.

O how I long to travel back,
And tread again that ancient track!
That I might once more reach that plain
Where first I left my glorious train;
From whence th' enlightened spirit sees
That shady City of Palm-trees.
But ah! my soul with too much stay
Is drunk, and staggers in the way!
Some men a forward motion love,
But I by backward steps would move;
And when this dust falls to the urn,
In that state I came, return.

FRIENDS DEPARTED

They are all gone into the world of light!
    And I alone sit ling'ring here;
Their very memory is fair and bright,
        And my sad thoughts doth clear.

It glows and glitters in my cloudy breast,
　　Like stars upon some gloomy grove,
Or those faint beams in which this hill is drest
　　　　After the sun's remove.

I see them walking in an air of glory,
　　Whose light doth trample on my days:
My days, which are at best but dull and hoary,
　　　　Mere glimmering and decays.

O holy Hope! and high Humility,
　　High as the heavens above!
These are your walks, and you have show'd them me,
　　　　To kindle my cold love.

Dear, beauteous Death! the jewel of the Just,
　　Shining nowhere, but in the dark;
What mysteries do lie beyond thy dust,
　　　　Could man outlook that mark!

He that found some fledg'd bird's nest may know,
　　At first sight, if the bird be flown;
But what fair well or grove he sings in now,
　　　　That is to him unknown.

And yet as Angels in some brighter dreams
　　Call to the soul, when man doth sleep:
So some strange thoughts transcend our wonted theme
　　　　And into glory peep.

If a star were confin'd into a tomb,
　　Her captive flames must needs burn there;
But when the hand that lock'd her up gives room,
　　　　She'll shine through all the sphere.

O Father of eternal life, and all
    Created glories under Thee!
Resume Thy spirit from this world of thrall
      Into true liberty.

Either disperse these mists, which blot and fill
    My perspective still as they pass:
Or else remove me hence unto that hill,
      Where I shall need no glass.

MAN

Weighing the steadfastness and state
  Of some mean things which here below reside,
Where birds like watchful clocks the noiseless date
  And intercourse of times divide,
Where bees at night get home and hive, and flowers
    Early as well as late,
Rise with the sun and set in the same bowers;

I would, said I, my God would give
  The staidness of these things to man! for these
To His divine appointments ever cleave,
  And no new business breaks their peace;
The birds nor sow nor reap, yet sup and dine,
    The flowers without clothes live,
  Yet Solomon was never drest so fine.

Man hath still either toys or care;
  He hath no root, nor to one place is tied,
But ever restless and irregular
  About the earth doth run and ride,

He knows he hath a home, but scarce knows where;
　　He says it is so far
That he hath quite forgot how to get there.

He knocks at all doors, strays and roams;
　　Nay hath not so much wit as some stones have
Which in the darkest nights point to their homes,
　　By some hid sense their Maker gave;
Man is the shuttle to whose winding quest
　　　　And passage through these looms
God ordered motion, but ordained no rest.

JOHN DRYDEN
(1631—1700)

A SONG FOR ST. CECILIA'S DAY, 1687

From harmony, from heavenly harmony,
　　This universal frame began:
　　When nature underneath a heap
　　　Of jarring atoms lay,
　　And could not heave her head,
The tuneful voice heard from high,
　　'Arise, ye more than dead!'
Then cold, and hot, and moist, and dry,
　　In order to their stations leap,
　　　And Music's power obey.
From harmony, from heavenly harmony,
　　This universal frame began:
　　From harmony to harmony
Through all the compass of the notes it ran,
The diapason closing full in Man.

What passion cannot Music raise and quell?
   When Jubal struck the chorded shell,
  His listening brethren stood around,
   And, wondering, on their faces fell
  To worship that celestial sound:
Less than a God they thought there could not dwell
   Within the hollow of that shell,
   That spoke so sweetly, and so well.
What passion cannot Music raise and quell?

   The trumpet's loud clangour
    Excites us to arms,
  With shrill notes of anger,
    And mortal alarms.

The double double double beat
   Of the thundering drum
   Cries Hark! the foes come;
Charge, charge, 'tis too late to retreat!

  The soft complaining flute,
  In dying notes, discovers
  The woes of hopeless lovers,
Whose dirge is whisper'd by the warbling lute.

  Sharp violins proclaim
Their jealous pangs and desperation,
Fury, frantic indignation,
Depth of pains, and height of passion.
  For the fair, disdainful dame.

But O, what art can teach,
What human voice can reach,
  The sacred organ's praise?
Notes inspiring holy love,
Notes that wing their heavenly ways
  To mend the choirs above.

Orpheus could lead the savage race;
And trees unrooted left their place,
  Sequacious of the lyre;
But bright Cecilia rais'd the wonder higher:
When to her organ vocal breath was given,
  An angel heard, and straight appear'd
  Mistaking Earth for Heaven.

GRAND CHORUS

As from the power of sacred lays
  The spheres began to move,
And sung the great Creator's praise
  To all the Blest above;
So when the last and dreadful hour
This crumbling pageant shall devour,
The trumpet shall be heard on high,
The dead shall live, the living die,
And Music shall untune the sky!

SONG

I feed a flame within, which so torments me
That it both pains my heart, and yet contents me:
'Tis such a pleasing smart, and I so love it,
That I had rather die than once remove it.

Yet he, for whom I grieve, shall never know it;
My tongue does not betray, nor my eyes show it.
Not a sigh, nor a tear. my pain discloses,
But they fall silently, like dew on roses.

Thus, to prevent my Love from being cruel,
My heart's the sacrifice, as 'tis the fuel;
And while I suffer this to give him quiet
My faith rewards my love, though he deny it.

On his eyes will I gaze, and there delight me;
While I conceal my love no frown can fright me.
To be more happy I dare not aspire,
Nor can I fall more low, mounting no higher.

THE DUKE OF BUCKINGHAM

... In the first rank of these did Zimri stand;
A man so various that he seem'd to be
Not one, but all Mankind's Epitome.
Stiff in opinions, always in the wrong;
Was everything by starts, and nothing long:
But, in the course of one revolving moon,
Was chymist, fiddler, statesman, and buffoon;
Then all for women, painting, rhyming, drinking,
Besides ten thousand freaks that died in thinking.
Blest madman, who could every hour employ
With something new to wish, or to enjoy!
Railing and praising were his usual themes,
And both (to show his judgment) in extremes:
So over violent, or over civil
That every man, with him, was God or Devil.

In squand'ring wealth was his peculiar art:
Nothing went unrewarded but desert.
Beggar'd by fools, whom still he found too late;
He had his jest, and they had his estate.
He laugh'd himself from court; then sought relief
By forming parties, but could ne'er be chief:
For, spite of him, the weight of business fell
On Absalom and wise Achitophel:
Thus, wicked but in will, of means bereft,
He left not faction, but of that was left...

Absalom and Achitophez.

THE LAUREATE OF DULNESS

...All human things are subject to decay,
And, when Fate summons, Monarchs must obey:
This Flecknoe found, who, like Augustus, young
Was call'd to empire and had govern'd long:
In prose and verse was own'd, without dispute
Through all the realms of Nonsense, absolute.
This aged Prince now flourishing in peace
And blest with issue of a large increase,
Worn out with business, did at length debate
To settle the succession of the state;
And pondering which of all his sons was fit
To reign, and wage immortal war with wit,
Cried ' 'Tis resolv'd; for Nature pleads that he
Should only rule, who most resembles me:
Shadwell alone my perfect image bears,
Mature in dulness from his tender years;
Shadwell alone of all my sons is he
Who stands confirm'd in full stupidity.

The rest to some faint meaning make pretence,
But Shadwell never deviates into sense.
Some beams of wit on other souls may fall,
Strike through and make a lucid interval;
But Shadwell's genuine night admits no ray,
His rising fogs prevail upon the day:
Besides, his goodly fabric fills the eye,
And seems design'd for thoughtless majesty:
Thoughtless as monarch oaks that shade the plain,
And spread in solemn state supinely reign...'

MacFlecknoe.

REASON AND REVELATION

...Dim, as the borrow'd beams of moon and stars
To lonely, weary, wand'ring travellers
Is Reason to the Soul; and as on high
Those rolling fires discover but the sky
Not light us here, so Reason's glimmering ray
Was lent, not to assure our doubtful way,
But guide us upward to a better day.
And as those nightly tapers disappear
When day's bright lord assumes the hemisphere,
So pale grows Reason at Religion's sight;
So dies, and so dissolves in supernatural light.
Some few, whose lamp shone brighter, have been led
From cause to cause to Nature's secret head;
And found that one first principle must be;
But what, or who, that universal He,
Whether some Soul encompassing this ball,
Unmade, unmov'd, yet making, moving all;

Or various atoms, interfering dance
Leapt into form (the noble work of chance),
Or this great All was from Eternity,
Not ev'n the Stagirite himself could see,
And Epicurus guess'd as well as he.
As blindly grop'd they for a future state,
As rashly judg'd of Providence and Fate:
But least of all could their endeavours find
What most concern'd the good of human kind:
For Happiness was never to be found,
But vanish'd from 'em, like enchanted ground.
One thought Content the good to be enjoy'd;
This, every little accident destroy'd:
The wiser madmen did for Virtue toil,
A thorny, or at best a barren soil:
In Pleasure some their glutton souls would steep,
But found their line too short, the well too deep,
And leaky vessels which no bliss could keep.
Thus, anxious thoughts in endless circles roll,
Without a centre where to fix the soul:
In this wild maze their vain endeavours end:
How can the less the greater comprehend?
Or finite Reason reach Infinity?
For what could fathom God were more than He. . . .

Religio Laici

TO THE MEMORY OF MR OLDHAM

Farewell, too little and too lately known,
Whom I began to think and call my own:
For sure our souls were near alli'd, and thine
Cast in the same poetic mould with mine.

One common note on either lyre did strike,
And knaves and fools we both abhorr'd alike.
To the same goal did both our studies drive;
The last set out the soonest did arrive.
Thus Nisus fell upon the slippery place,
Whilst his young friend perform'd and won the race.
O early ripe! to thy abundant store
What could advancing age have added more?
It might (what Nature never gives the young)
Have taught the numbers of thy native tongue.
But satire needs not these, and wit will shine
Through the harsh cadence of a rugged line.
A noble error, and but seldom made,
When poets are by too much force betray'd.
Thy gen'rous fruits, though gather'd ere their prime,
Still showed a quickness; and maturing Time
But mellows what we write to the dull sweets of rhyme.
Once more, hail, and farewell! farewell, thou young,
But ah! too short, Marcellus of our tongue!
Thy brows with ivy and with laurel bound;
But Fate and gloomy Night encompass thee around.

THE RUDE MILITIA

... The country rings around with loud alarms,
And raw in fields the rude militia swarms;
Mouths without hands; maintained at vast expense;
In peace a charge, in war a weak defence;
Stout once a month they march, a blustering band,
And ever, but in times of need, at hand.
This was the morn when, issuing on the guard,

Drawn up in rank and file they stood prepared
Of seeming arms to make a short essay,
Then hasten to be drunk, the business of the day ...

Cymon and Iphigenia.

UNKNOWN

BEAUTY EXTOLL'D

Gaze not on swans, in whose soft breast
A full-hatch'd beauty seems to nest,
Nor snow, which falling from the sky
Hovers in its virginity.

Gaze not on roses, though new-blown,
Grac'd with a fresh complexion;
Nor lilies, which no subtle bee
Hath robb'd by kissing chemistry.

Gaze not on that pure milky way,
Where night vies splendour with the day;
Nor pearl, whose silver walls confine
The riches of an Indian mine.

For if my Emperess appears,
Swans moulting die, snow melts to tears;
Roses do blush and hang their heads,
Pale lilies shrink into their beds.

The milky way rides post to shroud
Its baffled glory in a cloud;
And pearls do climb into her ear,
To hang themselves for envy there.

So have I seen stars big with light
Prove lanterns to the moon-eyed night,
Which, when Sol's rays were once display'd,
Sunk in their sockets, and decay'd.

SIR CHARLES SEDLEY
(1639?—1701)

SONG

Love still has something of the sea,
   From whence his mother rose;
No time his slaves from doubt can free,
   Nor give their thoughts repose;

They are becalmed in clearest days,
   And in rough weather toss'd;
They wither under cold delays,
   Or are in tempests lost.

One while they seem to touch the port,
   Then straight into the main
Some angry wind in cruel sport
   The vessel drives again.

At first disdain and pride they fear,
   Which if they chance to 'scape
Rivals and falsehood soon appear
   In a more dreadful shape.

By such degrees to joy they come,
   And are so long withstood,

So slowly they receive the sum,
  It hardly does them good.

'Tis cruel to prolong a pain;
  And to defer a joy,
Believe me, gentle Celemene,
  Offends the winged boy.

An hundred thousand oaths your fears
  Perhaps would not remove;
And if I gazed a thousand years
  I could no deeper love.

APHRA BEHN
(1640—1689)

SONG: LOVE ARM'D

Love in fantastic triumph sate
  Whilst bleeding hearts around him flow'd,
For whom fresh pains he did create
  And strange tyrannic power he show'd:
From thy bright eyes he took his fires,
  Which round about in sport he hurl'd;
But 'twas from mine he took desires
  Enough t' undo the amorous world.

From me he took his sighs and tears,
  From thee his pride and cruelty;
From me his languishments and fears,
  And every killing dart from thee.

Thus thou and I the god have arm'd
And set him up a deity;
But my poor heart alone is harm'd,
Whilst thine the victor is, and free!

JOHN WILMOT, EARL OF ROCHESTER

(1647—1680)

SONG

Absent from thee, I languish still;
Then ask me not, when I return;
The straying fool 'twill plainly kill
To wish all day, all night to mourn.

Dear, from thine arms then let me fly.
That my fantastic mind may prove
The torments it deserves to try,
That tears my fix'd heart from my love.

When, wearied with a world of woe,
To thy safe bosom I retire,
Where love, and peace, and truth does flow,
May I contented there expire!

Lest, once more wandering from that heaven,
I fall on some base heart unblest;
Faithless to thee, false, unforgiven—
And lose my everlasting rest.

A SATIRE AGAINST MANKIND

Were I, who to my cost already am,
One of those strange, prodigious creatures, Man,
A spirit free to choose for my own share
What sort of flesh and blood I pleased to wear,
I'd be a dog, a monkey, or a bear,
Or anything, but that vain animal
Who is so proud of being rational.
The senses are too gross; and he'll contrive
A sixth, to contradict the other five:
And before certain Instinct will prefer
Reason, which fifty times for one does err —
Reason, an *Ignus fatuus* of the mind,
Which leaves the light of nature, Sense, behind.
Pathless and dangerous, wandering ways it takes
Through Error's fenny bogs and thorny brakes:
While the misguided follower climbs with pain
Mountains of whimsies, heaped in his own brain;
Stumbling from thought to thought, falls headlong down
Into Doubt's boundless sea, where, like to drown,
Books bear him up awhile, and make him try
To swim with bladders of philosophy,
In hopes still to o'ertake the skipping light:
The vapour dances in his dazzled sight
Till, spent, it leaves him to eternal night.
Then Old Age and Experience, hand in hand,
Lead him to Death, and make him understand
After a search so painful and so long
That all his life he has been in the wrong...

EPITAPH ON CHARLES II

Here lies our Sovereign Lord the King,
   Whose word no man relies on,
Who never said a foolish thing,
   Nor ever did a wise one.

JONATHAN SWIFT
(1667—1745)

CRITICS

. . . Hobbes clearly proves that every creature
Lives in a state of war by nature.
The greater for the smallest watch,
But meddle seldom with their match.
A whale of moderate size will draw
A shoal of herrings down his maw.
A fox with geese his belly crams;
A wolf destroys a thousand lambs.
But search among the rhyming race,
The brave are worried by the base.
If on Parnassus' top you sit,
You rarely bite, are always bit:
Each poet of inferior size
On you shall rail and criticize;
And strive to tear you limb from limb,
While others do as much for him.
   The vermin only tease and pinch
Their foes superior by an inch.

So, naturalists observe, a flea
Hath smaller fleas that on him prey,
And these have smaller fleas to bite 'em,
And so proceed *ad infinitum:*
Thus ev'ry poet in his kind
Is bit by him that comes behind;
Who, though too little to be seen,
Can tease and gall and give the spleen;
Call dunces, fools, and sons of whores,
Lay Grubstreet at each others' doors:
Extol the Greek and Roman masters,
And curse our modern poetasters.
Complain, as many an ancient bard did,
How genius is no more rewarded;
How wrong a taste prevails among us;
How much our ancestors out-sung us;
Can personate an awkward scorn
For those who are not poets born,
And all their brother dunces lash,
Who crowd the press with hourly trash. ...

On Poetry: A Rhapsody

ISAAC WATTS

(1674—1748)

THE DAY OF JUDGEMENT

When the fierce North-wind with his airy forces
Rears up the Baltic to a foaming fury;
And the red lightning with a storm of hail comes
Rushing amain down;

How the poor sailors stand amazed and tremble,
While the hoarse thunder, like a bloody trumpet,
Roars a loud onset to the gaping waters
                              Quick to devour them.

Such shall the noise be, and the wild disorder
(If things eternal may be like these earthly),
Such the dire terror when the great Archangel
                              Shakes the creation;

Tears the strong pillars of the vault of Heaven,
Breaks up old marble, the repose of princes,
Sees the graves open, and the bones arising,
                              Flames all around them.

Hark, the shrill outcries of the guilty wretches!
Lively bright horror and amazing anguish
Stare thro' their eyelids, while the living worm lies
                              Gnawing within them.

Thoughts, like old vultures, prey upon their heart-strings,
And the smart twinges, when the eye beholds the
Lofty Judge frowning, and a flood of vengeance
                              Rolling afore him.

Hopeless immortals! how they scream and shiver,
While devils push them to the pit wide-yawning
Hideous and gloomy, to receive them headlong
                              Down to the centre!

Stop here, my fancy: (all away, ye horrid
Doleful ideas!) come, arise to Jesus,
How He sits God-like! and the saints around Him
                              Throned, yet adoring!

O may I sit there when He comes triumphant,
Dooming the nations! then ascend to glory,
While our Hosannas all along the passage
                              Shout the Redeemer!

HYMN

Our God, our help in ages past,
  Our hope for years to come,
Our shelter from the stormy blast,
  And our eternal home.

Beneath the shadow of thy throne
  Thy Saints have dwelt secure;
Sufficient is thine arm alone,
  And our defence is sure.

Before the hills in order stood,
  Or Earth receiv'd her frame,
From everlasting thou art God,
  To endless years the same.

Thy Word commands our flesh to dust,
  Return, ye sons of men:
All nations rose from Earth at first,
  And turn to Earth again.

A thousand ages in thy sight
  Are like an evening gone;
Short as the watch that ends the night
  Before the rising Sun.

The busy tribes of flesh and blood
  With all their lives and cares
Are carried downwards by thy flood,
  And lost in following years.

Time like an ever-rolling stream
  Bears all its sons away;
They fly forgotten as a dream
  Dies at the opening day.

Like flow'ry fields the nations stand
  Pleas'd with the morning-light;
The flowers beneath the mower's hand
  Lie withering ere 'tis night.

Our God, our help in ages past,
  Our hope for years to come,
Be thou our guard while troubles last,
  And our eternal home

JOHN GAY
(1685—1732)

WEET WILLIAM'S FAREWELL TO BLACK-EYED SUSAN

All in the Downs the fleet was moor'd,
  The streamers waving in the wind,
When black-ey'd Susan came aboard.
  'Oh, where shall I my true love find?
Tell me, ye jovial sailors, tell me true,
If my sweet William sails among the crew.'

William, who high upon the yard
 Rock'd with the billow to and fro,
Soon as her well-known voice he heard
 He sigh'd, and cast his eyes below:
The cord slides swiftly through his glowing hands,
And, quick as lightning, on the deck he stands.

So the sweet lark, high pois'd in air,
 Shuts close his pinions to his breast,
If, chance, his mate's shrill call he hear,
 And drops at once into her nest.
The noblest captain in the British fleet
Might envy William's lip those kisses sweet.

'Oh Susan, Susan, lovely dear,
 My vows shall ever true remain;
Let me kiss off that falling tear,
 We only part to meet again.
Change as ye list, ye winds; my heart shall be
The faithful compass that still points to thee.

Believe not what the landmen say,
 Who tempt with doubts thy constant mind:
They'll tell thee sailors when away
 In ev'ry port a mistress find.
Yes, yes, believe them when they tell thee so,
For thou art present wheresoe'er I go.

If to far India's coast we sail,
 Thy eyes are seen in diamonds bright,
Thy breath is Afric's spicy gale,
 Thy skin is ivory, so white.

Thus ev'ry beauteous object that I view
Wakes in my soul some charm of lovely Sue.

Though battle call me from thy arms,
    Let not my pretty Susan mourn;
Though cannons roar, yet safe from harms
    William shall to his dear return.
Love turns aside the balls that round me fly,
Lest precious tears should drop from Susan's eye.'

The boatswain gave the dreadful word,
    The sails their swelling bosom spread,
No longer must she stay aboard:
    They kiss'd, she sigh'd, he hung his head.
Her less'ning boat unwilling rows to land:
'Adieu!' she cries, and wav'd her lily hand.

ALEXANDER POPE
(1688—1744)

A LITTLE LEARNING

... A little learning is a dang'rous thing;
Drink deep, or taste not the Pierian spring:
There shallow draughts intoxicate the brain,
And drinking largely sobers us again.
Fir'd at first sight with what the Muse imparts,
In fearless youth we tempt the heights of arts,
While from the bounded level of our mind
Short views we take, nor see the lengths behind;
But more advanc'd, behold with strange surprise
New distant scenes of endless science rise

So pleas'd at first the tow'ring Alps we try,
Mount o'er the vales, and seem to tread the sky,
Th' eternal snows appear already past,
And the first clouds and mountains seem the last:
But those attain'd, we tremble to survey
The growing labours of the lengthen'd way,
Th' increasing prospect tires our wand'ring eyes
Hills peep o'er hills, and Alps on Alps arise...

An Essay on Criticism.

THE TOILET

... And now, unveil'd, the toilet stands display'd,
Each silver vase in mystic order laid.
First, rob'd in white, the nymph intent adores,
With head uncover'd, the cosmetic pow'rs.
A heav'nly image in the glass appears,
To that she bends, to that her eyes she rears;
Th' inferior priestess, at her altar's side,
Trembling begins the sacred rites of pride.
Unnumber'd treasures ope at once, and here
The various off'rings of the world appear;
From each she nicely culls with curious toil,
And decks the goddess with the glitt'ring spoil.
This casket India's glowing gems unlocks,
And all Arabia breathes from yonder box.
The tortoise here and elephant unite,
Transform'd to combs, the speckled, and the white.
Here files of pins extend their shining rows,
Puffs, powders, patches, Bibles, billet-doux.
Now awful Beauty puts on all its arms;
The fair each moment rises in her charms,

Repairs her smiles, awakens ev'ry grace,
And calls forth all the wonders of her face;
Sees by degrees a purer blush arise,
And keener lightnings quicken in her eyes.
The busy sylphs surround their darling care,
These set the head, and those divide the hair,
Some fold the sleeve, whilst others plait the gown;
And Betty's prais'd for labours not her own. . . .

The Rape of the Lock.

ELEGY TO THE MEMORY OF AN UNFORTUNATE LADY

What beck'ning ghost, along the moonlight shade
Invites my steps, and points to yonder glade?
'Tis she!—but why that bleeding bosom gored,
Why dimly gleams the visionary sword?
O, ever beauteous, ever friendly! tell,
Is it, in Heav'n, a crime to love too well?
To bear too tender or too firm a heart,
To act a lover's or a Roman's part?
Is there no bright reversion in the sky
For those who greatly think, or bravely die?

Why bade ye else, ye Pow'rs! her soul aspire
Above the vulgar flight of low desire?
Ambition first sprung from your blest abodes;
The glorious fault of angels and of gods;
Thence to their images on earth it flows,
And in the breasts of kings and heroes glows.
Most souls, 'tis true, but peep out once an age,
Dull sullen pris'ners in the body's cage:

Dim lights of life, that burn a length of years,
Useless, unseen, as lamps in sepulchres;
Like Eastern kings a lazy state they keep,
And close confined to their own palace, sleep.

    From these perhaps (ere Nature bade her die)
Fate snatch'd her early to the pitying sky.
As into air the purer spirits flow,
And sep'rate from their kindred dregs below,
So flew the soul to its congenial place,
Nor left one virtue to redeem her race.

    But thou, false guardian of a charge too good!
Thou, mean deserter of thy brother's blood!
See on these ruby lips the trembling breath,
These cheeks now fading at the blast of Death
Cold is that breast which warm'd the world before,
And those love- darting eyes must roll no more.
Thus, if eternal Justice rules the ball,
Thus shall your wives, and thus your children fall;
On all the line a sudden vengeance waits,
And frequent hearses shall besiege your gates.
There passengers shall stand, and pointing say
(While the long fun'rals blacken all the way),
'Lo! these were they whose souls the Furies steel'd
And cursed with hearts unknowing how to yield.'
Thus unlamented pass the proud away,
The gaze of fools, and pageant of a day!
So perish all whose breast ne'er learn'd to glow
For others' good, or melt at others' woe!

    What can atone (O ever-injured shade!)
Thy fate unpitied, and thy rites unpaid?
No friend's complaint, no kind domestic tear
Pleased thy pale ghost, or graced thy mournful bier.

By foreign hands thy dying eyes were closed,
By foreign hands thy decent limbs composed,
By foreign hands thy humble grave adorn'd,
By strangers honour'd and by strangers mourn'd!
What tho' no friends in sable weeds appear,
Grieve for an hour, perhaps, then mourn a year,
And bear about the mockery of woe
To midnight dances, and the public show?
What tho' no weeping Loves thy ashes grace,
Nor polish'd marble emulate thy face?
What tho' no sacred earth allow thee room,
Nor hallow'd dirge be mutter'd o'er thy tomb?
Yet shall thy grave with rising flow'rs be drest,
And the green turf lie lightly on thy breast:
There shall the morn her earliest tears bestow,
There the first roses of the year shall blow;
While angels with their silver wings o'ershade
The ground now sacred by thy reliques made.

So peaceful rests, without a stone, a name
What once had beauty, titles, wealth, and fame.
How loved, how honour'd once, avails thee not,
To whom related, or by whom begot;
A heap of dust alone remains of thee,
Tis all thou art, and all the proud shall be!

Poets themselves must fall, like those they sung,
Deaf the praised ear, and mute the tuneful tongue.
Ev'n he, whose soul now melts in mournful lays,
Shall shortly want the gen'rous tear he pays;
Then from his closing eyes thy form shall part,
And the last pang shall tear thee from his heart;
Life's idle business at one gasp be o'er,
The Muse forgot, and thou beloved no more!

HOPE SPRINGS ETERNAL

... Heav'n from all creatures hides the book of fate,
All but the page prescrib'd, their present state,
From brutes what men, from men what spirits know
Or who could suffer Being here below?
The lamb thy riot dooms to bleed to-day,
Had he thy reason, would he skip and play?
Pleas'd to the last, he crops the flow'ry food,
And licks the hand just rais'd to shed his blood.
Oh blindness to the future! kindly giv'n,
That each may fill the circle mark'd by Heav'n:
Who sees with equal eye, as God of all,
A hero perish, or a sparrow fall,
Atoms or systems into ruin hurl'd,
And now a bubble burst, and now a world.

Hope humbly then; with trembling pinions soar;
Wait the great teacher, Death; and God adore!
What future bliss, he gives not thee to know,
But gives that hope to be thy blessing now.
Hope springs eternal in the human breast—
Man never is, but always to be blest:
The soul uneasy, and confin'd at home,
Rests, and expatiates, in a life to come.

Lo! the poor Indian, whose untutor'd mind
Sees God in clouds, or hears him in the wind;
His soul, proud Science never taught to stray
Far as the solar walk, or milky way;
Yet simple Nature to his hope has giv'n,
Behind the cloud-topt hill, an humbler heav'n;

Some safer world in depth of woods embrac'd,
Some happier island in the wat'ry waste,
Where slaves once more their native land behold,
No fiends torment, no Christians thirst for gold.
To be, contents his natural desire,
He asks no angel's wing, no seraph's fire;
But thinks, admitted to that equal sky,
His faithful dog shall bear him company ...

An Essay on Man.

LORD HERVEY

P .. Let Sporus tremble—A. What? that thing of silk,
Sporus, that mere white curd of ass's milk?
Satire or sense, alas! can Sporus feel?
Who breaks a butterfly upon a wheel?
P. Yet let me flap this bug with gilded wings,
This painted child of dirt, that stinks and stings;
Whose buzz the witty and the fair annoys,
Yet wit ne'er tastes, and beauty ne'er enjoys:
So well-bred spaniels civilly delight
In mumbling of the game they dare not bite.
Eternal smiles his emptiness betray,
As shallow streams run dimpling all the way.
Whether in florid impotence he speaks,
And, as the prompter breathes, the puppet squeaks;
Or at the ear of Eve, familiar toad,
Half froth, half venom, spits himself abroad,
In puns, or politics, or tales, or lies,
Or spite, or smut, or rhymes, or blasphemies.
His wit all see-saw, between that and this,

Now high, now low, now master up, now miss,
And he himself one vile antithesis.
Amphibious thing! that acting either part,
The trifling head or the corrupted heart,
Fop at the toilet, flatt'rer at the board,
Now trips a lady, and now struts a lord.
Eve's tempter thus the Rabbins have exprest,
A cherub's face, a reptile all the rest;
Beauty that shocks you, parts that none will trust;
Wit that can creep, and pride that licks the dust . . .

Epistle to Dr. Arbuthnot.

VERBAL CRITICS

. . . Pains, reading, study, are their just pretence,
And all they want is spirit, taste, and sense.
Comma's and points they set exactly right,
And 'twere a sin to rob them of their mite.
Yet ne'er one sprig of laurel grac'd these ribalds,
From slashing Bentley down to pidling Tibalds
Each wight who reads not, and but scans and spells,
Each word-catcher that lives on syllables,
Ev'n such small critics some regard may claim,
Preserv'd in Milton's or in Shakespear's name.
Pretty! in amber to observe the forms
Of hairs, or straws, or dirt, or grubs, or worms!
The things, we know, are neither rich nor rare,
But wonder how the devil they got there . . .

Epistle to Dr. Arbuthno

THE SECOND DUKE OF BUCKINGHAM

... In the worst inn's worst room, with mat half-hung,
The floors of plaster, and the walls of dung,
On once a flock-bed, but repair'd with straw,
With tape-ty'd curtains, never meant to draw,
The George and Garter dangling from that bed
Where tawdry yellow strove with dirty red,
Great Villiers lies—alas! how chang'd from him,
That life of pleasure, and that soul of whim!
Gallant and gay, in Cliveden's proud alcove,
The bow'r of wanton Shrewsbury and love;
Or just as gay, at council, in a ring
Of mimic'd statesmen, and their merry king.
No wit to flatter left of all his store!
No fool to laugh at, which he valu'd more.
There, victor of his health, of fortune, friends,
And fame, this lord of useless thousands ends ...

Moral Essays.

TIMON'S VILLA

... At Timon's Villa let us pass a day,
Where all cry out, 'What sums are thrown away!'
So proud, so grand; of that stupendous air,
Soft and Agreeable come never there.
Greatness, with Timon, dwells in such a draught
As brings all Brobdignag before your thought.
To compass this, his building is a town,
His pond an ocean, his parterre a down:
Who but must laugh, the master when he sees,
A puny insect, shiv'ring at a breeze!

Lo, what huge heaps of littleness around!
The whole, a labour'd quarry above ground:
Two Cupids squirt before: a lake behind
Improves the keenness of the northern wind.
His gardens next your admiration call,
On ev'ry side you look, behold the wall!
No pleasing intricacies intervene,
No artful wildness to perplex the scene:
Grove nods at grove, each alley has a brother,
And half the platform just reflects the other.
The suff'ring eye inverted Nature sees,
Trees cut to statues, statues thick as trees;
With here a fountain, never to be play'd;
And there a summer-house, that knows no shade:
Here Amphitrite sails thro' myrtle bow'rs;
There gladiators fight, or die, in flow'rs;
Unwatered see the drooping sea-horse mourn,
And swallows roost in Nilus' dusty urn.

My Lord advances with majestic mien,
Smit with the mighty pleasure, to be seen;
But soft—by regular approach—not yet—
First thro' the length of yon hot terrace sweat;
And when up ten steep slopes you've dragg'd your thigh
Just at his study-door he'll bless your eyes.

His study! with what authors is it stor'd?
In books, not authors, curious is my Lord;
To all their dated backs he turns you round:
These Aldus printed, those Du Sueil has bound.
Lo, some are vellum, and the rest as good
For all his Lordship knows, but they are wood.
For Locke or Milton 'tis in vain to look,
These shelves admit not any modern book.

And now the chapel's silver bell you hear,
That summons you to all the pride of pray'r:
Light quirks of music, broken and uneven,
Make the soul dance upon a jig to Heav'n.
On painted ceilings you devoutly stare,
Where sprawl the Saints of Verrio or Laguerre,
On gilded clouds in fair expansion lie,
And bring all Paradise before your eye.
To rest, the cushion and soft Dean invite,
Who never mentions Hell to ears polite.

But hark! the himing clocks to dinner call;
A hundred footsteps scrape the marble hall:
The rich buffet well-colour'd serpents grace,
And gaping Tritons spew to wash your face.
Is this a dinner? this a genial room?
No, 'tis a temple, and a hecatomb.
A solemn sacrifice, perform'd in state,
You drink by measure, and to minutes eat.
So quick retires each flying course, you'd swear
Sancho's dread doctor and his wand were there.
Between each act the trembling salvers ring,
From soup to sweet-wine, and God bless the King.
In plenty starving, tantaliz'd in state,
And complaisantly help'd to all I hate,
Treated, caress'd, and tir'd, I take my leave,
Sick of his civil pride from morn to eve;
I curse such lavish cost, and little skill,
And swear no day was ever past so ill.

Yet hence the poor are cloth'd, the hungry fed;
Health to himself, and to his infants bread,
The lab'rer bears: What his hard heart denies,
His charitable vanity supplies.

Another age shall see the golden ear
Imbrown the slope, and nod on the parterre,
Deep harvests bury all his pride has plann'd,
And laughing Ceres re-assume the land . . .

Moral Essay

THE TRIUMPH OF DULNESS

. . . O Muse! relate (for you can tell alone,
Wits have short memories, and dunces none)
Relate who first, who last, resign'd to rest;
Whose heads she partly, who completely bless'd;
What charms could Faction, what Ambition lull,
The venal quiet and entrance the dull;
Till drown'd was sense and shame and right
                       and wrong —
O sing, and hush the nations with thy song!

In vain, in vain, — the all-composing hour
Relentless falls; the Muse obeys the pow'r.
She comes! She comes! The sable throne behold
Of Night primaeval and of Chaos old!
Before her, Fancy's gilded clouds decay,
And all its vaying rainbows die away.
Wit shoots in vain its momentary fires,
The meteor drops and in a flash expires.
As one by one, at dread Medea's strain,
The sick'ning stars fade off th'ethereal plain;
As Argus' eyes, by Hermes' wand oppress'd,
Clos'd one by one to everlasting rest;
Thus at her felt approach and secret might
Art after art goes out, and all is night.

See skulking Truth to her old cavern fled,
Mountains of cauistry heap'd o'er her head!
Philosophy, that lean'd on heav'n before,
Shrinks to her second cause, and is no more.
Physic of Metaphysic begs defence,
And Metaphysic calls for aid on Sense!
See Mystery to Mathematics fly —
In vain! They gaze, turn giddy, rave and die.
Religion blushing veils her sacred fires,
And unawares Morality expires.
Nor public flame, nor private, dares to shine;
Nor human spark is left, nor glimpse divine.
Lo! Thy dread empire, Chaos, is restor'd;
Light dies before thy uncreating word:
Thy hand, great Anarch! lets the curtain fall;
And Universal Darkness buries All.

The Dunciad.

SAMUEL WESLEY
(1691—1739)

ON THE SETTING-UP OF MR BUTLER'S MONUMENT
IN WESTMINSTER ABBEY

While Butler, needy wretch, was yet alive
No gen'rous patron would a dinner give.
See him, when starv'd to death and turn'd to dust,
Presented with a monumental bust!
The poet's fate is here in emblem shown;
He ask'd for bread, and he receiv'd a stone.

MATTHEW GREEN
(1696—1737)

ON EVEN KEEL

... Thus, thus I steer my bark, and sail
On even keel with gentle gale;
At helm I make my reason sit,
My crew of passions all submit.
If dark and blustering prove some nights,
Philosophy puts forth her lights;
Experience holds the cautious glass,
To shun the breakers, as I pass,
And frequent throws the wary lead,
To see what dangers may be hid:
And once in seven years I'm seen
At Bath or Tunbridge, to careen.
Though pleased to see the dolphins play,
I mind my compass and my way.
With store sufficient for relief,
And wisely still prepared to reef,
Nor wanting the dispersive bowl
Of cloudy weather in the soul,
I make (may heaven propitious send
Such wind and weather to the end)
Neither becalmed, nor over-blown,
Life's voyage to the world unknown. ...

The Spleen

JAMES THOMSON
(1700—1748)

PRELUDE

... The north-east spends his rage; and now, shut up
Within his iron caves, the effusive south
Warms the wide air, and o'er the void of heaven
Breathes the big clouds with vernal showers distent...
At first a dusky wreath they seem to rise,
Scarce staining ether; but by fast degrees,
In heaps on heaps, the doubling vapour sails
Along the loaded sky, and, mingling deep,
Sits on the horizon round a settled gloom:
Not such as wintry storms on mortals shed,
Oppressing life; but lovely, gentle, kind,
And full of every hope and every joy;
The wish of Nature. Gradual sinks the breeze
Into a perfect calm; that not a breath
Is heard to quiver through the closing woods,
Or rustling turn the many-twinkling leaves
Of aspen tall. The uncurling floods, diffused
In glassy breadth, seem through delusive lapse
Forgetful of their course. 'Tis silence all,
And pleasing expectation...

FROST AT NIGHT

... With the fierce rage of winter deep suffus'd,
An icy gale, oft shifting, o'er the pool
Breathes a blue film, and in its mid career

Arrests the bickering stream. The loosen'd ice
Let down the flood, and half dissolv'd by day,
Rustles no more; but to the sedgy bank
Fast grows, or gathers round the pointed stone,
A crystal pavement, by the breath of heaven
Cemented firm; till, seiz'd from shore to shore,
The whole imprison'd river growls below.
Loud rings the frozen earth, and hard reflects
A double noise; while, at his evening watch,
The village dog deters the nightly thief;
The heifer lows; the distant water-fall
Swells in the breeze; and with the hasty tread
Of traveller, the hollow-sounding plain
Shakes from afar. The full ethereal round,
Infinite worlds disclosing to the view,
Shines out intensely keen; and, all one cope
Of starry glitter, glows from pole to pole.
From pole to pole the rigid influence falls,
Thro' the still night, incessant, heavy strong,
And seizes nature fast. It freezes on;
Till Morn, late-rising o'er the drooping world
Lifts her pale eye unjoyous. Then appears
The various labour of the silent night
Prone from the dripping eave, and dumb cascade,
Whose idle torrents only seem to roar,
The pendant icicle; the frost-work fair,
Where transient hues, and fancy'd figures rise;
Wide-spouted o'er the hill, the frozen brook,
A livid tract, cold-gleaming on the morn;
The forest bent beneath the plumy wave;
And by the frost refin'd the whiter snow,
Incrusted hard, and sounding to the tread

Of early shepherd, as he pensive seeks
His pining flock, or from the mountain-top,
Pleas'd with the slippery surface, swift descends . . .

Winter.

VERSES OCCASIONED BY THE DEATH
OF DR. AIKMAN

As those we love decay, we die in part,
String after string is sever'd from the heart;
Till loosen'd life, at last, but breathing clay,
Without one pang is glad to fall away.
Unhappy he, who latest feels the blow,
Whose eyes have wept o'er every friend laid low,
Drag'd ling'ring on from partial death to death,
Till, dying, all he can resign is breath.

JOHN DYER
(1700—1758)

LINES FROM GRONGAR HILL

. . . See on the mountain's southern side,
Where the prospect opens wide,
Where the ev'ning gilds the sky,
How close and small the hedges lie!
What streaks of meadows cross the eye!
A step, methinks, may pass the stream,
So little distant dangers seem;
So we mistake the future's face,
Eyed through Hope's deluding glass;
As yon summits soft and fair,

Clad in colours of the air,
Which, to those who journey near,
Barren and brown and rough appear.
Still we tread tired the same coarse way;
The present's still a cloudy day...

Grongar Hill

ENGLISH WEATHER

...How erring oft the judgment in its hate,
Or fond desire! Those slow-descending show'rs,
Those hov'ring fogs, that bathe our growing vales
In deep November (loath'd by trifling Gaul,
Effeminate), are gifts the Pleiads shed,
Britannia's handmaids. As the bev'rage falls,
Her hills rejoice, her vallies laugh and sing.

Hail noble Albion! where no golden mines,
No soft perfumes, nor oils, nor myrtle bow'rs
The vig'rous frame and lofty heart of man
Enervate: round whose stern cerulean brows
White-winged snow, and cloud, and pearly rain,
Frequent attend, with solemn majesty:
Rich queen of mists and vapours!...

The Fleece

CHARLES WESLEY
(1707—1788)

A MORNING HYMN

Christ, Whose glory fills the skies,
    Christ, the true, the only Light,
Sun of Righteousness, arise,
    Triumph o'er the shades of night!

Day-spring from on high, be near!
Day-star, in my heart appear!

Dark and cheerless is the morn
    Unaccompanied by Thee;
Joyless is the day's return,
    Till Thy mercy's beams I see;
Till they inward light impart,
Glad my eyes, and warm my heart.

Visit then this soul of mine,
    Pierce the gloom of sin and grief!
Fill me, Radiancy Divine,
    Scatter all my unbelief!
More and more Thyself display,
Shining to the perfect day!

SAMUEL JOHNSON
(1709—1784)

POVERTY IN LONDON

. . . By numbers here from shame or censure free,
All crimes are safe, but hated poverty.
This, only this, the rigid law pursues,
This, only this, provokes the snarling Muse;
The sober trader at a tatter'd cloak,
Wakes from his dream, and labours for a joke;
With brisker air the silken courtiers gaze,
And turn the varied taunt a thousand ways.
Of all the griefs that harrass the distrest,
Sure the most bitter is a scornful jest;

Fate never wounds more deep the gen'rous heart
Than when a blockhead's insult points the dart.
　　Has Heaven reserv'd, in pity to the poor
No pathless waste, or undiscover'd shore?
No secret island in the boundless main
No peaceful desert yet unclaim'd by Spain?
Quick let us rise, the happy seats explore,
And bear oppression's insolence no more.
This mournful truth is ev'ry where confest,
Slow rises worth, by poverty deprest:
But here more slow, where all are slaves to gold,
Where looks are merchandise, and smiles are sold,
Where won by bribes, by flatteries implor'd,
The groom retails the favours of his lord . . .

London

CHARLES XII OF SWEDEN

. . . On what foundation stands the warrior's pride?
How just his hopes let Swedish Charles decide;
A frame of adamant, a soul of fire,
No dangers fright him and no labours tire;
O'er love, o'er fear, extends his wide domain,
Unconquer'd lord of pleasure and of pain;
No joys to him pacific sceptres yield,
War sounds the trump, he rushes to the field;
Behold surrounding Kings their pow'rs combine,
And one capitulate, and one resign:
Peace courts his hand, but spreads her charms in vain
'Think nothing gain'd', he cries, 'till nought remain,
'On Moscow's walls till Gothic standards fly,
'And all be mine beneath the polar sky.'

The march begins in military state,
And nations on his eye suspended wait;
Stern famine guards the solitary coast,
And winter barricades the realms of frost;
He comes, nor want nor cold his course delay;—
Hide, blushing Glory, hide Pultowa's day:
The vanquish'd hero leaves his broken bands,
And shows his miseries in distant lands;
Condemn'd a needy supplicant to wait,
While ladies interpose, and slaves debate.
But did not chance at length her error mend?
Did no subverted empire mark his end?
Did rival monarchs give the fatal wound?
Or hostile millions press him to the ground?
His fall was destin'd to a barren strand,
A petty fortress, and a dubious hand;
He left the name, at which the world grew pale,
To point a moral, or adorn a tale...

                                 The Vanity of Human Wishes.

PRAYER

...Where then shall Hope and Fear their objects find?
Must dull Suspense corrupt the stagnant mind?
Must helpless man, in ignorance sedate,
Roll darkling down the torrent of his fate?
Must no dislike alarm, no wishes rise,
No cries attempt the mercies of the skies?
Inquirer, cease! petitions yet remain,
Which Heav'n may hear, nor deem religion vain
Still raise for good the supplicating voice,
But leave to Heav'n the measure and the choice;

Safe in His pow'r, whose eyes discern afar
The secret ambush of a specious pray'r.
Implore his aid, in his decisions rest,
Secure whate'er he gives, he gives the best.
Yet when the sense of sacred presence fires,
And strong devotion to the skies aspires,
Pour forth thy fervours for a healthful mind,
Obedient passions, and a will resign'd;
For love, which scarce collective man can fill;
For patience, sovereign o'er transmuted ill;
For faith, that panting for a happier seat,
Counts death kind Nature's signal of retreat:
These goods for man the laws of Heav'n ordain,
These goods He grants, who grants the pow'r to gain;
With these celestial Wisdom calms the mind,
And makes the happiness she does not find ...

The Vanity of Human Wishes.

THOMAS GRAY
(1716—1771)

ELEGY WRITTEN IN A COUNTRY CHURCHYARD

The curfew tolls the knell of parting day,
   The lowing herd wind slowly o'er the lea,
The plowman homeward plods his weary way,
   And leaves the world to darkness and to me.

Now fades the glimmering landscape on the sight,
   And all the air a solemn stillness holds,
Save where the beetle wheels his droning flight,
   And drowsy tinklings lull the distant folds;

Save that from yonder ivy-mantled tow'r
  The moping owl does to the moon complain
Of such as, wand'ring near her secret bow'r,
  Molest her ancient solitary reign.

Beneath those rugged elms, that yew-tree's shade,
  Where heaves the turf in many a mould'ring heap,
Each in his narrow cell for ever laid,
  The rude forefathers of the hamlet sleep.

The breezy call of incense-breathing Morn,
  The swallow twitt'ring from the straw-built shed,
The cock's shrill clarion, or the echoing horn,
  No more shall rouse them from their lowly bed.

For them no more the blazing hearth shall burn,
  Or busy housewife ply her evening care:
No children run to lisp their sire's return,
  Or climb his knees the envied kiss to share.

Oft did the harvest to their sickle yield,
  Their furrow oft the stubborn glebe has broke:
How jocund did they drive their team afield!
  How bow'd the woods beneath their sturdy stroke!

Let not Ambition mock their useful toil,
  Their homely joys, and destiny obscure;
Nor Grandeur hear with a disdainful smile
  The short and simple annals of the poor.

The boast of heraldry, the pomp of pow'r,
  And all that beauty, all that wealth e'er gave,
Awaits alike th' inevitable hour:
  The paths of glory lead but to the grave.

Nor you, ye proud, impute to these the fault,
  If Memory o'er their tomb no trophies raise,
Where through the long-drawn aisle and fretted vault
  The pealing anthem swells the note of praise.

Can storied urn or animated bust
  Back to its mansion call the fleeting breath?
Can Honour's voice provoke the silent dust,
  Or Flatt'ry soothe the dull cold ear of death?

Perhaps in this neglected spot is laid
  Some heart once pregnant with celestial fire;
Hands, that the rod of empire might have sway'd,
  Or waked to ecstasy the living lyre.

But Knowledge to their eyes her ample page
  Rich with the spoils of time did ne'er unroll;
Chill Penury repress'd their noble rage,
  And froze the genial current of the soul.

Full many a gem of purest ray serene
  The dark unfathom'd caves of ocean bear:
Full many a flower is born to blush unseen,
  And waste its sweetness on the desert air.

Some village Hampden that with dauntless breast
  The little tyrant of his fields withstood,
Some mute inglorious Milton, here may rest,
  Some Cromwell guiltless of his country's blood.

Th' applause of list'ning senates to command
  The threats of pain and ruin to despise,

To scatter plenty o'er a smiling land,
  And read their history in a nation's eyes,

Their lot forbade: nor circumscribed alone
  Their growing virtues, but their crimes confined;
Forbade to wade through slaughter to a throne,
  And shut the gates of mercy on mankind,

The struggling pangs of conscious truth to hide,
  To quench the blushes of ingenuous shame,
Or heap the shrine of Luxury and Pride
  With incense kindled at the Muse's flame.

Far from the madding crowd's ignoble strife
  Their sober wishes never learn'd to stray;
Along the cool sequester'd vale of life
  They kept the noiseless tenor of their way.

Yet ev'n these bones from insult to protect
  Some frail memorial still erected nigh,
With uncouth rhymes and shapeless sculpture deck'd,
  Implores the passing tribute of a sigh.

Their name, their years, spelt by th' unletter'd muse,
  The place of fame and elegy supply:
And many a holy text around she strews,
  That teach the rustic moralist to die.

For who, to dumb Forgetfulness a prey,
  This pleasing anxious being e'er resign'd,
Left the warm precincts of the cheerful day,
  Nor cast one longing ling'ring look behind?

On some fond breast the parting soul relies,
  Some pious drops the closing eye requires;
E'en from the tomb the voice of Nature cries,
  E'en in our ashes live their wonted fires.

For thee, who, mindful of th' unhonour'd dead,
  Dost in these lines their artless tale relate;
If chance, by lonely contemplation led,
  Some kindred spirit shall inquire thy fate,

Haply some hoary-headed swain may say,
  'Oft have we seen him at the peep of dawn
Brushing with hasty steps the dews away
  To meet the sun upon the upland lawn.

'There at the foot of yonder nodding beech
  That wreathes its old fantastic roots so high,
His listless length at noontide would he stretch
  And pore upon the brook that babbles by.

'Hard by yon wood, now smiling as in scorn,
  Mutt'ring his wayward fancies he would rove,
Now drooping, woeful wan, like one forlorn,
  Or crazed with care, or cross'd in hopeless love

'One morn I miss'd him on the custom'd hill,
  Along the heath and near his fav'rite tree;
Another came, nor yet beside the rill,
  Nor up the lawn, nor at the wood was he;

'The next with dirges due in sad array
  Slow through the church-way path we saw him borne
Approach and read (for thou canst read) the lay
  Graved on the stone beneath yon aged thorn.'

IMPROMPTU,

SUGGESTED BY A VIEW, IN 1766, OF THE SEAT AND RUINS OF A NOBLEMAN, AT KINGSGATE, KENT

Old, and abandon'd by each venal friend,
   Here Holland form'd the pious resolution
To smuggle a few years, and strive to mend
   A broken character and constitution.

On this congenial spot he fix'd his choice;
   Earl Goodwin trembled for his neighbouring sand;
Here sea-gulls scream, and cormorants rejoice,
   And mariners, though shipwreck'd, dread to land.

Here reign the blustering North and blighting East,
   No tree is heard to whisper, bird to sing;
Yet Nature could not furnish out the feast,
   Art he invokes new horrors still to bring.

Here mouldering fanes and battlements arise,
   Turrets and arches nodding to their fall,
Unpeopled monast'ries delude our eyes,
   And mimic desolation covers all.

"Ah!" said the sighing peer, "had Bute been true,
   Nor Mungo's Rigby's, Bradshaw's friendship vain,
Far better scenes than these had blest our view,
   And realis'd the beauties which we feign:

"Purg'd by the sword, and purified by fire,
   Then had we seen proud London's hated walls;
Owls would have hooted in St Peter's choir,
   And foxes stunk and litter'd in St Paul's."

THE EPITAPH

Here rests his head upon the lap of Earth
   A Youth to Fortune and to Fame unknown.
Fair Science frown'd not on his humble birth,
   And Melancholy mark'd him for her own.

Large was his bounty, and his soul sincere,
   Heav'n did a recompense as largely send:
He gave to Mis'ry all he had, a tear,
   He gain'd from Heav'n ('twas all he wish'd) a friend

No farther seek his merits to disclose,
   Or draw his frailties from their dread abode,
(There they alike in trembling hope repose,)
   The bosom of his Father and his God.

WILLIAM COLLINS
(1721—1759)

ODE,
WRITTEN IN THE BEGINNING OF THE YEAR 1746

How sleep the brave, who sink to rest
By all their country's wishes blest!
When Spring, with dewy fingers cold,
Returns to deck their hallow'd mould,
She there shall dress a sweeter sod
Than Fancy's feet have ever trod.

By fairy hands their knell is rung;
By forms unseen their dirge is sung;

There Honour comes, a pilgrim grey,
To bless the turf that wraps their clay;
And Freedom shall awhile repair
To dwell, a weeping hermit, there!

ODE TO EVENING

If aught of oaten stop, or pastoral song,
May hope, chaste Eve, to soothe thy modest ear,
    Like thy own solemn springs,
    Thy springs and dying gales;

O nymph reserved, while now the bright-hair'd sun
Sits in yon western tent, whose cloudy skirts,
    With brede ethereal wove,
    O'erhang his wavy bed:

Now air is hush'd save where the weak-eyed bat
With short shrill shriek flits by on leathern wing,
    Or where the beetle winds
    His small but sullen horn,

As oft he rises, 'midst the twilight path
Against the pilgrim borne in heedless hum:
    Now teach me, maid composed,
    To breathe some soften'd strain,

Whose numbers, stealing through thy darkening vale,
May not unseemly with its stillness suit,
    As, musing slow, I hail
    Thy genial loved return!

For when thy folding-star arising shows
His paly circlet, at his warning lamp
    The fragrant hours, and elves
    Who slept in buds the day,

And many a nymph who wreathes her brows with s
And sheds the freshening dew, and, lovelier still,
    The pensive pleasures sweet,
    Prepare thy shadowy car:

Then lead, calm votaress, where some sheety lake
Cheers the lone heath, or some time-hallow'd pile
    Or upland fallows grey
    Reflect its last cool gleam.

Or if chill blustering winds, or driving rain,
Prevent my willing feet, be mine the hut
    That from the mountain's side
    Views wilds and swelling floods,

And hamlets brown, and dim-discover'd spires,
And hears their simple bell, and marks o'er all
    Thy dewy fingers draw
    The gradual dusky veil.

While Spring shall pour his show'rs, as oft he wont,
And bathe thy breathing tresses, meekest Eve!
    While Summer loves to sport
    Beneath thy lingering light;

While sallow Autumn fills thy lap with leaves,
Or Winter, yelling through the troublous air,
    Affrights thy shrinking train,
    And rudely rends thy robes:

So long, regardful of thy quiet rule,
Shall Fancy, Friendship, Science, rose-lipp'd Health
    Thy gentlest influence own,
    And hymn thy favourite name!

CHRISTOPHER SMART
(1722—1771)

STANZAS FROM 'A SONG TO DAVID'

    ... For Adoration all the ranks
Of angels yield eternal thanks,
    And David in the midst;
With God's good poor, which, last and least
In man's esteem, thou to thy feast,
    O blessed bride-groom, bidst.

For Adoration seasons change,
And order, truth, and beauty range,
    Adjust, attract, and fill:
The grass the polyanthus checks;
And polish'd porphyry reflects,
    By the descending rill.

Rich almonds colour to the prime
For Adoration; tendrils climb,
    And fruit-trees pledge their gems;
And Ivis with her gorgeous vest
Builds for her eggs her cunning nest,
    And bell-flowers bow their stems.

With vinous syrup cedars spout;
From rocks pure honey gushing out,

For Adoration springs:
All scenes of painting crowd the map
Of nature; to the mermaid's pap
   The scalèd infant clings.

The spotted ounce and playsome cubs
Run rustling 'mongst the flow'ring shrubs,
   And lizards feed the moss;
For Adoration beasts embark,
   While waves upholding halcyon's ark
   No longer roar and toss.

While Israel sits beneath his fig,
With coral root and amber sprig
   The wean'd advent'rer sports;
Where to the palm the jasmin cleaves,
For Adoration 'mongst the leaves
   The gale his peace reports.

Increasing days their reign exalt,
Nor in the pink and mottled vault
   Th' opposing spirits tilt;
And, by the coasting reader spied,
The silverlings and crusions glide
   For Adoration gilt.

For Adoration rip'ning canes
And cocoa's purest milk detains
   The western pilgrim's staff;
Where rain in clasping boughs inclos'd,
And vines with oranges dispos'd,
   Embow'r the social laugh.

Now labour his reward receives,
For Adoration counts his sheaves
  To peace, her bounteous prince;
The nectarine his strong tint imbibes,
And apples of ten thousand tribes,
  And quick peculiar quince.

The wealthy crops of whit'ning rice,
'Mongst thyine woods and groves of spice,
  For Adoration grow;
And, marshall'd in the fencèd land,
The peaches and pomegranates stand,
  Where wild carnations blow.

The laurels with the winter strive;
The crocus burnishes alive
  Upon the snow-clad earth:
For Adoration myrtles stay
To keep the garden from dismay,
  And bless the sight from dearth.

The pheasant shows his pompous neck;
And ermine, jealous of a speck,
  With fear eludes offence:
The sable, with his glossy pride,
For Adoration is descried,
  Where frosts the wave condense.

The cheerful holly, pensive yew,
And holy thorn, their trim renew;
  The squirrel hoards his nuts:

All creatures batten o'er their stores,
And careful nature all her doors
  For Adoration shuts.

Sweet is the dew that falls betimes,
And drops upon the leafy limes;
  Sweet Hermon's fragrant air:
Sweet is the lily's silver bell,
And sweet the wakeful tapers smell
  That watch for early pray'r.

Sweet the young nurse with love intense,
Which smiles o'er sleeping innocence;
  Sweet when the lost arrive:
Sweet the musician's ardour beats,
While his vague mind's in quest of sweets
  The choicest flow'rs to hive.

Sweeter in all the strains of love,
The language of thy turtle dove,
  Pair'd to thy swelling chord;
Sweeter with ev'ry grace endu'd,
The glory of thy gratitude,
  Respir'd unto the Lord.

Strong is the horse upon his speed;
Strong in pursuit the rapid glede,
  Which makes at once his game:
Strong the tall ostrich on the ground;
Strong thro' the turbulent profound
  Shoots xiphias to his aim.

Strong is the lion—like a coal
His eye-ball—like a bastion's mole
   His chest against the foes:
Strong, the gier-eagle on his sail,
Strong against tide, th' enormous whale
   Emerges as he goes.

But stronger still, in earth and air,
And in the sea, the man of pray'r;
   And far beneath the tide;
And in the seat to faith assign'd,
Where ask is have, where seek is find,
   Where knock is open wide.

Beauteous the fleet before the gale;
Beauteous the multitudes in mail,
   Rank'd arms and crested heads:
Beauteous the garden's umbrage mild,
Walk, water, meditated wild,
   And all the bloomy beds.

Beauteous the moon full on the lawn;
And beauteous, when the veil's withdrawn,
   The virgin to her spouse:
Beauteous the temple deck'd and fill'd,
When to the heav'n of heav'ns they build
   Their heart-directed vows.

Beauteous, yea beauteous more than these,
The shepherd king upon his knees,
   For his momentous trust;

With wish of infinite conceit,
For man, beast, mute, the small and great,
  And prostrate dust to dust.

Precious the bounteous widow's mite;
  And precious, for extreme delight,
  The largess from the churl:
Precious the ruby's blushing blaze,
And alba's blest imperial rays,
  And pure cerulean pearl.

Precious the penitential tear;
And precious is the sigh sincere,
  Acceptable to God:
And precious are the winning flow'rs,
In gladsome Israel's feast of bow'rs,
  Bound on the hallow'd sod.

More precious that diviner part
Of David, ev'n the Lord's own heart,
  Great, beautiful, and new:
In all things where it was intent,
In all extremes, in each event,
  Proof—answ'ring true to true.

Glorious the sun in mid career;
Glorious th' assembled fires appear;
  Glorious the comet's train:
Glorious the trumpet and alarm;
Glorious th' almighty stretch'd-out arm;
  Glorious th' enraptur'd main:

Glorious the northern lights astream;
Glorious the song, when God's the theme
  Glorious the thunder's roar:
Glorious hosanna from the den;
Glorious the catholic amen;
  Glorious the martyr's gore:

Glorious—more glorious is the crown
Of Him that brought salvation down
  By meekness, call'd thy Son;
Thou that stupendous truth believ'd,
And now the matchless deed's achiev'd,
  DETERMINED, DARED and DONE.

A Song to David.

OLIVER GOLDSMITH
(1728—1774)

THE VILLAGE PARSON

... Near yonder copse, where once the garden smiled,
And still where many a garden flower grows wild;
There, where a few torn shrubs the place disclose,
The village preacher's modest mansion rose.
A man he was, to all the country dear,
And passing rich with forty pounds a year;
Remote from towns he ran his godly race,
Nor e'er had changed, nor wished to change his place;
Unpractised he to fawn, or seek for power,
By doctrines fashioned to the varying hour;
Far other aims his heart had learned to prize,
More skilled to raise the wretched than to rise.

His house was known to all the vagrant train,
He chid their wanderings, but relieved their pain;
The long remembered beggar was his guest,
Whose beard descending swept his aged breast;
The ruined spendthrift, now no longer proud,
Claimed kindred there, and had his claims allowed;
The broken soldier, kindly bade to stay,
Sate by his fire, and talked the night away;
Wept o'er his wounds, or tales of sorrow done,
Shouldered his crutch, and shewed how fields were won
Pleased with his guests, the good man learned to glow,
And quite forgot their vices in their woe;
Careless their merits, or their faults to scan,
His pity gave ere charity began.

Thus to relieve the wretched was his pride,
And even his failings leaned to Virtue's side;
But in his duty prompt at every call,
He watched and wept, he prayed and felt, for all.
And, as a bird each fond endearment tries,
To tempt its new fledged offspring to the skies;
He tried each art, reproved each dull delay,
Allured to brighter worlds, and led the way.

Beside the bed where parting life was laid,
And sorrow, guilt, and pain, by turns dismayed
The reverend champion stood. At his control,
Despair and anguish fled the struggling soul;
Comfort came down the trembling wretch to raise,
And his last faltering accents whispered praise.

At church, with meek and unaffected grace,
His looks adorned the venerable place;
Truth from his lips prevailed with double sway,
And fools, who came to scoff, remained to pray.

The service past, around the pious man,
With steady zeal each honest rustic ran;
Even children followed with endearing wile,
And plucked his gown, to share the good man's smile.
His ready smile a parent's warmth exprest,
Their welfare pleased him, and their cares distrest;
To them his heart, his love, his griefs were given,
But all his serious thoughts had rest in Heaven.
As some tall cliff that lifts its awful form,
Swells from the vale, and midway leaves the storm,
Tho' round its breast the rolling clouds are spread,
Eternal sunshine settles on its head ...

The Deserted Village.

EDMUND BURKE

... Here lies our good Edmund, whose genius was such,
We scarcely can praise it, or blame it too much;
Who, born for the Universe, narrow'd his mind,
And to party gave up, what was meant for mankind.
Tho' fraught with all learning, yet straining his throat,
To persuade Tommy Townsend to lend him a vote;
Who, too deep for his hearers, still went on refining,
And thought of convincing, while they thought of dining;
Tho' equal to all things, for all things unfit,
Too nice for a statesman, too proud for a wit:
For a patriot too cool; for a drudge, disobedient,
And too fond of the right to pursue the expedient.
In short, 'twas his fate, unemploy'd, or in play, Sir,
To eat mutton cold, and cut blocks with a razor ...

Retaliation.

WILLIAM COWPER
(1731—1800)

HYMN

God moves in a mysterious way,
   His wonders to perform;
He plants his footsteps in the sea,
   And rides upon the storm.

Deep in unfathomable mines
   Of never failing skill,
He treasures up his bright designs,
   And works his sovereign will.

Ye fearful saints, fresh courage take.
   The clouds ye so much dread
Are big with mercy, and shall break
   In blessings on your head.

Judge not the Lord by feeble sense,
   But trust him for his grace;
Behind a frowning providence,
   He hides a smiling face.

His purposes will ripen fast,
   Unfolding ev'ry hour;
The bud may have a bitter taste,
   But sweet will be the flow'r.

Blind unbelief is sure to err,
  And scan his work in vain;
God is his own interpreter,
  And he will make it plain.

THE POSTMAN

... Hark! 'tis the twanging horn! O'er yonder bridge,
That with its wearisome but needful length
Bestrides the wintry flood, in which the moon
Sees her unwrinkled face reflected bright,
He comes, the herald of a noisy world,
With spattered boots, strapped waist, and frozen locks,
News from all nations lumbering at his back.
True to his charge, the close-packed load behind,
Yet careless what he brings, his one concern
Is to conduct it to the destined inn,
And having dropped the expected bag—pass on.
He whistles as he goes, light-hearted wretch,
Cold and yet cheerful: messenger of grief
Perhaps to thousands, and of joy to some,
To him indifferent whether grief or joy.
Houses in ashes, and the fall of stocks,
Births, deaths, and marriages, epistles wet
With tears that trickled down the writer's cheeks
Fast as the periods from his fluent quill,
Or charged with amorous sighs of absent swains,
Or nymphs responsive, equally affect
His horse and him, unconscious of them all.
But oh the important budget! ushered in
With such heart-shaking music, who can say

What are its tidings? have our troops awaked?
Or do they still, as if with opium drugged,
Snore to the murmurs of the Atlantic wave?
Is India free? and does she wear her plumed
And jewelled turban with a smile of peace,
Or do we grind her still? The grand debate,
The popular harangue, the tart reply,
The logic, and the wisdom, and the wit,
And the loud laugh—I long to know them all;
I burn to set the imprisoned wranglers free,
And give them voice and utterance once again.
    Now stir the fire, and close the shutters fast,
Let fall the curtains, wheel the sofa round,
And while the bubbling and loud hissing urn
Throws up a steamy column, and the cups
That cheer but not inebriate, wait on each,
So let us welcome peaceful evening in...

The Task.

ENGLAND

...England, with all thy faults, I love thee still—
My country! and, while yet a nook is left,
Where English minds and manners may be found,
Shall be constrain'd to love thee. Though thy clime
Be fickle, and thy year most part deform'd
With dripping rains, or wither'd by a frost—
I would not yet exhange thy sullen skies,
And fields without a flower, for warmer France
With all her vines; nor for Ausonia's groves
Of golden fruitage, and her myrtle bowers.
To shake thy senate, and from heights sublime

Of patriot eloquence to flash down fire
Upon thy foes, was never meant my task:
But I can feel thy fortunes, and partake
Thy joys and sorrows, with as true a heart
As any thunderer there. And I can feel
Thy follies too; and with a just disdain
Frown at effeminates, whose very looks
Reflect dishonour on the land I love.
How, in the name of soldiership and sense,
Should England prosper, when such things, as smooth
And tender as a girl, all essenced o'er
With odours, and as profligate as sweet—
Who sell their laurel for a myrtle wreath,
And love when they should fight; when such as these
Presume to lay their hand upon the ark
Of her magnificent and awful cause?
Time was when it was praise and boast enough
In every clime, and travel where we might,
That we were born her children. Praise enough
To fill th' ambition of a private man,
That Chatham's language was his mother tongue
And Wolfe's great name compatriot with his own.
Farewell those honours, and farewell with them
The hope of such hereafter! They have fall'n
Each in his field of glory; one in arms,
And one in council—Wolfe upon the lap
Of smiling Victory that moment won,
And Chatham, heart-sick of his country's shame!
They made us many soldiers. Chatham still
Consulting England's happiness at home,
Secured it by an unforgiving frown,
If any wrong'd her. Wolfe, where'er he fought,

Put so much of his heart into his act
That his example had a magnet's force,
And all were swift to follow whom all loved.
Those suns are set. Oh, rise some other such!
Or all that we have left is empty talk
Of old achievements, and despair of new...

The Task.

THE CASTAWAY

Obscurest night involv'd the sky,
　Th' Atlantic billows roar'd,
When such a destin'd wretch as I,
　Wash'd headlong from on board,
Of friends, of hope, of all bereft,
His floating home for ever left.

No braver chief could Albion boast
　Than he with whom he went,
Nor ever ship left Albion's coast,
　With warmer wishes sent.
He lov'd them both, but both in vain,
Nor him beheld, nor her again.

Not long beneath the whelming brine,
　Expert to swim, he lay;
Nor soon he felt his strength decline,
　Or courage die away;
But wag'd with death a lasting strife,
Supported by despair of life.

He shouted: nor his friends had fail'd
　To check the vessel's course,

But so the furious blast prevail'd,
  That, pitiless perforce,
They left their outcast mate behind,
And scudded still before the wind.

Some succour yet they could afford;
  And, such as storms allow,
The cask, the coop, the floated cord,
  Delay'd not to bestow.
But he (they knew) nor ship, nor shore,
Whate'er they gave, should visit more.

Nor, cruel as it seem'd, could he
  Their haste himself condemn,
Aware that flight, in such a sea,
  Alone could rescue them;
Yet bitter felt it still to die
Deserted, and his friends so nigh.

He long survives, who lives an hour
  In ocean, self-upheld:
And so long he, with unspent pow'r,
  His destiny repell'd;
And ever, as the minutes flew,
Entreated help, or cried—Adieu!

At length, his transient respite past,
  His comrades, who before
Had heard his voice in ev'ry blast,
  Could catch the sound no more.
For then, by toil subdued, he drank
The stifling wave, and then he sank.

No poet wept him: but the page
   Of narrative sincere,
That tells his name, his worth, his age,
   Is wet with Anson's tear.
And tears by bards or heroes shed
Alike immortalize the dead.

I therefore purpose not, or dream,
   Descanting on his fate,
To give the melancholy theme
   A more enduring date:
But misery still delights to trace
Its semblance in another's case.

No voice divine the storm allay'd,
   No light propitious shone;
When, snatch'd from all effectual aid,
   We perish'd, each alone:
But I beneath a rougher sea,
And whelm'd in deeper gulfs than he.

JOHN WOLCOT ("PETER PINDAR")
(1738—1819)

LINES ON DR. JOHNSON

I own I like not Johnson's turgid style
That gives an inch the importance of a mile,
Casts of manure a wagon-load around,
To raise a simple daisy from the ground;

Uplifts the club of Hercules—for what?
To crush a butterfly or brain a gnat;
Creates a whirlwind from the earth, to draw
A goose's feather or exalt a straw;
Sets wheels on wheels in motion—such a clatter—
To force up one poor nipperkin of water;
Bids ocean labour with tremendous roar,
To heave a cockle-shell upon the shore;
Alike in every theme his pompous art,
Heaven's awful thunder or a rumbling cart!

GEORGE CRABBE
(1754—1832)

THE PAUPER'S FUNERAL

... Now to the church behold the mourners come,
Sedately torpid and devoutly dumb;
The village children now their games suspend,
To see the bier that bears their ancient friend.
For he was one in all their idle sport,
And like a monarch ruled their little court;
The pliant bow he formed, the flying ball,
The bat, the wicker, were his labours all.
Him now they follow to his grave, and stand
Silent and sad, and gazing hand in hand;
While bending low, their eager eyes explore
The mingled relics of the parish poor.
The bell tolls late, the moping owl flies round,
Fear marks the flight and magnifies the sound;

The busy priest, detain'd by weightier care,
Defers his duty till the day of prayer;
And waiting long, the crowd retire distrest
To think a poor man's bones should lie unblest. ...

The Village

THE FORESHORE

... Thus by himself compell'd to live each day,
To wait for certain hours the tide's delay;
At the same times the same dull views to see,
The bounding marsh-bank and the blighted tree;
The water only, when the tides were high;
When low, the mud half-cover'd and half-dry;
The sun-burnt tar that blisters on the planks,
And bank-side stakes in their uneven ranks;
Heaps of entangled weeds that slowly float,
As the tide rolls by the impeded boat.

   When tides were neap, and, in the sultry day,
Through the tall bounding mud-banks made their way
Which on each side rose swelling, and below
The dark warm flood ran silently and slow;
There anchoring, Peter chose from man to hide,
There hang his head, and view the lazy tide
In its hot slimy channel slowly glide;
Where the small eels that left the deeper way
For the warm shore, within the shallows play;
Where gaping mussels, left upon the mud,
Slope their slow passage to the fallen flood; —
Here dull and hopeless he'd lie down and trace
How sidelong crabs had scrawl'd their crooked race;

Or sadly listen to the tuneless cry
Of fishing gull or clanging golden-eye;
What time the sea-birds to the marsh would come,
And the loud bittern, from the bullrush home,
Gave from the salt-ditch side the bellowing boom;
He nursed the feelings these dull scenes produce,
And loved to stop beside the opening sluice;
Where the small stream, confined in narrow bound,
Ran with a dull, unvaried, sadd'ning sound;
Where all, presented to the eye or ear,
Oppress'd the soul with misery, grief, and fear ...

The Borough.

WILLIAM BLAKE
(1757—1827)

THE LITTLE BLACK BOY

My mother bore me in the southern wild,
And I am black, but O! my soul is white;
White as an angel is the English child,
But I am black, as if bereav'd of light.

My mother taught me underneath a tree,
And sitting down before the heat of day,
She took me on her lap and kissed me,
And pointing to the east, began to say:

"Look on the rising sun: there God does live,
And gives his light, and gives his heat away;
And flowers and trees and beasts and men receive
Comfort in morning, joy in the noonday.

"And we are put on earth a little space,
That we may learn to bear the beams of love;
And these black bodies and this sunburnt face
Is but a cloud, and like a shady grove.

"For when souls have learn'd the heat to bear,
The cloud will vanish; we shall hear his voice,
Saying: 'Come out from the grove, my love & care,
And round my golden tent like lambs rejoice."

Thus did my mother say, and kissed me;
And thus I say to little English boy:
When I from black and he from white cloud free,
And round the tent of God like lambs we joy,

I'll shade him from the heat, till he can bear
To lean in joy upon our father's knee;
And then I'll stand and stroke his silver hair,
And be like him, and he will then love me.

THE DIVINE IMAGE

To Mercy, Pity, Peace, and Love
All pray in their distress;
And to these virtues of delight
Return their thankfulness.

For Mercy, Pity, Peace, and Love
Is God, our father dear,
And Mercy, Pity, Peace, and Love
Is Man, his child and care.

For Mercy has a human heart,
Pity a human face,
And Love, the human form divine,
And Peace, the human dress.

Then every man, of every clime,
That prays in his distress,
Prays to the human form divine,
Love, Mercy, Pity, Peace.

And all must love the human form,
In heathen, turk, or jew;
Where Mercy, Love, & Pity dwell
There God is dwelling too.

THE TIGER

Tiger! Tiger! burning bright
In the forests of the night,
What immortal hand or eye
Could frame thy fearful symmetry?

In what distant deeps or skies
Burnt the fire of thine eyes?
On what wings dare he aspire?
What the hand dare seize the fire?

And what shoulder, & what art,
Could twist the sinews of thy heart?
And when thy heart began to beat,
What dread hand? & what dread feet?

What the hammer? what the chain?
In what furnace was thy brain?
What the anvil? what dread grasp
Dare its deadly terrors clasp?

When the stars threw down their spears,
And water'd heaven with their tears,
Did he smile his work to see?
Did he who made the Lamb make thee?

Tiger! Tiger! burning bright
In the forests of the night,
What immortal hand or eye,
Dare frame thy fearful symmetry?

LONDON

I wander thro' each charter'd street,
Near where the charter'd Thames does flow,
And mark in every face I meet
Marks of weakness, marks of woe.

In every cry of every Man,
In every Infant's cry of fear,
In every voice, in every ban,
The mind-forg'd manacles I hear.

How the Chimney-sweeper's cry
Every black'ning Church appalls;
And the hapless Soldier's sigh
Runs in blood down Palace walls.

But most thro' midnight streets I hear
How the youthful Harlot's curse
Blasts the new born Infant's tear,
And blights with plagues the Marriage hearse.

THE CLOD AND THE PEBBLE

'Love seeketh not Itself to please
Nor for itself hath any care,
But for another gives its ease,
And builds a Heaven in Hell's despair.'

So sung a little Clod of Clay
Trodden with the cattle's feet,
But a Pebble of the brook
Warbled out these metres meet:

'Love seeketh only Self to please,
To bind another to Its delight,
Joys in another's loss of ease,
And builds a Hell in Heaven's despite.'

JERUSALEM

And did those feet in ancient time
Walk upon England's mountains green?
And was the holy Lamb of God
On England's pleasant pastures seen?

And did the Countenance Divine
Shine forth upon our clouded hills?
And was Jerusalem builded here
Among these dark Satanic Mills?

Bring me my Bow of burning gold:
Bring me my Arrows of desire:
Bring me my Spear: O clouds unfold!
Bring me my Chariot of fire.

I will not cease from Mental Fight,
Nor shall my Sword sleep in my hand
Till we have built Jerusalem
In England's green & pleasant Land.

Milton

THE ARTS OF DEATH

... Then left the sons of Urizen the plow & harrow, the loom
The hammer & the chisel & the rule & compasses.
They forg'd the sword, the chariot of war, the battle ax,
The trumpet fitted to the battle & the flute of summer,
And all the arts of life they chang'd into the arts of death
The hour glass contemn'd because its simple workmanship
Was as the workmanship of the plowman, & the water whee
That raises water into Cisterns, broken & burn'd in fire
Because its workmanship was like the workmanship of the
                                        shepherd,
And in their stead intricate wheels invented, Wheel withou
                                        wheel,
To perplex youth in their outgoings & to bind to labours
Of day & night the myriads of Eternity, that they might fil
And polish brass & iron hour after hour, laborious work-
                                        manship,
Kept ignorant of the use that they might spend the days
                                        of wisdom

In sorrowful drudgery to obtain a scanty pittance of bread,
In ignorance to view a small portion & think that All,
And call it demonstration, blind to all the simple rules of
life . . .

The Four Zoas.

BROTHERHOOD

. . . Jesus replied: 'Fear not Albion: unless I die thou canst
not live;
But if I die I shall arise again & thou with me.
This is Friendship & Brotherhood: without it Man Is Not.'

So Jesus spoke: the Covering Cherub coming on in darkness
Overshadow'd them, & Jesus said: 'Thus do Men in Eternity
One for another to put off, by forgiveness, every sin.'

Albion reply'd: 'Cannot Man exist without Mysterious
Offering of Self for Another? is this Friendship & Brotherhood?
I see thee in the likeness & similitude of Los my Friend.'

  Jesus said: 'Wouldest thou love one who never died
For thee, or ever die for one who had not died for thee?
And if God dieth not for Man & giveth not himself
Eternally for Man, Man could not exist; for Man is Love
As God is Love: every kindness to another is a little Death
In the Divine Image, nor can Man exist but by Brotherhood.'

So saying the Cloud overshadowing divided them asunder.
Albion stood in terror, not for himself but for his Friend
Divine; & Self was lost in the contemplation of faith
And wonder at the Divine Mercy & at Los's sublime honour.

'Do I sleep amidst danger to Friends? O my Cities & Counties,
Do you sleep? rouze up, rouze up! Eternal Death is abroad!'

So Albion spoke & threw himself into the Furnaces of affliction.
All was a Vision, all a Dream: the Furnaces became
Fountains of Living Waters flowing from the Humanity Divine.
And all the Cities of Albion rose from their Slumbers, and All
The Sons & Daughters of Albion on soft clouds, waking
                                        from Sleep...

Jerusalem IV.

ROBERT BURNS
(1759—1796)

MY LOVE IS LIKE A RED RED ROSE

My love is like a red red rose
    That's newly sprung in June:
My love is like the melodie
    That's sweetly play'd in tune.

So fair art thou, my bonnie lass,
    So deep in love am I:
And I will love thee still, my dear,
    Till a' the seas gang dry.

Till a' the seas gang dry, my dear,
    And the rocks melt wi' the sun:
And I will love thee still, my dear,
    While the sands o' life shall run.

And fare thee weel, my only love,
    And fare, thee weel awhile!
And I will come again, my love,
    Tho' it were ten thousand mile.

BONNIE DOON

Ye flowery banks o' bonnie Doon,
   How can ye blume sae fair?
How can ye chant, ye little birds,
   And I sae fu' o' care?

Thou'll break my heart, thou bonnie bird,
   That sings upon the bough;
Thou minds me o' the happy days,
   When my fause luve was true.

Thou'll break my heart, thou bonnie bird,
   That sings beside thy mate;
For sae I sat, and sae I sang,
   And wist na o' my fate.

Aft hae I rov'd by bonnie Doon,
   To see the wood-bine twine,
And ilka bird sang o' its love,
   And sae did I o' mine.

JOHN BARLEYCORN

A BALLAD

There was three Kings into the east,
   Three Kings both great and high,
And they hae sworn a solemn oath
   John Barleycorn should die.

They took a plough and plough'd him down,
   Put clods upon his head,

And they hae sworn a solemn oath
  John Barleycorn was dead.

But the cheerfu' Spring came kindly on,
  And show'rs began to fall;
John Barleycorn got up again,
  And sore surpris'd them all.

The sultry suns of Summer came,
  And he grew thick and strong,
His head weel arm'd wi' pointed spears,
  That no one should him wrong.

The sober Autumn enter'd mild,
  When he grew wan and pale;
His bending joints and drooping head
  Show'd he began to fail.

His colour sicken'd more and more,
  He faded into age;
And then his enemies began
  To shew their deadly rage.

They've ta'en a weapon, long and sharp,
  And cut him by the knee;
Then tied him fast upon a cart,
  Like a rogue for forgerie.

They laid him down upon his back,
  And cudgell'd him full sore;

They hung him up before the storm,
   And turn'd him o'er and o'er.

They fillèd up a darksome pit
   With water to the brim,
They heavèd in John Barleycorn,
   There let him sink or swim.

They laid him out upon the floor,
   To work him farther woe,
And still, as signs of life appear'd,
   They toss'd him to and fro.

They wasted, o'er a scorching flame,
   The marrow of his bones;
But a miller us'd him worst of all,
   For he crush'd him between two stones.

And they hae ta'en his very heart's blood,
   And drank it round and round;
And still the more and more they drank,
   Their joy did more abound.

John Barleycorn was a hero bold,
   Of noble enterprise,
For if you do but taste his blood,
   'Twill make your courage rise;

'Twill make a man forget his woe;
   'Twill heighten all his joy:
'Twill make the widow's heart to sing,
   Tho' the tear were in her eye.

Then let us toast John Barleycorn,
    Each man a glass in hand;
And may his great posterity
    Ne'er fail in old Scotland!

EPISTLE TO JOHN LAPRAIK, AN OLD SCOTTISH
BARD

While briers an' woodbines budding green,
An' paitricks[1] scraichin' loud at e'en,
An' morning poussie whiddin'[2] seen,
            Inspire my Muse,
This freedom, in an unknown frien',
            I pray excuse.

On Fasten-een we had a rockin',[3]
To ca' the crack[4] and weave our stockin';
And there was muckle fun and jokin',
            Ye need na doubt;
At length we had a hearty yokin'
            At sang about.

There was ae sang, amang the rest,
Aboon them a' it pleas'd me best,
That some kind husband had addrest
            To some sweet wife:
It thirl'd the heart-strings thro' the breast,
            A' to the life.

I've scarce heard ought describ'd sae weel,
What gen'rous, manly bosoms feel;

[1] partridges. [2] a hare running. [3] social gathering. [4] tell stories.

Thought I 'Can this be Pope, or Steele,
      Or Beattie's wark!'
They tauld me 'twas an odd kind chiel
      About Muirkirk.

It pat me fidgin' fain[1] to hear't,
And sae about him there I spier'd;[2]
Then a' that kenn'd him round declar'd
      He had ingine,[3]
That nane excell'd it, few cam near't,
      It was sae fine.

That, set him to a pint of ale,
An' either douce or merry tale,
Or rhymes an' sangs he'd made himsel,
      Or witty catches,
'Tween Inverness and Teviotdale,
      He had few matches.

Then up I gat, an' swoor an aith,
Tho' I should pawn my pleugh and graith,[4]
Or die a cadger pownie's[5] death,
      At some dyke-back,
A pint an' gill I'd gie them baith
      To hear your crack.

But, first an' foremost, I should tell,
Amaist as soon as I could spell,
I to the crambo-jingle fell;
      Tho' rude an' rough,
Yet crooning to a body's sel,
      Does weel eneugh.

[1] fidgeting with eagerness. [2] asked. [3] genius. [4] harness. [5] carrier pony.

I am nae poet, in a sense,
But just a rhymer, like, by chance,
An' hae to learning nae pretence,
   Yet what the matter?
Whene'er my Muse does on me glance,
   I jingle at her.

Your critic-folk may cock their nose,
And say 'How can you e'er propose,
You wha ken hardly verse frae prose,
   To mak a sang?'
But, by your leaves, my learnèd foes,
   Y'ere maybe wrang.

What's a' your jargon o' your schools,
Your Latin names for horns an' stools;
If honest nature made you fools,
   What sairs[1] your grammars?
Ye'd better ta'en up spades and shools,
   Or knappin'-hammers.[2]

A set o' dull conceited hashes
Confuse their brains in college classes!
They gang in stirks,[3] and come out asses,
   Plain truth to speak;
An' syne they think to climb Parnassus
   By dint o' Greek!

Gie me ae spark o' Nature's fire,
That's a' the learning I desire;

---

[1] serves.   [2] stone-breaking hammers.   [3] young cattle.

Then tho' I drudge thro' dub[1] an' mire
   At pleugh or cart,
My Muse, though hamely in attire,
   May touch the heart.

O for a spunk[2] o' Allan's glee,
Or Fergusson's, the bauld an' slee,
Or bright Lapraik's my friend to be,
   If I can hit it!
That would be lear[3] eneugh for me,
   If I could get it.

Now, sir, if ye hae friends enow,
Tho' real friends, I b'lieve, are few,
Yet, if your catalogue be fou,
   I'se no insist,
But gif ye want ae friend that's true,
   I'm on your list.

I winna blaw about mysel,
As ill I like my fauts to tell;
But friends, an' folks that wish me well,
   They sometimes roose[4] me;
Tho' I maun own, as mony still
   As far abuse me.

There's ae wee faut they whiles lay to me,
I like the lasses—Gude forgie me!
For mony a plack[5] they wheedle frae me,
   At dance or fair;
Maybe some ither thing they gie me
   They weel can spare.

[1] puddle. [2] fiery spark. [3] learning. [4] commend. [5] small coin.

English Verse

But Mauchline race, or Mauchline fair,
I should be proud to meet you there;
We'se gie ae night's discharge to care,
            If we forgather,
An' hae a swap o' rhymin'-ware
                Wi' ane anither.

The four-gill chap, we'se gar him clatter,
An' kirsen him wi' reekin water;
Syne we'll sit down an' tak our whitter,[1]
            To cheer our heart;
An' faith, we'se be acquainted better
                Before we part.

Awa, ye selfish warly[2] race,
Wha think that havins,[3] sense, an' grace,
Ev'n love an' friendship, should give place
            To catch-the-plack!
I dinna like to see your face,
                Nor hear your crack.

But ye whom social pleasure charms,
Whose hearts the tide of kindness warms,
Who hold your being on the terms,
            'Each aid the others,'
Come to my bowl, come to my arms,
                My friends, my brothers!

But to conclude my lang epistle,
As my auld pen's worn to the gristle;

[1] drink. [2] worldly. [3] good manners.

Twa lines frae you wad gar me fissle,[1]
       Who am, most fervent,
While I can either sing, or whistle,
       Your friend and servant.

GEORGE CANNING
(1770—1827)

SAPPHICS

THE FRIEND OF HUMANITY AND THE KNIFE-GRINDER

Friend of humanity

'Needy Knife-grinder! whither are you going?
Rough is the road, your wheel is out of order—
Bleak blows the blast;—your hat has got a hole in't,
       So have your breeches!

'Weary Knife-grinder! little think the proud ones,
Who in their coaches roll along the turnpike-
-road, what hard work 'tis crying all day "Knives and
       Scissors to grind O!'

'Tell me, Knife-grinder, how you came to grind knives?
Did some rich man tyrannically use you?
Was it the 'Squire? or Parson of the Parish?
       Or the Attorney?

'Was it the 'Squire for killing of his Game? or
Covetous Parson for his Tithes distraining?
Or roguish Lawyer made you lose your little
       All in a law-suit?

[1] bustle.

'(Have you not read the Rights of Man, by Tom Paine?)
Drops of compassion tremble on my eye-lids,
Ready to fall, as soon as you have told your
                                        Pitiful story.'

Knife-grinder

'Story! God bless you! I have none to tell, Sir,
Only last night a-drinking at the Chequers,
This poor old hat and breeches, as you see, were
                                        Torn in a scuffle.

'Constables came up for to take me into
Custody; they took me before the Justice;
Justice Oldmixon put me in the Parish-
                                        -Stocks for a Vagrant.

'I should be glad to drink your Honour's health in
A Pot of Beer, if you would give me Sixpence;
But for my part, I never love to meddle
                                        With Politics, Sir.'

Friend of humanity

'*I* give thee Sixpence! I will see thee damn'd first—
Wretch! whom no sense of wrongs can rouse to vengeance—
Sordid, unfeeling, reprobate, degraded,
                                        Spiritless outcast!'

(*Kicks the Knife-grinder, overturns his Wheel, and exit in
    a transport of republican enthusiasm and universal
    philanthropy.*)

                                        The Anti-Jacobin

WILLIAM WORDSWORTH
(1770—1850)

SONNETS

(i)

Earth has not anything to show more fair:
   Dull would he be of soul who could pass by
   A sight so touching in its majesty:
This City now doth like a garment wear
The beauty of the morning; silent, bare,
   Ships, towers, domes, theatres, and temples lie
   Open unto the fields, and to the sky;
All bright and glittering in the smokeless air.
Never did sun more beautifully steep
   In his first splendour valley, rock, or hill;
Ne'er saw I, never felt, a calm so deep!
   The river glideth at his own sweet will:
   Dear God! the very houses seem asleep;
   And all that mighty heart is lying still!

(ii)

The world is too much with us; late and soon,
   Getting and spending, we lay waste our powers:
   Little we see in Nature that is ours;
We have given our hearts away, a sordid boon!
This sea that bares her bosom to the moon;
   The winds that will be howling at all hours,
   And are up-gather'd now like sleeping flowers;

For this, for everything, we are out of tune;
It moves us not.—Great God! I'd rather be
  A Pagan suckled in a creed outworn;
So might I, standing on this pleasant lea,
  Have glimpses that would make me less forlorn;
Have sight of Proteus rising from the sea;
  Or hear old Triton blow his wreathèd horn.

(iii)

Surprised by joy—impatient as the Wind
  I turned to share the transport—O! with whom
  But Thee, deep buried in the silent tomb,
That spot which no vicissitude can find?
Love, faithful love, recall'd thee to my mind—
  But how could I forget thee? Through what power,
  Even for the least division of an hour,
Have I been so beguiled as to be blind
To my most grievous loss?—That thought's return
  Was the worst pang that sorrow ever bore,
Save one, one only, when I stood forlorn,
  Knowing my heart's best treasure was no more;
That neither present time, nor years unborn
  Could to my sight that heavenly face restore.

(iv)

I thought of thee, my partner and my guide,
  As being pass'd away.—Vain sympathies!
  For, backward, Duddon! as I cast my eyes,
I see what was, and is, and will abide;
Still glides the stream, and shall for ever glide;

The form remains, the function never dies;
　　While we, the brave, the mighty, and the wise,
We men, who in our morn of youth defied
The elements, must vanish;—be it so!
　　Enough, if something from our hands have power
　　To live, and act, and serve the future hour;
And if, as toward the silent tomb we go,　　　[dower,
　　Through love, through hope, and faith's transcendent
We feel that we are greater than we know.

(v)

From low to high doth dissolution climb,
　　And sink from high to low, along a scale
　　Of awful notes, whose concord shall not fail;
A musical but melancholy chime,
Which they can hear who meddle not with crime,
　　Nor avarice, nor over-anxious care.
　　Truth fails not; but her outward forms that bear
The longest date do melt like frosty rime,
That in the morning whiten'd hill and plain
And is no more; drop like the tower sublime
　　Of yesterday, which royally did wear
His crown of weeds, but could not even sustain
　　Some casual shout that broke the silent air,
Or the unimaginable touch of Time.

LUCY

　　A slumber did my spirit seal;
　　　　I had no human fears:
　　She seem'd a thing that could not feel
　　　　The touch of earthly years.

No motion has she now, no force;
　She neither hears nor sees;
Roll'd round in earth's diurnal course,
　With rocks, and stones, and trees.

A LESSON

There is a flower, the lesser Celandine,
That shrinks like many more from cold and rain,
And the first moment that the sun may shine,
Bright as the sun himself, 'tis out again!

When hailstones have been falling, swarm on swarm,
Or blasts the green field and the trees distress'd,
Oft have I seen it muffled up from harm
In close self-shelter, like a thing at rest.

But lately, one rough day, this flower I pass'd,
And recognized it, though an alter'd form,
Now standing forth an offering to the blast
And buffeted at will by rain and storm.

I stopp'd and said, with inly-mutter'd voice,
'It doth not love the shower, nor seek the cold;
This neither is its courage nor its choice,
But its necessity in being old.

The sunshine may not cheer it, nor the dew;
It cannot help itself in its decay;
Stiff in its members, wither'd, changed of hue,' —
And, in my spleen, I smiled that it was grey.

To be a prodigal's favourite — then, worse truth,
A miser's pensioner — behold our lot!
O Man! that from thy fair and shining youth
Age might but take the things Youth needed not!

THE SOLITARY REAPER

Behold her, single in the field,
    Yon solitary Highland Lass!
Reaping and singing by herself;
    Stop here, or gently pass!
Alone she cuts and binds the grain,
And sings a melancholy strain;
O listen! for the Vale profound
Is overflowing with the sound.

No Nightingale did ever chaunt
    More welcome notes to weary bands
Of travellers in some shady haunt,
    Among Arabian sands:
A voice so thrilling ne'er was heard
In spring-time from the Cuckoo-bird,
Breaking the silence of the seas
Among the farthest Hebrides.

Will no one tell me what she sings?—
    Perhaps the plaintive numbers flow
For old, unhappy, far-off things,
    And battles long ago:
Or is it some more humble lay,
Familiar matter of to-day?

Some natural sorrow, loss, or pain,
That has been, and may be again?

Whate'er the theme, the Maiden sang
    As if her song could have no ending;
I saw her singing at her work,
    And o'er the sickle bending;–
I listen'd, motionless and still;
And, as I mounted up the hill,
The music in my heart I bore,
Long after it was heard no more.

PASSAGES FROM 'THE PRELUDE'

(i)

... Wisdom and Spirit of the universe!
Thou Soul that art the eternity of thought,
That givest to forms and images a breath
And everlasting motion, not in vain
By day or star-light thus from my first dawn
Of childhood didst thou intertwine for me
The passions that build up our human soul;
Not with the mean and vulgar works of man,
But with high objects, with enduring things—
With life and nature, purifying thus
The elements of feeling and of thought,
And sanctifying, by such discipline,
Both pain and fear, until we recognize
A grandeur in the beatings of the heart.
Nor was this fellowship vouchsafed to me
With stinted kindness. In November days,

When vapours rolling down the valley made
A lonely scene more lonesome, among woods,
At noon and 'mid the calm of summer nights,
When, by the margin of the trembling lake,
Beneath the gloomy hills homeward I went
In solitude, such intercourse was mine;
Mine was it in the fields both day and night,
And by the waters, all the summer long.

   And in the frosty season, when the sun
Was set, and visible for many a mile
The cottage windows blazed through twilight gloom,
I heeded not their summons: happy time
It was indeed for all of us—for me
It was a time of rapture! Clear and loud
The village clock tolled six,—I wheeled about,
Proud and exulting like an untired horse
That cares not for his home. All shod with steel,
We hissed along the polished ice in games
Confederate, imitative of the chase
And woodland pleasures,—the resounding horn,
The pack loud chiming, and the hunted hare.
So through the darkness and the cold we flew,
And not a voice was idle: with the din
Smitten, the precipices rang aloud:
The leafless trees and every icy crag
Tinkled like iron; while far distant hills
Into the tumult sent an alien sound
Of melancholy not unnoticed, while the stars
Eastward were sparkling clear, and in the west
The orange sky of evening died away.

Not seldom from the uproar I retired
Into a silent bay, or sportively
Glanced sideway, leaving the tumultuous throng,
To cut across the reflex of a star
That fled, and, flying still before me, gleamed
Upon the glassy plain; and oftentimes,
When we had given our bodies to the wind,
And all the shadowy banks on either side
Came sweeping through the darkness, spinning still
The rapid line of motion, then at once
Have I, reclining back upon my heels,
Stopped short; yet still the solitary cliffs
Wheeled by me—even as if the earth had rolled
With visible motion her diurnal round!
Behind me did they stretch in solemn train,
Feebler and feebler, and I stood and watched
Till all was tranquil as a dreamless sleep . . .

Book I

(ii)

. . . Dust as we are, the immortal spirit grows
Like harmony in music; there is a dark
Inscrutable workmanship that reconciles
Discordant elements, makes them cling together
In one society. How strange that all
The terrors, pains, and early miseries,
Regrets, vexations, lassitudes interfused
Within my mind, should e'er have borne a part,
And that a needful part, in making up
The calm existence that is mine when I
Am worthy of myself! Praise to the end!
Thanks to the means which Nature deigned to employ:

Whether her fearless visitings, or those
That came with soft alarms, like hurtless light
Opening the peaceful clouds; or she may use
Severer interventions, ministry
More palpable, as best might suit her aim.

One summer evening (led by her) I found
A little boat tied to a willow tree
Within a rocky cave, its usual home.
Straight I unloosed her chain, and stepping in
Pushed from the shore. It was an act of stealth
And troubled pleasure, nor without the voice
Of mountain-echoes did my boat move on;
Leaving behind her still, on either side,
Small circles glittering idly in the moon,
Until they melted all into one track
Of sparkling light. But now, like one who rows,
Proud of his skill, to reach a chosen point
With a unswerving line, I fixed my view
Upon the summit of a craggy ridge,
The horizon's utmost boundary; far above
Was nothing but the stars and the grey sky.
She was an elfin pinnace; lustily
I dipped my oars into the silent lake,
And, as I rose upon the stroke, my boat
Went heaving through the water like a swan;
When, from behind that craggy steep till then
The horizon's bound, a huge peak, black and huge,
As if with voluntary power instinct
Upreared its head. I struck and struck again,
And growing still in stature the grim shape
Towered up between me and the stars, and still,

For so it seemed, with purpose of its own
And measured motion like a living thing,
Strode after me. With trembling oars I turned,
And through the silent water stole my way
Back to the covert of the willow tree;
There in her mooring-place I left my bark,—
And through the meadows homeward went, in grave
And serious mood; but after I had seen
That spectacle, for many days, my brain
Worked with a dim and undetermined sense
Of unknown modes of being; o'er my thoughts
There hung a darkness, call it solitude
Or blank desertion. No familiar shapes
Remained, no pleasant images of trees,
Of sea or sky, no colours of green fields;
But huge and mighty forms, that do not live
Like living men, moved slowly through the mind
By day, and were a trouble to my dreams . . .

Book

(iii)

. . . There was a Boy: ye knew him well, ye cliffs
And islands of Winander!—many a time
At evening, when the earliest stars began
To move along the edges of the hills,
Rising or setting, would he stand alone
Beneath the trees or by the glimmering lake,
And there, with fingers interwoven, both hands
Pressed closely palm to palm, and to his mouth
Uplifted, he, as through an instrument,
Blew mimic hootings to the silent owls,
That they might answer him; and they would shout

Across the watery vale, and shout again,
Responsive to his call, with quivering peals,
And long halloos and screams, and echoes loud,
Redoubled and redoubled, concourse wild
Of jocund din; and, when a lengthened pause
Of silence came and baffled his best skill,
Then sometimes, in that silence while he hung
Listening, a gentle shock of mild surprise
Has carried far into his heart the voice
Of mountain torrents; or the visible scene
Would enter unawares into his mind,
With all its solemn imagery, its rocks,
Its woods, and that uncertain heaven, received
Into the bosom of the steady lake . . .

Book V.

(iv)

. . . There, 'tis the shepherd's task the winter long
To wait upon the storms: of their approach
Sagacious, into sheltering coves he drives
His flock, and thither from the homestead bears
A toilsome burden up the craggy ways,
And deals it out, their regular nourishment
Strewn on the frozen snow. And when the spring
Looks out, and all the pastures dance with lambs,
And when the flock, with warmer weather, climbs
Higher and higher, him his office leads
To watch their goings, whatsoever track
The wanderers choose. For this he quits his home
At day-spring, and no sooner doth the sun
Begin to strike him with a fire-like heat,
Than he lies down upon some shining rock,

And breakfasts with his dog. When they have stolen,
As is their wont, a pittance from strict time,
For rest not needed or exchange of love,
Then from his couch he starts: and now his feet
Crush out a livelier fragrance from the flowers
Of lowly thyme, by Nature's skill enwrought
In the wild turf: the lingering dews of morn
Smoke round him, as from hill to hill he hies,
His staff protending like a hunter's spear,
Or by its aid leaping from crag to crag,
And o'er the brawling beds of unbridged streams...

                                                Book VIII

SIR WALTER SCOTT
(1771—1832)

PROUD MAISIE

Proud Maisie is in the wood,
  Walking so early;
Sweet Robin sits on the bush,
  Singing so rarely.

'Tell me, thou bonny bird,
  When shall I marry me?'
—'When six braw gentlemen
  Kirkward shall carry ye.'

'Who makes the bridal bed,
  Birdie, say truly?'
—'The grey-headed sexton
  That delves the grave duly.

'The glow-worm o'er grave and stone
Shall light thee steady;
The owl from the steeple sing
Welcome, proud lady!'

SAMUEL TAYLOR COLERIDGE
(1772—1834)

THE RIME OF THE ANCIENT MARINER

PART I

It is an ancient Mariner,
And he stoppeth one of three.
'By thy long grey beard and glittering eye,
Now wherefore stopp'st thou me?

An ancient Mariner meeteth three gallants bidden to a wedding feast, and detaineth one.

The Bridegroom's doors are open'd wide,
And I am next of kin;
The guests are met, the feast is set:
May'st hear the merry din.'

He holds him with his skinny hand,
'There was a ship,' quoth he.
'Hold off! unhand me, grey-beard loon!'
Eftsoons his hand dropt he.

He holds him with his glittering eye—
The Wedding-Guest stood still,
And listens like a three years' child:
The Mariner hath his will.

The Wedding-Guest is spell-bound by the eye of the old seafaring man, and constrained to hear his tale.

The Wedding-Guest sat on a stone:
He cannot choose but hear;
And thus spake on that ancient man,
The bright-eyed Mariner.

'The ship was cheer'd, the harbour clear'd,
Merrily did we drop
Below the kirk, below the hill,
Below the lighthouse top.

The Mariner
tells how the
ship sailed
southward with
a good wind
and fair
weather, till
it reached the
Line.

The Sun came up upon the left,
Out of the sea came he!
And he shone bright, and on the right
Went down into the sea.

Higher and higher every day,
Till over the mast at noon—'
The Wedding-Guest here beat his breast,
For he heard the loud bassoon.

The Wedding-
Guest heareth
the bridal
music; but the
Mariner con-
tinueth his tale.

The bride hath paced into the hall,
Red as a rose is she;
Nodding their heads before her goes
The merry minstrelsy.

The Wedding-Guest he beat his breast,
Yet he cannot choose but hear;
And thus spake on that ancient man,
The bright-eyed Mariner.

The ship driven
by a storm to-
ward the South
Pole.

'And now the Storm-blast came, and he
Was tyrannous and strong:
He struck with his o'ertaking wings,
And chased us south along.

With sloping masts and dipping prow,
As who pursued with yell and blow
Still treads the shadow of his foe,
And forward bends his head,
The ship drove fast, loud roar'd the blast,
And southward aye we fled.

And now there came both mist and snow,
And it grew wondrous cold:
And ice, mast-high, came floating by,
As green as emerald.

And through the drifts the snowy clifts
Did send a dismal sheen:
Nor shapes of men nor beasts we ken—
The ice was all between.

The land of ice, and of fearful sounds, where no living thing was to be seen.

The ice was here, the ice was there,
The ice was all around:
It crack'd and growl'd, and roar'd and howl'd,
Like noises in a swound!

At length did cross an Albatross,
Thorough the fog it came;
As if it had been a Christian soul,
We hail'd it in God's name.

Till a great sea-bird, called the Albatross, came through the snow-fog, and was received with great joy and hospitality.

It ate the food it ne'er had eat,
And round and round it flew.
The ice did split with a thunder-fit;
The helmsman steer'd us through!

And lo! the Albatross proveth a bird of good omen, and followeth the ship as it returned northward through fog and floating ice.

And a good south wind sprung up behind;
The Albatross did follow,
And every day, for food or play,
Came to the mariners' hollo!

In mist or cloud, on mast or shroud,
It perch'd for vespers nine;
Whiles all the night, through fog-smoke white,
Glimmer'd the white moonshine.'

The ancient Mariner inhospitably killeth the pious bird of good omen.

'God save thee, ancient Mariner,
From the fiends, that plague thee thus!—
Why look'st thou so?'—'With my crossbow
I shot the Albatross.

PART II

'The Sun now rose upon the right:
Out of the sea came he,
Still hid in mist, and on the left
Went down into the sea.

And the good south wind still blew behind,
But no sweet bird did follow,
Nor any day for food or play
Came to the mariners' hollo!

His shipmates cry out against the ancient Mariner for killing the bird of good luck.

And I had done a hellish thing,
And it would work 'em woe:
For all averr'd I had kill'd the bird
That made the breeze to blow.
Ah wretch! said they, the bird to slay,
That made the breeze to blow!

Nor dim nor red, like God's own head,
The glorious Sun uprist:
Then all averr'd I had kill'd the bird
That brought the fog and mist.
'Twas right, said they, such birds to slay,
That bring the fog and mist.

But when the fog cleared off, they justify the same, and thus make themselves accomplices in the crime.

The fair breeze blew, the white foam flew,
The furrow follow'd free;
We were the first that ever burst
Into that silent sea.

The fair breeze continues; the ship enters the Pacific Ocean, and sails northward, even till it reaches the Line.

Down dropt the breeze, the sails dropt down,
'Twas sad as sad could be;
And we did speak only to break
The silence of the sea!

The ship hath been suddenly becalmed.

All in a hot and copper sky,
The bloody Sun, at noon,
Right up above the mast did stand,
No bigger than the Moon.

Day after day, day after day,
We stuck, nor breath nor motion;
As idle as a painted ship
Upon a painted ocean.

Water, water, everywhere,
And all the boards did shrink;
Water, water, everywhere
Nor any drop to drink.

And the Albatross begins to be avenged.

The very deep did rot: O Christ!
That ever this should be!
Yea, slimy things did crawl with legs
Upon the slimy sea.

About, about, in reel and rout
The death-fires danced at night;
The water, like a witch's oils,
Burnt green, and blue, and white.

A Spirit had
followed them,
one of the in-
visible inhabit-
ants of this
planet, neither
departed souls
nor angels; con-

And some in dreams assurèd were
Of the Spirit that plagued us so;
Nine fathom deep he had follow'd us
From the land of mist and snow

cerning whom the learned Jew, Josephus, and the Platonic Constantinopolitan,
Michael Psellus may be consulted. They are very numerous, and there is no climate
or element without one or more.

And every tongue, through utter drought,
Was wither'd at the root;
We could not speak, no more than if
We had been choked with soot.

The shipmates
in their sore
distress, would
fain throw the
whole guilt on
the ancient
Mariner in
sign whereof
they hang the
dead sea-bird
round his neck.

Ah! well a-day! what evil looks
Had I from old and young!
Instead of the cross, the Albatross
About my neck was hung.

PART III

'There passed a weary time. Each throat
Was parch'd, and glazed each eye.
A weary time! a weary time!

How glazed each weary eye!
When, looking westward, I beheld
A something in the sky.

The ancient
Mariner be-
holdeth a sign
in the element
afar off.

At first it seem'd a little speck,
And then it seem'd a mist;
It moved and moved, and took at last
A certain shape, I wist.

A speck, a mist, a shape, I wist!
And still it near'd and near'd;
As if it dodged a water-sprite,
It plunged, and tack'd and veer'd.

With throats unslaked, with black lips baked,
We could nor laugh nor wail;
Through utter drought all dumb we stood!
I bit my arm, I suck'd the blood,
And cried, A sail! a sail!

At its nearer
approach, it
seemeth him
to be a ship;
and at a dear
ransom he
freeth his
speech from
the bonds of
thirst.

With throats unslaked, with black lips baked,
Agape they heard me call:
Gramercy! they for joy did grin,
And all at once their breath drew in,
As they were drinking all.

A flash of joy;

See! see! (I cried) she tacks no more!
Hither to work us weal—
Without a breeze, without a tide,
She steadies with upright keel!

And horror
follows. For
can it be a
ship that comes
onward without
wind or tide?

The western wave was all aflame,
The day was wellnigh done!

Almost upon the western wave
Rested the broad, bright Sun;
When that strange shape drove suddenly
Betwixt us and the Sun.

It seemeth him but the skeleton of a ship.

And straight the Sun was fleck'd with bars
(Heaven's Mother send us grace!),
As if through a dungeon-grate he peer'd
With broad and burning face.

Alas (thought I, and my heart beat loud)
How fast she nears and nears!
Are those her sails that glance in the Sun,
Like restless gossameres?

And its ribs are seen as bars on the face of the setting Sun. The Spectre-Woman and her Death-mate, and no other, on board the skeleton ship. Like vessel, like crew!

Are those her ribs through which the Sun
Did peer, as through a grate?
And is that Woman all her crew?
Is that a Death? and are there two?
Is Death that Woman's mate?

Her lips were red, her looks were free,
Her locks were yellow as gold:
Her skin was as white as leprosy,
The Nightmare Life-in-Death was she,
Who thicks man's blood with cold.

Death and Life-in-Death have diced for the ship's crew, and she (the latter) winneth the ancient Mariner.

The naked hulk alongside came,
And the twain were casting dice;
"The game is done! I've won! I've won!"
Quoth she, and whistles thrice.

The Sun's rim dips; the stars rush out,
At one stride comes the dark;
With far-heard whisper, o'er the sea,
Off shot the spectre-bark.

No twilight within the courts of the Sun.

We listen'd and look'd sideways up!
Fear at my heart, as at a cup,
My life-blood seem'd to sip!
The stars were dim, and thick the night,
The steersman's face by his lamp gleam'd white;
From the sails the dew did drip—
Till clomb above the eastern bar
The hornèd Moon, with one bright star
Within the nether tip.

At the rising of the Moon,

One after one, by the star-dogg'd Moon,
Too quick for groan or sigh,
Each turn'd his face with a ghastly pang,
And cursed me with his eye.

One after another,

Four times fifty living men
(And I heard nor sigh nor groan),
With heavy thump, a lifeless lump,
They dropp'd down one by one.

His shipmates drop down dead.

The souls did from their bodies fly—
They fled to bliss or woe!
And every soul, it pass'd me by
Like the whizz of my crossbow!'

But Life-in-Death begins her work on the ancient Mariner.

PART IV

The Wedding-Guest feareth that a spirit is talking to him.

'I fear thee, ancient Mariner!
I fear thy skinny hand!
And thou art long, and lank, and brown,
As is the ribb'd sea-sand.

I fear thee and thy glittering eye,
And thy skinny hand so brown.'—
'Fear not, fear not, thou Wedding-Guest!
This body dropt not down.

But the ancient Mariner assureth him of his bodily life, and proceedeth to relate his horrible penance.

Alone, alone, all, all alone
Alone on a wide, wide sea!
And never a saint took pity on
My soul in agony.

He despiseth the creatures of the calm.

The many men, so beautiful!
And they all dead did lie:
And a thousand thousand slimy things
Lived on; and so did I.

And envieth that they should live, and so many lie dead.

I look'd upon the rotting sea,
And drew my eyes away;
I look'd upon the rotting deck,
And there the dead men lay.

I look'd to heaven, and tried to pray;
But or ever a prayer had gusht,
A wicked whisper came, and made
My heart as dry as dust.

I closed my lids, and kept them close,
And the balls like pulses beat;
But the sky and the sea, and the sea and the sky,
Lay like a load on my weary eye,
And the dead were at my feet.

The cold sweat melted from their limbs,
Nor rot nor reek did they:
The look with which they look'd on me
Had never pass'd away.

> But the curse
> liveth for him
> in the eye of the
> dead men.

An orphan's curse would drag to hell
A spirit from on high;
But oh! more horrible than that
Is the curse in a dead man's eye!
Seven days, seven nights, I saw that curse,
And yet I could not die.

The moving Moon went up the sky,
And nowhere did abide;
Softly she was going up,
And a star or two beside—

> In his loneli-
> ness and
> fixedness he
> yearneth
> towards the
> journeying
> Moon, and the
> stars, that still
> sojourn, yet still move onward: and everywhere the blue sky belongs to them,
> and is their appointed rest and their native country and their own natural homes,
> which they enter unannounced, as lords that are certainly expected, and yet there
> is a silent joy at their arrival.

Her beams bemock'd the sultry main,
Like April hoar-frost spread;
But where the ship's huge shadow lay,
The charmèd water burnt alway
A still and awful red.

Beyond the shadow of the ship,
I watch'd the water-snakes:
They moved in tracks of shining white,
And when they rear'd, the elfish light
Fell off in hoary flakes.

Within the shadow of the ship
I watch'd their rich attire:
Blue, glossy green, and velvet black,
They coil'd and swam; and every track
Was a flash of golden fire.

O happy living things! no tongue
Their beauty might declare:
A spring of love gush'd from my heart,

And I bless'd them unaware:
Sure my kind saint took pity on me,
And I bless'd them unaware.

The selfsame moment I could pray;
And from my neck so free
The Albatross fell off, and sank
Like lead into the sea.

Part V

'O sleep! it is a gentle thing,
Beloved from pole to pole!
To Mary Queen the praise be given!
She sent the gentle sleep from Heaven,
That slid into my soul.

The silly buckets on the deck,
That had so long remain'd,
I dreamt that they were fill'd with dew;
And when I awoke, it rain'd.

By grace of
the holy
Mother, the
ancient
Mariner is
refreshed
with rain.

My lips were wet, my throat was cold.
My garments all were dank;
Sure I had drunken in my dreams,
And still my body drank.

I moved, and could not feel my limbs:
I was so light—almost
I thought that I had died in sleep,
And was a blessèd ghost.

And soon I heard a roaring wind:
It did not come anear;
But with its sound it shook the sails,
That were so thin and sere.

He heareth
sounds and
seeth strange
sights and
commotions
in the sky and
the element.

The upper air burst into life;
And a hundred fire-flags sheen;
To and fro they were hurried about!
And to and fro, and in and out,
The wan stars danced between.

And the coming wind did roar more loud,
And the sails did sigh like sedge;
And the rain pour'd down from one black cloud;
The Moon was at its edge.

The thick black cloud was cleft, and still
The Moon was at its side;
Like waters shot from some high crag,
The lightning fell with never a jag,
A river steep and wide.

The loud wind never reach'd the ship,
Yet now the ship moved on!
Beneath the lightning and the Moon
The dead men gave a groan.

They groan'd, they stirr'd, they all uprose,
Nor spake, nor moved their eyes;
It had been strange, even in a dream,
To have seen those dead men rise.

The helmsman steer'd, the ship moved on;
Yet never a breze up-blew;
The mariners all 'gan work the ropes,
Where they were wont to do;
They raised their limbs like lifeless tools—
We were a ghastly crew.

The body of my brother's son
Stood by me, knee to knee:
The body and I pull'd at one rope,
But he said naught to me.'

'I fear thee, ancient Mariner!'
'Be calm, thou Wedding-Guest:
'Twas not those souls that fled in pain,
Which to their corses came again,
But a troop of spirits blest:

The bodies of the ship's crew are inspired, and the ship moves on;

But not by the souls of the men, nor by demons of earth or middle air, but by a blessed troop of angelic spirits, sent down by the invocation of the guardian saint.

For when it dawn'd—they dropp'd their arms,
And cluster'd round the mast;
Sweet sounds rose slowly through their mouths,
And from their bodies pass'd.

Around, around, flew each sweet sound,
Then darted to the Sun;
Slowly the sounds came back again,
Now mix'd, now one by one.

Sometimes a-dropping from the sky
I heard the skylark sing;
Sometimes all little birds that are,
How they seem'd to fill the sea and air
With their sweet jargoning!

And now 'twas like all instruments,
Now like a lonely flute;
And now it is an angel's song,
That makes the Heavens be mute.

It ceased; yet still the sails made on
A pleasant noise till noon,
A noise like of a hidden brook
In the leafy month of June,
That to the sleeping woods all night
Singeth a quiet tune.

Till noon we quietly sail'd on,
Yet never a breeze did breathe:
Slowly and smoothly went the ship,
Moved onward from beneath.

The lonesome Spirit from the South Pole carries on the ship as far as the Line, in obedience to the angelic troop, but still requireth vengeance.

Under the keel nine fathom deep,
From the land of mist and snow,
The Spirit slid: and it was he
That made the ship to go.
The sails at noon left off their tune,
And the ship stood still also.

The Sun, right up above the mast,
Had fix'd her to the ocean:
But in a minute she 'gan stir,
With a short uneasy motion—
Backwards and forwards half her length
With a short uneasy motion.

Then like a pawing horse let go,
She made a sudden bound:
It flung the blood into my head,
And I fell down in a swound.

The Polar Spirit's fellow demons, the invisible inhabitants of the element, take part in his wrong; and two of them relate, one to the other, that penance long and heavy for the ancient Mariner hath been accorded to the Polar Spirit, who returneth southward.

How long in that same fit I lay,
I have not to declare;
But ere my living life return'd,
I heard, and in my soul discern'd
Two voices in the air.

"Is it he?" quoth one, "is this the man?
By Him who died on cross,
With his cruel bow he laid full low
The harmless Albatross.

The Spirit who bideth by himself
In the land of mist and snow,

He loved the bird that loved the man
Who shot him with his bow."

The other was a softer voice,
As soft as honey-dew:
Quoth he, "The man hath penance done,
And penance more will do."

PART VI

First Voice:
"But tell me, tell me! speak again,
Thy soft response renewing—
What makes that ship drive on so fast?
What is the Ocean doing?"

Second Voice:
"Still as a slave before his lord,
The Ocean hath no blast;
His great bright eye most silently
Up to the Moon is cast—

If he may know which way to go;
For she guides him smooth or grim.
See, brother, see! how graciously
She looketh down on him."

First Voice:
"But why drives on that ship so fast,
Without or wave or wind?"

Second Voice:
"The air is cut away before,
And closes from behind.

The Mariner
hath been cast
into a trance;
for the angelic
power causeth
the vessel to
drive north-
ward faster
than human life
could endure.

Fly, brother, fly! more high, more high!
Or we shall be belated:
For slow and slow that ship will go,
When the Mariner's trance is abated."

The super-
natural motion
is retarded;
the Mariner
awakes, and
his penance
begins anew.

I woke, and we were sailing on
As in a gentle weather:
'Twas night, calm night, the Moon was high;
The dead men stood together.

All stood together on the deck,
For a charnel-dungeon fitter:
All fix'd on me their stony eyes,
That in the Moon did glitter.

The pang, the curse, with which they died,
Had never pass'd away:
I could not draw my eyes from theirs,
Nor turn them up to pray.

The curse is
finally expiated.

And now this spell was snapt: once more
I viewed the ocean green,
And look'd far forth, yet little saw
Of what had else been seen—

Like one that on a lonesome road
Doth walk in fear and dread,
And having once turn'd round, walks on,
And turns no more his head;
Because he knows a frightful fiend
Doth close behind him tread.

But soon there breathed a wind on me,
Nor sound nor motion made:
Its path was not upon the sea,
In ripple or in shade.

It raised my hair, it fann'd my cheek
Like a meadow-gale of spring—
It mingled strangely with my fears,
Yet it felt like a welcoming.

Swiftly, swiftly flew the ship,
Yet she sail'd softly too:
Sweetly, sweetly blew the breeze—
On me alone it blew.

O dream of joy! is this indeed
The lighthouse top I see?
Is this the hill? is this the kirk?
Is this mine own countree?

And the ancient Mariner beholdeth his native country.

We drifted o'er the harbour-bar,
And I with sobs did pray—
O let me be awake, my God!
Or let me sleep alway.

The harbour-bay was clear as glass,
So smoothly it was strewn!
And on the bay the moonlight lay,
And the shadow of the Moon.

The rock shone bright, the kirk no less
That stands above the rock:

The moonlight steep'd in silentness
The steady weathercock.

The angelic
spirits leave the
dead bodies,

And the bay was white with silent light
Till rising from the same,
Full many shapes, that shadows were,
In crimson colours came.

And appear in
their own forms
of light.

A little distance from the prow
Those crimson shadows were:
I turn'd my eyes upon the deck—
O Christ! what saw I there!

Each corse lay flat, lifeless and flat,
And, by the holy rood!
A man all light, a seraph-man,
On every corse there stood.

This seraph-band, each waved his hand:
It was a heavenly sight!
They stood as signals to the land,
Each one a lovely light;

This seraph-band, each waved his hand,
No voice did they impart—
No voice; but O, the silence sank
Like music on my heart.

But soon I heard the dash of oars,
I heard the Pilot's cheer;
My head was turn'd perforce away,
And I saw a boat appear.

The Pilot and the Pilot's boy,
I heard them coming fast:
Dear Lord in Heaven! it was a joy
The dead men could not blast.

I saw a third—I heard his voice:
It is the Hermit good!
He singeth loud his godly hymns
That he makes in the wood.
He'll shrieve my soul, he'll wash away
The Albatross's blood.

PART VII

'This Hermit good lives in that wood
Which slopes down to the sea.
How loudly his sweet voice he rears!
He loves to talk with marineres
That come from a far countree.

He kneels at morn, and noon, and eve—
He hath a cushion plump.
It is the moss that wholly hides
The rotted old oak-stump.

The skiff-boat near'd: I heard them talk,
"Why, this is strange, I trow!
Where are those lights so many and fair,
That signal made but now?"

"Strange, by my faith!" the Hermit said—
"And they answer'd not our cheer!

The Hermit of the Wood.

Approacheth the ship with wonder.

The planks look warp'd! and see those sails,
How thin they are and sere!
I never saw aught like to them,
Unless perchance it were

Brown skeletons of leaves that lag
My forest-brook along;
When the ivy-tod is heavy with snow,
And the owlet whoops to the wolf below,
That eats the she-wolf's young."

"Dear Lord! it hath a fiendish look—
(The Pilot made reply)
I am a-fear'd."—"Push on, push on!"
Said the Hermit cheerily.

The boat came closer to the ship,
But I nor spake nor stirr'd;
The boat came close beneath the ship,
And straight a sound was heard.

The ship suddenly sinketh.

Under the water it rumbled on
Still louder and more dread:
It reach'd the ship, it split the bay;
The ship went down like lead.

The ancient Mariner is saved in the Pilot's boat.

Stunn'd by that loud and dreadful sound,
Which sky and ocean smote,
Like one that hath been seven days drown'd
My body lay afloat;
But swift as dreams, myself I found
Within the Pilot's boat.

Upon the whirl, where sank the ship,
The boat spun round and round;
And all was still, save that the hill
Was telling of the sound.

I moved my lips—the Pilot shriek'd
And fell down in a fit;
The holy Hermit raised his eyes,
And pray'd where he did sit.

I took the oars: the Pilot's boy,
Who now doth crazy go,
Laugh'd loud and long, and all the while
His eyes went to and fro.
"Ha! ha!" quoth he, "full plain I see
The Devil knows how to row."

And now, all in my own countree,
I stood on the firm land!
The Hermit stepp'd forth from the boat,
And scarcely he could stand.

The ancient Mariner earnestly entreateth the Hermit to shrieve him; and the penance of life falls on him.

"O shrieve me, shrieve me, holy man!"
The Hermit cross'd his brow.
"Say quick," quoth he, "I bid thee say—
What manner of man art thou?"

Forthwith this frame of mine was wrench'd
With a woful agony,
Which forced me to begin my tale;
And then it left me free.

And ever and anon throughout his future life an agony constraineth him to travel from land to land;

Since then, at an uncertain hour,
That agony returns:
And till my ghastly tale is told,
This heart within me burns.

I pass, like night, from land to land;
I have strange power of speech;
That moment that his face I see,
I know the man that must hear me:
To him my tale I teach.

What loud uproar bursts from that door!
The wedding-guests are there:
But in the garden-bower the bride
And bride-maids singing are:
And hark, the little vesper bell,
Which biddeth me to prayer!

O Wedding-Guest! this soul hath been
Alone on a wide, wide sea:
So lonely 'twas, that God Himself
Scarce seemèd there to be.

O sweeter than the marriage-feast,
'Tis sweeter far to me,
To walk together to the kirk
With a goodly company!—

To walk together to the kirk,
And all together pray,
While each to his great Father bends,
Old men, and babes, and loving friends,
And youths and maidens gay!

Farewell, farewell! but this I tell
To thee, thou Wedding-Guest!
He prayeth well, who loveth well
Both man and bird and beast.

And to teach, by his own example, love and reverence to all things that God made and loveth.

He prayeth best, who loveth best
All things both great and small;
For the dear God who loveth us,
He made and loveth all.'

The Mariner, whose eye is bright,
Whose beard with age is hoar,
Is gone: and now the Wedding-Guest
Turn'd from the bridegroom's door.

He went like one that hath been stunn'd,
And is of sense forlorn:
A sadder and a wiser man
He rose the morrow morn.

KUBLA KHAN

In Xanadu did Kubla Khan
    A stately pleasure-dome decree:
Where Alph, the sacred river, ran
Through caverns measureless to man
    Down to a sunless sea.
So twice five miles of fertile ground
    With walls and towers were girdled round:
And there were gardens bright with sinuous rills
Where blossom'd many an incense-bearing tree;
And here were forests ancient as the hills,
Enfolding sunny spots of greenery.

But O, that deep romantic chasm which slanted
Down the green hill athwart a cedarn cover!
A savage place! as holy and enchanted
As e'er beneath a waning moon was haunted
By woman wailing for her demon-lover!
And from this chasm, with ceaseless turmoil seething,
As if this earth in fast thick pants were breathing,
A mighty fountain momently was forced;
Amid whose swift half-intermitted burst
Huge fragments vaulted like rebounding hail,
Or chaffy grain beneath the thresher's flail:
And 'mid these dancing rocks at once and ever
It flung up momently the sacred river.
Five miles meandering with a mazy motion
Through wood and dale the sacred river ran,
Then reach'd the caverns measureless to man,
And sank in tumult to a lifeless ocean:
And 'mid this tumult Kubla heard from far
Ancestral voices prophesying war!

    The shadow of the dome of pleasure
      Floated midway on the waves;
    Where was heard the mingled measure
      From the fountain and the caves.
  It was a miracle of rare device,
  A sunny pleasure-dome with caves of ice!

    A damsel with a dulcimer
      In a vision once I saw:
    It was an Abyssinian maid,
      And on her dulcimer she play'd,
    Singing of Mount Abora.

Could I revive within me,
    Her symphony and song,
To such a deep delight 'twould win me,
That with music loud and long,
I would build that dome in air,
That sunny dome! those caves of ice!
And all who heard should see them there,
And all should cry, Beware! Beware!
His flashing eyes, his floating hair!
Weave a circle round him thrice,
    And close your eyes with holy dread,
    For he on honey-dew hath fed,
And drunk the milk of Paradise.

WALTER SAVAGE LANDOR
(1775—1864)

DIRCE

Stand close around, ye Stygian set,
    With Dirce in one boat convey'd!
Or Charon, seeing, may forget
    That he is old and she a shade.

ON HIS SEVENTY-FIFTH BIRTHDAY

I strove with none, for none was worth my strife.
Nature I loved and, next to Nature, Art:
I warm'd both hands before the fire of life;
It sinks, and I am ready to depart.

THOMAS LOVE PEACOCK
(1785—1866)

THREE MEN OF GOTHAM

Seamen three! What men be ye?
Gotham's three wise men we be.
Whither in your bowl so free?
To rake the moon from out the sea.
The bowl goes trim. The moon doth shine.
And our ballast is old wine.—
And your ballast is old wine.

Who art thou, so fast adrift?
I am he they call Old Care.
Here on board we will thee lift.
No: I may not enter there.
Wherefore so? 'Tis Jove's decree,
In a bowl Care may not be.—
In a bowl Care may not be.

Fear ye not the waves that roll?
No: in charmèd bowl we swim.
What the charm that floats the bowl?
Water may not pass the brim.
The bowl goes trim. The moon doth shine.
And our ballast is old wine.—
And your ballast is old wine.

LORD BYRON
(1788—1824)

SONG

So, we'll go no more a-roving
    So late into the night,
Though the heart be still as loving,
    And the moon be still as bright.

For the sword outwears its sheath,
    And the soul wears out the breast,
And the heart must pause to breathe,
    And love itself have rest.

Though the night was made for loving,
    And the day returns too soon,
Yet we'll go more a-roving
    By the light of the moon.

VOLTAIRE AND GIBBON

cvi

... The one was fire and fickleness, a child
Most mutable in wishes, but in mind
A wit as various,—gay, grave, sage, or wild,—
Historian, bard, philosopher, combined;
He multiplied himself among mankind,

The Proteus of their talents: But his own
Breathed most in ridicule,—which, as the wind,
Blew where it listed, laying all things prone,—
Now to o'erthrow a fool, and now to shake a throne.

cvii

The other, deep and slow, exhausting thought,
And hiving wisdom with each studious year,
In meditation dwelt—with learning wrought,
And shaped his weapon with an edge severe,
Sapping a solemn creed with solemn sneer;
The lord of irony,—that master spell,
Which stung his foes to wrath, which grew from fear,
And doomed him to the zealot's ready Hell,
Which answers to all doubts so eloquently well...

Childe Harold.

THE OCEAN

CLXXIX

... Roll on, thou deep and dark blue Ocean—roll!
Ten thousand fleets sweep over thee in vain;
Man marks the earth with ruin—his control
Stops with the shore;—upon the watery plain
The wrecks are all thy deed, nor doth remain
A shadow of man's ravage, save his own,
When, for a moment, like a drop of rain,
He sinks into thy depths with bubbling groan—
Without a grave—unknelled, uncoffined, and unknown.

CLXXX

His steps are not upon thy paths,—thy fields
Are not a spoil for him,—thou dost arise

And shake him from thee; the vile strength he wields
For Earth's destruction thou dost all despise,
Spurning him from thy bosom to the skies—
And send'st him, shivering in thy playful spray
And howling, to his Gods, where haply lies
His petty hope in some near port or bay,
And dashest him again to Earth:—there let him lay.

CLXXXI

The armaments which thunderstrike the walls
Of rock-built cities, bidding nations quake,
And Monarchs tremble in their Capitals,
The oak Leviathans, whose huge ribs make
Their clay creator the vain title take
Of Lord of thee, and Arbiter of War—
These are thy toys, and, as the snowy flake,
They melt into thy yeast of waves, which mar
Alike the Armada's pride, or spoils of Trafalgar.

CLXXXII

Thy shores are empires, changed in all save thee—
Assyria—Greece—Rome—Carthage—what are they?
Thy waters washed them power while they were free,
And many a tyrant since; their shores obey
The stranger, slave, or savage; their decay
Has dried up realms to deserts:—not so thou,
Unchangeable save to thy wild waves' play;
Time writes no wrinkle on thine azure brow —
Such as Creation's dawn beheld, thou rollest now ...

Childe Harold.

STANZAS FROM 'THE VISION OF JUDGMENT'

Saint Peter sat by the celestial gate:
　His keys were rusty, and the lock was dull,
So little trouble had been given of late;
　Not that the place by any means was full,
But since the Gallic era "eighty-eight"
　The Devils had ta'en a longer, stronger pull,
And "a pull altogether," as they say
At sea—which drew most souls another way.

The Angels all were singing out of tune,
　And hoarse with having little else to do,
Excepting to wind up the sun and moon,
　Or curb a runaway young star or two,
Or wild colt of a comet, which too soon
　Broke out of bounds o'er the ethereal blue,
Splitting some planet with its playful tail,
As boats are sometimes by a wanton whale.

The Guardian Seraphs had retired on high,
　Finding their charges past all care below;
Terrestrial business filled nought in the sky
　Save the Recording Angel's black bureau;
Who found, indeed, the facts to multiply
　With such rapidity of vice and woe,
That he had stripped off both his wings in quills,
And yet was in arrear of human ills.

His business so augmented of late years,
　That he was forced, against his will, no doubt,

(Just like those cherubs, earthly ministers,)
  For some resource to turn himself about,
And claim the help of his celestial peers,
  To aid him ere he should be quite worn out
By the increased demand for his remarks:
Six Angels and twelve Saints were named his clerks.

This was a handsome board—at least for Heaven;
  And yet they had even then enough to do,
So many Conquerors' cars were daily driven,
  So many kingdoms fitted up anew;
Each day, too, slew its thousands six or seven,
  Till at the crowning carnage, Waterloo,
They threw their pens down in divine disgust—
The page was so besmeared with blood and dust.

This by the way; 'tis not mine to record
  What Angels shrink from: even the very Devil
On this occasion his own work abhorred,
  So surfeited with the infernal revel:
Though he himself had sharpened every sword,
  It almost quenched his innate thirst of evil.
(Here Satan's sole good work deserves insertion—
'Tis, that he has both Generals in reversion.)

Let's skip a few short years of hollow peace,
  Which peopled earth no better, Hell as wont,
And Heaven none—they form the tyrant's lease,
  With nothing but new names subscribed upon't;

'Twill one day finish: meantime they increase,
  "With seven heads and ten horns," and all in front,
Like Saint John's foretold beast; but ours are born
  Less formidable in the head than horn.

In the first year of Freedom's second dawn
  Died George the Third; although no tyrant, one
Who shielded tyrants, till each sense with-drawn
  Left him nor mental nor external sun:
A better farmer ne'er brushed dew from lawn,
  A worse king never left a realm undone!
He died—but left his subjects still behind,
One half as mad—and t'other no less blind.

He died! his death made no great stir on earth:
  His burial made some pomp; there was profusion
Of velvet—gilding—brass—and no great dearth
  Of aught but tears—save those shed by collusion:
For these things may be bought at their true worth;
  Of elegy there was the due infusion—
Bought also; and the torches, cloaks and banners,
Heralds, and relics of old Gothic manners,

Formed a sepulchral melodrame. Of all
  The fools who flocked to swell or see the show,
Who cared about the corpse? The funeral
  Made the attraction, and the black the woe.
There throbbed not there a thought which pierced the pall
  And when the gorgeous coffin was laid low,

It seemed the mockery of hell to fold
The rottenness of eighty years in gold.

So mix his body with the dust! It might
   Return to what it *must* far sooner, were
The natural compound left alone to fight
   Its way back into earth, and fire, and air;
But the unnatural balsams merely blight
   What Nature made him at his birth, as bare
As the mere million's base unmummied clay—
Yet all his spices but prolong decay.

He's dead—and upper earth with him has done;
   He's buried; save the undertaker's bill,
Or lapidary scrawl, the world is gone
   For him, unless he left a German will:
But where's the proctor who will ask his son?
   In whom his qualities are reigning still,
Except that household virtue, most uncommon,
Of constancy to a bad, ugly woman.

"God save the king!" It is a large economy
   In God to save the like; but if he will
Be saving, all the better; for not one am I
   Of those who think damnation better still:
I hardly know too if not quite alone am I
   In this small hope of bettering future ill
By circumscribing, with some slight restriction,
The eternity of Hell's hot jurisdiction ...

THE POWER OF MONEY

Why call the miser miserable? as
  I said before: the frugal life is his,
Which in a saint or cynic ever was
  The theme of praise: a hermit would not miss
Canonization for the self-same cause,
  And wherefore blame gaunt Wealth's austerities?
Because, you'll say, nought calls for such a trial;—
Then there's more merit in his self-denial.

He is your only poet;—Passion, pure
  And sparkling on from heap to heap, displays,
Possessed, the ore, of which *mere hopes* allure
  Nations athwart the deep: the golden rays
Flash up in ingots from the mine obscure:
  On him the Diamond pours its brilliant blaze,
While the mild Emerald's beam shades down the dyes
Of other stones, to soothe the miser's eyes.

The lands on either side are his; the ship
  From Ceylon, Inde, or far Cathay, unloads
For him the fragrant produce of each trip;
  Beneath his cars of Ceres groan the roads,
And the vine blushes like Aurora's lip;
  His very cellars might be King's abodes;
While he, despising every sensual call,
Commands—the intellectual Lord of *all*.

Perhaps he hath great projects in his mind,
  To build a college, or to found a race,

A hospital, a church,—and leave behind
  Some dome surmounted by his meagre face:
Perhaps he fain would liberate Mankind
  Even with the very ore which makes them base;
Perhaps he would be wealthiest of his nation,
Or revel in the joys of calculation.

But whether all, or each, or none of these
  May be the hoarder's principle of action,
The fool will call such mania a disease:—
  What is his *own*? Go—look at each transaction,
Wars, revels, loves—do these bring men more ease
  Than the mere plodding through each "vulgar fraction"?
Or do they benefit Mankind? Lean Miser!
Let spendthrifts' heirs inquire of yours—who's wiser?

How beauteous are rouleaus! how charming chests
  Containing ingots, bags of dollars, coins
(Not of old victors, all whose heads and crests
  Weigh not the thin ore where their visage shines,
But) of fine unclipped gold, where dully rests
  Some likeness, which the glittering cirque confines,
Of modern, reigning, sterling, stupid stamp!—
Yes! ready money *is* Aladdin's lamp.

"Love rules the Camp, the Court, the Grove,—for Love
  Is Heaven, and Heaven is Love:"—so sings the bard;
Which it were rather difficult to prove
  (A thing with poetry in general hard).
Perhaps there may be something in "the Grove,"
  At least it rhymes to "Love": but I'm prepared

To doubt (no less than landlords of their rental)
If "Courts" and "Camps" be quite so sentimental.

But if Love don't *Cash* does, and Cash alone:
  Cash rules the Grove, and fells it too besides;
Without cash, camps were thin, and courts were none;
  Without cash, Malthus tells you—"take no brides."
So Cash rules Love the ruler, on his own
  High ground, as virgin Cynthia sways the tides:
And as for "Heaven being Love," why not say honey
Is wax? Heaven is not Love, 'tis Matrimony.

Don Juan, XII

PERCY BYSSHE SHELLEY
(1792—1822)

FROM

THE MASK OF ANARCHY

WRITTEN ON THE OCCASION OF THE MASSACRE AT MANCHESTER

As I lay asleep in Italy
There came a voice from over the Sea,
And with great power it forth led me
To walk in the visions of Poesy.

I met Murder on the way—
He had a mask like Castlereagh—
Very smooth he looked, yet grim;
Seven blood-hounds followed him:

All were fat; and well they might
Be in admirable plight,
For one by one, and two by two,
He tossed them human hearts to chew
Which from his wide cloak he drew.

Next came Fraud, and he had on,
Like Eldon, an ermined gown;
His big tears, for he wept well,
Turned to mill-stones as they fell.

And the little children, who
Round his feet played to and fro,
Thinking every tear a gem,
Had their brains knocked out by them.

Clothed with the Bible, as with light,
And the shadows of the night,
Like Sidmouth, next, Hypocrisy
On a crocodile rode by.

And many more Destructions played
In this ghastly masquerade,
All disguised, even to the eyes,
Like Bishops, lawyers, peers, or spies.

Last came Anarchy: he rode
On a white horse, splashed with blood;
He was pale even to the lips,
Like Death in the Apocalypse.

And he wore a kingly crown;
And in his grasp a sceptre shone;
On his brow this mark I saw—
'I am **God**, and King and Law!'

With a pace stately and fast,
Over English land he passed,
Trampling to a mire of blood
The adoring multitude.

And a mighty troop around,
With their trampling shook the ground,
Waving each a bloody sword,
For the service of their Lord.

And with glorious triumph, they
Rode through England proud and gay,
Drunk as with intoxication
Of the wine of desolation.

O'er fields and towns, from sea to sea,
Passed the Pageant swift and free,
Tearing up, and trampling down;
Till they came to London town.

And each dweller, panic-stricken,
Felt his heart with terror sicken
Hearing the tempestuous cry
Of the triumph of Anarchy.

For with pomp to meet him came,
Clothed in arms like blood and flame,

The hired murderers, who did sing
'Thou art God, and Law, and King.

'We have waited, weak and lone
For thy coming, Mighty One!
Our purses are empty, our swords are cold,
Give us glory, and blood, and gold.'

Lawyers and priests, a motley crowd,
To the earth their pale brows bowed;
Like a bad prayer not over loud,
Whispering—'Thou art Law and God.'—

Then all cried with one accord,
'Thou art King, and God, and Lord;
Anarchy, to thee we bow,
Be thy name made holy now!'

And Anarchy, the Skeleton,
Bowed and grinned to every one,
As well as if his education
Had cost ten millions to the nation.

For he knew the Palaces
Of our Kings were rightly his;
His the sceptre, crown, and globe,
And the gold-inwoven robe.

So he sent his slaves before
To seize upon the Bank and Tower,
And was proceeding with intent
To meet his pensioned Parliament

When one fled past, a maniac maid,
And her name was Hope, she said:
But she looked more like Despair,
And she cried out in the air:

'My father Time is weak and gray
With waiting for a better day;
See how idiot-like he stands,
Fumbling with his palsied hands!

'He has had child after child,
And the dust of death is piled
Over every one but me—
Misery, oh, Misery!'

Then she lay down in the street,
Right before the horses' feet,
Expecting, with a patient eye,
Murder, Fraud, and Anarchy.

When between her and her foes
A mist, a light, an image rose,
Small at first, and weak, and frail
Like the vapour of a vale:

Till as clouds grow on the blast,
Like tower-crowned giants striding fast,
And glare with lightnings as they fly,
And speak in thunder to the sky,

It grew—a Shape arrayed in mail
Brighter than the viper's scale,
And upborne on wings whose grain
Was as the light of sunny rain.

On its helm, seen far away,
A planet, like the Morning's, lay;
And those plumes its light rained through
Like a shower of crimson dew.

With step as soft as wind it passed
O'er the heads of men—so fast
That they knew the presence there,
And looked,—but all was empty air.

As flowers beneath May's footstep waken,
As stars from Night's loose hair are shaken,
As waves arise when loud winds call,
Thoughts sprung where'er that step did fall.

And the prostrate multitude
Looked—and ankle-deep in blood,
Hope, that maiden most serene,
Was walking with a quiet mien:

And Anarchy, the ghastly birth,
Lay dead earth upon the earth;
The Horse of Death tameless as wind
Fled, and with his hoofs did grind
To dust the murderers thronged behind.

A rushing light of clouds and splendour,
A sense awakening and yet tender
Was heard and felt—and at its close
These words of joy and fear arose

As if their own indignant Earth
Which gave the sons of England birth
Had felt their blood upon her brow,
And shuddering with a mother's throe

Had turnèd every drop of blood
By which her face had been bedewed
To an accent unwithstood,—
As if her heart had cried aloud:

'Men of England, heirs of Glory,
Heroes of unwritten story,
Nurslings of one mighty Mother,
Hopes of her, and one another;

'Rise like Lions after slumber
In unvanquishable number,
Shake your chains to earth like dew
Which in sleep had fallen on you—
Ye are many—they are few. . . .

ENGLAND IN 1819

An old, mad, blind, despised, and dying king,—
Princes, the dregs of their dull race, who flow
Through public scorn,—mud from a muddy spring,—
Rulers who neither see, nor feel, nor know,

But leech-like to their fainting country cling,
Till they drop, blind in blood, without a blow,—
A people starved and stabbed in the untilled field,—
An army, which liberticide and prey
Makes as a two-edged sword to all who wield,—
Golden and sanguine laws which tempt and slay;
Religion Christless, Godless—a book sealed;
A Senate,—Time's worst statute unrepealed,—
Are graves, from which a glorious Phantom may
Burst, to illumine our tempestuous day.

ODE TO THE WEST WIND

I

O Wild West Wind, thou breath of Autumn's being
  Thou from whose unseen presence the leaves dead
Are driven like ghosts from an enchanter fleeing,

  Yellow, and black, and pale, and hectic red,
Pestilence-stricken multitudes! O thou
  Who chariotest to their dark wintry bed

The wingèd seeds, where they lie cold and low,
  Each like a corpse within its grave, until
Thine azure sister of the Spring shall blow

  Her clarion o'er the dreaming earth, and fill
(Driving sweet buds like flocks to feed in air)
  With living hues and odours plain and hill;

Wild Spirit, which art moving everywhere;
Destroyer and preserver; hear, O hear!

II

Thou on whose stream, 'mid the steep sky's commotion
 Loose clouds like earth's decaying leaves are shed,
Shook from the tangled boughs of heaven and ocean,

 Angels of rain and lightning! there are spread
On the blue surface of thine airy surge,
 Like the bright hair uplifted from the head

Of some fierce Mænad, even from the dim verge
 Of the horizon to the zenith's height,
The locks of the approaching storm. Thou dirge

 Of the dying year, to which this closing night
Will be the dome of a vast sepulchre,
 Vaulted with all thy congregated might

Of vapours, from whose solid atmosphere
Black rain, and fire, and hail, will burst: O hear!

III

Thou who didst waken from his summer dreams
 The blue Mediterranean, where he lay,
Lull'd by the coil of his crystalline streams,

 Beside a pumice isle in Baiæ's bay,
And saw in sleep old palaces and towers
 Quivering within the wave's intenser day,

All overgrown with azure moss, and flowers
 So sweet, the sense faints picturing them! Thou
For whose path the Atlantic's level powers

Cleave themselves into chasms, while far below
The sea-blooms and the oozy woods which wear
  The sapless foliage of the ocean, know

Thy voice, and suddenly grow gray with fear,
And tremble and despoil themselves: O hear!

IV

If I were a dead leaf thou mightest bear;
  If I were a swift cloud to fly with thee;
A wave to pant beneath thy power, and share

  The impulse of thy strength, only less free
Than thou, O uncontrollable! if even
  I were as in my boyhood, and could be

The comrade of thy wanderings over heaven,
  As then, when to outstrip thy skiey speed
Scarce seem'd a vision—I would ne'er have striven

  As thus with thee in prayer in my sore need.
O! lift me as a wave, a leaf, a cloud!
  I fall upon the thorns of life! I bleed!

A heavy weight of hours has chain'd and bow'd
One too like thee—tameless, and swift, and proud.

V

Make me thy lyre, even as the forest is:
  What if my leaves are falling like its own?
The tumult of thy mighty harmonies

Will take from both a deep autumnal tone,
Sweet though in sadness. Be thou, Spirit fierce,
    My spirit! Be thou me, impetuous one!

Drive my dead thoughts over the universe,
    Like wither'd leaves, to quicken a new birth;
And, by the incantation of this verse,

    Scatter, as from an unextinguish'd hearth
Ashes and sparks, my words among mankind!
    Be through my lips to unawaken'd earth

The trumpet of a prophecy! O Wind,
If Winter comes, can Spring be far behind?

STANZAS FROM 'ADONAIS',

AN ELEGY ON THE DEATH

of

JOHN KEATS

. . . He has outsoared the shadow of our night;
Envy and calumny and hate and pain,
And that unrest which men miscall delight,
Can touch him not and torture not again;
From the contagion of the world's slow stain
He is secure, and now can never mourn
A heart grown cold, a head grown gray in vain;
    Nor, when the spirit's self has ceased to burn,
With sparkless ashes load an unlamented urn.

He lives, he wakes—'tis Death is dead, not he;
Mourn not for Adonais.—Thou young Dawn,
Turn all thy dew to splendour, for from thee
The spirit thou lamentest is not gone;
Ye caverns and ye forests, cease to moan!
Cease, ye faint flowers and fountains, and thou Air,
Which like a mourning veil thy scarf hadst thrown
O'er the abandoned Earth, now leave it bare
Even to the joyous stars which smile on its despair!

He is made one with Nature: there is heard
His voice in all her music, from the moan
Of thunder, to the song of night's sweet bird;
He is a presence to be felt and known
In darkness and in light, from herb and stone,
Spreading itself where'er that Power may move
Which has withdrawn his being to its own;
Which wields the world with never-wearied love,
Sustains it from beneath, and kindles it above

He is a portion of the loveliness
Which once he made more lovely: he doth bear
His part, while the one Spirit's plastic stress
Sweeps through the dull dense world, compelling there,
All new successions to the forms they wear;
Torturing th' unwilling dross that checks its flight
To its own likeness, as each mass may bear;
And bursting in its beauty and its might
From trees and beasts and men into the Heaven's light . . .

CHORUS FROM 'HELLAS'

The world's great age begins anew,
 The golden years return,
The earth doth like a snake renew
 Her winter weeds outworn:
Heaven smiles, and faiths and empires gleam,
Like wrecks of a dissolving dream.

A brighter Hellas rears its mountains
 From waves serener far;
A new Peneus rolls his fountains
 Against the morning star.
Where fairer Tempes bloom, there sleep
Young Cyclads on a sunnier deep.

A loftier Argo cleaves the main,
 Fraught with a later prize;
Another Orpheus sings again,
 And loves, and weeps, and dies.
A new Ulysses leaves once more
Calypso for his native shore.

Oh, write no more the tale of Troy,
 If earth Death's scroll must be!
Nor mix with Laian rage the joy
 Which dawns upon the free:
Although a subtler Sphinx renew
Riddles of death Thebes never knew.

Another Athens shall arise,
  And to remoter time
Bequeath, like sunset to the skies,
  The splendour of its prime;
And leave, if nought so bright may live,
All earth can take or Heaven can give.

Saturn and Love their long repose
  Shall burst, more bright and good
Than all who fell, than One who rose,
  Than many unsubdued:
Not gold, not blood, their altar dowers,
But votive tears and symbol flowers.

Oh, cease! must hate and death return?
  Cease! must men kill and die?
Cease! drain not to its dregs the urn
  Of bitter prophecy.
The world is weary of the past,
Oh, might it die or rest at last!

STANZAS FROM 'THE TRIUMPH OF LIFE'

   . . . The old anatomies
Sate hatching their bare broods under the shade

'Of daemon wings, and laughed from their dead eyes
To reassume the delegated power,
Arrayed in which those worms did monarchize,

'Who made this earth their charnel. Others more
Humble, like falcons, sate upon the fist
Of common men, and round their heads did soar;

'Or like small gnats and flies, as thick as mist
On evening marshes, thronged about the brow
Of lawyers, statesmen, priest and theorist;—

'And others, like discoloured flakes of snow
On fairest bosoms and the sunniest hair,
Fell, and were melted by the youthful glow

'Which they extinguished; and, like tears, they were
A veil to those from whose faint lids they rained
In drops of sorrow. I became aware

'Of whence those forms proceeded which thus stained
The track in which we moved. After brief space,
From every form the beauty slowly waned;

'From every firmest limb and fairest face
The strength and freshness fell like dust, and left
The action and the shape without the grace

'Of life. The marble brow of youth was cleft
With care; and in those eyes where once hope shone,
Desire, like a lioness bereft

'Of her last cub, glared ere it died; each one
Of that great crowd sent forth incessantly
These shadows, numerous as the dead leaves blown

'In autumn evening from a poplar tree.
Each like himself and like each other were
At first; but some distorted seemed to be

'Obscure clouds, moulded by the casual air;
And of this stuff the car's creative ray
Wrought all the busy phantoms that were there,

'As the sun shapes the clouds; thus on the way
Mask after mask fell from the countenance
And form of all; and long before the day

'Was old, the joy which waked like heaven's glance
The sleepers in the oblivious valley, died;
And some grew weary of the ghastly dance,

'And fell, as I have fallen, by the wayside;—
Those soonest from whose forms most shadows passed,
And least of strength and beauty did abide.

'Then, what is life? I cried.' —

JOHN CLARE
(1793—1864)

STANZAS FROM 'SUMMER IMAGES'

... I see the wild flowers, in their summer morn
  Of beauty, feeding on joy's luscious hours;
The gay convolvulus, wreathing round the thorn,
  Agape for honey showers;

And slender kingcup, burnished with the dew
  Of morning's early hours,
    Like gold yminted new;

And mark by rustic bridge, o'er shallow stream,
  Cow-tending boy, to toil unreconciled,
Absorbed as in some vagrant summer dream;
  Who now, in gestures wild,
Starts dancing to his shadow on the wall,
  Feeling self-gratified,
    Nor fearing human thrall:

Then thread the sunny valley laced with streams,
  Or forests rude, and the oershadowed brims
Of simple ponds, where idle shepherd dreams,
  And streaks his listless limbs;
Or trace hay-scented meadows, smooth and long,
  Where joy's wild impulse swims
    In one continued song.

I love at early morn, from new mown swath,
  To see the startled frog his route pursue;
To mark while, leaping oer the dripping path,
  His bright sides scatter dew,
The early lark that from its bustle flies,
  To hail his matin new;
    And watch him to the skies:

To note on hedgerow baulks, in moisture sprent,
  The jetty snail creep from the mossy thorn,
With earnest heed, and tremulous intent,
  Frail brother of the morn,

That from the tiny bents and misted leaves
  Withdraws his timid horn,
    And fearful vision weaves:

Or swallow heed on smoke-tanned chimney top,
  Wont to be first unsealing morning's eye,
Ere yet the bee hath gleaned one wayward drop
  Of honey on his thigh;
To see him seek morn's airy couch to sing,
  Until the golden sky
    Bepaint his russet wing:

And sawning boy by tanning corn espy,
  With clapping noise to startle birds away,
And hear him bawl to every passer by
  To know the hour of day;
And see the uncradled breeze, refreshed and strong,
  With waking blossoms play,
    And breathe eolian song.

I love the south-west wind, or low or loud,
  And not the less when sudden drops of rain
Moisten my pallid cheek from ebon cloud,
  Threatening soft showers again,
That over lands new ploughed and meadow grounds,
  Summer's sweet breath unchain,
    And wake harmonious sounds.

Rich music breathes in summer's every sound;
  And in her harmony of varied greens,
Woods, meadows, hedge-rows, corn-fields, all around
  Much beauty intervenes,

Filling with harmony the ear and eye;
   While o'er the mingling scenes
     Far spreads the laughing sky.

And wind-enamoured aspen—mark the leaves
   Turn up their silver lining to the sun,
And list! the brustling noise, that oft deceives,
   And makes the sheep-boy run:
The sound so mimics fast-approaching showers,
   He thinks the rain begun,
     And hastes to sheltering bowers.

But now the evening curdles dank and grey,
   Changing her watchet hue for sombre weed;
And moping owls, to close the lids of day,
   On drowsy wing proceed;
While chickering crickets, tremulous and long,
   Light's farewell inly heed,
     And give it parting song.

The pranking bat its flighty circlet makes;
   The glow-worm burnishes its lamp anew
Oer meadows dew-besprent; and beetle wakes
   Enquiries ever new,
Teazing each passing ear with murmurs vain,
   As wanting to pursue
     His homeward path again.

Hark to the melody of distant bells
   That on the wind with pleasing hum rebounds
By fitful starts, then musically swells
   O'er the dun stilly grounds;

While on the meadow bridge the pausing boy
  Listens the mellow sounds,
    And hums in vacant joy.

Now homeward-bound, the hedger bundles round
  His evening faggot, and with every stride
His leathern doublet leaves a rustling sound.
  Till silly sheep beside
His path start tremulous, and once again
  Look back dissatisfied,
    Then scour the dewy plain.

How sweet the soothing calm that smoothly stills
  O'er the heart's every sense its opiate dews,
In meek-eyed moods and ever balmy trills!
  That softens and subdues,
With gentle quiet's bland and sober train,
  Which dreamy eve renews
    In many a mellow strain.

I love to walk the fields, they are to me
  A legacy no evil can destroy;
They, like a spell, set every rapture free
  That cheered me when a boy.
Play—pastime—all time's blotting pen concealed,
  Comes like a new-born joy,
    To greet me in the field.

For nature's objects ever harmonize
  With emulous taste, that vulgar deed annoys;

It loves in quiet moods to sympathize,
   And meet vibrating joys
O'er nature's pleasant things; nor will it deem
   Pastime the muse employs
     A vain obtrusive theme.

JOHN KEATS
(1795—1821)

ODE TO A NIGHTINGALE

My heart aches, and a drowsy numbness pains
   My sense, as though of hemlock I had drunk,
Or emptied some dull opiate to the drains
   One minute past, and Lethe-wards had sunk:
'Tis not through envy of thy happy lot,
   But being too happy in thy happiness,
     That thou, light-wingèd Dryad of the trees,
       In some melodious plot
   Of beechen green, and shadows numberless,
     Singest of summer in full-throated ease.

O for a draught of vintage! that hath been
   Cool'd a long age in the deep-delvèd earth,
Tasting of Flora and the country-green,
   Dance, and Provençal song, and sunburnt mirth!
O for a beaker full of the warm South!
   Full of the true, the blushful Hippocrene,
     With beaded bubbles winking at the brim,
       And purple-stainèd mouth;
   That I might drink, and leave the world unseen,
     And with thee fade away into the forest dim:

Fade far away, dissolve, and quite forget
  What thou among the leaves hast never known,
The weariness, the fever, and the fret
  Here, where men sit and hear each other groan;
Where palsy shakes a few, sad, last grey hairs,
    Where youth grows pale, and spectre-thin, and dies;
      Where but to think is to be full of sorrow
        And leaden-eyed despairs;
    Where beauty cannot keep her lustrous eyes,
  Or new Love pine at them beyond to-morrow.

Away! away! for I will fly to thee,
  Not charioted by Bacchus and his pards,
But on the viewless wings of Poesy,
  Though the dull brain perplexes and retards:
Already with thee! tender is the night,
    And haply the Queen-Moon is on her throne,
      Cluster'd around by all her starry Fays;
        But here there is no light,
  Save what from heaven is with the breezes blown
    Through verdurous glooms and winding mossy ways.

I cannot see what flowers are at my feet,
  Nor what soft incense hangs upon the boughs,
But, in embalmèd darkness, guess each sweet
  Wherewith the seasonable month endows
The grass, the thicket, and the fruit-tree wild;
    White hawthorn, and the pastoral eglantine;
      Fast-fading violets cover'd up in leaves;
        And mid-May's eldest child,
  The coming musk-rose, full of dewy wine,
    The murmurous haunt of flies on summer eves.

Darkling I listen; and, for many a time
  I have been half in love with easeful Death,
Call'd him soft names in many a musèd rhyme,
  To take into the air my quiet breath;
Now more than ever seems it rich to die,
  To cease upon the midnight with no pain,
    While thou art pouring forth thy soul abroad
      In such an ecstasy!
  Still wouldst thou sing, and I have ears in vain—
    To thy high requiem become a sod.

Thou wast not born for death, immortal Bird!
  No hungry generations tread thee down;
The voice I hear this passing night was heard
  In ancient days by emperor and clown:
Perhaps the self-same song that found a path
  Through the sad heart of Ruth, when, sick for home
    She stood in tears amid the alien corn;
      The same that ofttimes hath
  Charm'd magic casements, opening on the foam
  Of perilous seas, in faery lands forlorn.

Forlorn! the very word is like a bell
  To toll me back from thee to my sole self!
Adieu! the fancy cannot cheat so well
  As she is famed to do, deceiving elf.
Adieu! adieu! thy plaintive anthem fades
  Past the near meadows, over the still stream,
    Up the hill-side; and now 'tis buried deep
      In the next valley-glades:
  Was it a vision, or a waking dream?
    Fled is that music:—do I wake or sleep?

ODE ON A GRECIAN URN

Thou still unravish'd bride of quietness,
　　Thou foster-child of Silence and slow Time,
Sylvan historian, who canst thus express
　　A flowery tale more sweetly than our rhyme:
What leaf-fringed legend haunts about thy shape
　　Of deities or mortals, or of both,
　　　In Tempe or the dales of Arcady?
　　What men or gods are these? What maidens loth?
What mad pursuit? What struggle to escape?
　　　What pipes and timbrels? What wild ecstasy?

Heard melodies are sweet, but those unheard
　　Are sweeter, therefore, ye soft pipes, play on;
Not to the sensual ear, but, more endear'd,
　　Pipe to the spirit ditties of no tone:
Fair youth, beneath the trees, thou canst not leave
　　Thy song, nor ever can those trees be bare;
　　　Bold Lover, never, never canst thou kiss,
Though winning near the goal—yet, do not grieve;
　　　She cannot fade, though thou hast not thy bliss,
　　For ever wilt thou love, and she be fair!

Ah, happy, happy boughs! that cannot shed
　　Your leaves, nor ever bid the Spring adieu;
And, happy melodist, unwearièd,
　　For ever piping songs for ever new;
More happy love! more happy, happy love!
　　For ever warm and still to be enjoy'd,
　　　For ever panting and for ever young;

All breathing human passion far above,
  That leaves a heart high-sorrowful and cloy'd,
    A burning forehead, and a parching tongue.

Who are these coming to the sacrifice?
  To what green altar, O mysterious priest,
Lead'st thou that heifer lowing at the skies,
  And all her silken flanks with garlands drest?
What little town by river or sea-shore,
  Or mountain-built with peaceful citadel,
    Is emptied of its folk, this pious morn?
And, little town, thy streets for evermore
  Will silent be; and not a soul, to tell
    Why thou art desolate, can e'er return.

O Attic shape! fair attitude! with brede
  Of marble men and maidens overwrought,
With forest branches and the trodden weed;
  Thou, silent form! dost tease us out of thought
As doth eternity. Cold Pastoral!
  When old age shall this generation waste,
    Thou shalt remain, in midst of other woe
Than ours, a friend to man, to whom thou say'st,
'Beauty is truth, truth beauty,—that is all
  Ye know on earth, and all ye need to know.'

TO AUTUMN

Season of mists and mellow fruitfulness!
  Close bosom-friend of the maturing sun;
Conspiring with him how to load and bless
  With fruit the vines that round the thatch-eaves r

To bend with apples the moss'd cottage-trees,
  And fill all fruit with ripeness to the core;
    To swell the gourd, and plump the hazel shells
  With a sweet kernel; to set budding more,
And still more, later flowers for the bees,
Until they think warm days will never cease,
  For Summer has o'er-brimm'd their clammy cells.

Who hath not seen thee oft amid thy store?
  Sometimes whoever seeks abroad may find
Thee sitting careless on a granary floor,
  Thy hair soft-lifted by the winnowing wind,
Or on a half-reap'd furrow sound asleep,
  Drowsed with the fume of poppies, while thy hook
    Spares the next swath and all its twinèd flowers;
And sometimes like a gleaner thou dost keep
  Steady thy laden head across a brook;
  Or by a cider-press, with patient look,
    Thou watchest the last oozings hours by hours.

Where are the songs of Spring? Ay, where are they?
  Think not of them, thou hast thy music too,—
While barrèd clouds bloom the soft-dying day,
  And touch the stubble-plains with rosy hue;
Then in a wailful choir the small gnats mourn
  Among the river sallows, borne aloft
    Or sinking as the light wind lives or dies;
And full-grown lambs loud bleat from hilly bourn;
Hedge-crickets sing; and now with treble soft
The redbreast whistles from a garden-croft;
  And gathering swallows twitter in the skies.

LA BELLE DAME SANS MERCI

'O what can ail thee, knight-at-arms,
    Alone and palely loitering?
The sedge is wither'd from the lake,
        And no birds sing.

'O what can ail thee, knight-at-arms,
    So haggard and so woe-begone?
The squirrel's granary is full,
        And the harvest's done.

'I see a lily on thy brow
With anguish moist and fever dew;
And on thy cheek a fading rose
        Fast withereth too.'

'I met a lady in the meads,
    Full beautiful—a faery's child,
Her hair was long, her foot was light,
        And her eyes were wild.

'I made a garland for her head,
    And bracelets too, and fragrant zone;
She look'd at me as she did love,
        And made sweet moan.

'I set her on my pacing steed
    And nothing else saw all day long,
For sideways would she lean, and sing
        A faery's song.

'She found me roots of relish sweet,
   And honey wild and manna dew,
And sure in language strange she said,
     "I love thee true!"

'She took me to her elfin grot,
   And there she wept and sigh'd full sore;
And there I shut her wild, wild eyes
     With kisses four.

'And there she lullèd me asleep,
   And there I dream'd—Ah! woe betide!
The latest dream I ever dream'd
     On the cold hill's side.

'I saw pale kings and princes too,
   Pale warriors, death-pale were they all;
Who cried—"La belle Dame sans Merci
     Hath thee in thrall!"

'I saw their starved lips in the gloam
   With horrid warning gapèd wide,
And I awoke and found me here
     On the cold hill's side.

'And this is why I sojourn here
   Alone and palely loitering,
Though the sedge is wither'd from the lake,
     And no birds sing.'

ON FIRST LOOKING INTO CHAPMAN'S HOMER

Much have I travell'd in the realms of gold,
   And many goodly states and kingdoms seen;
   Round many western islands have I been
Which bards in fealty to Apollo hold.
Oft of one wide expanse had I been told
   That deep-brow'd Homer ruled as his demesne:
   Yet did I never breathe its pure serene
Till I heard Chapman speak out loud and bold:
Then felt I like some watcher of the skies
   When a new planet swims into his ken;
Or like stout Cortez, when with eagle eyes
   He stared at the Pacific—and all his men
Look'd at each other with a wild surmise—
   Silent, upon a peak in Darien.

PASSAGES FROM 'THE FALL OF HYPERION'

(i)

... Fanatics have their dreams, wherewith they weave
A paradise for a sect; the savage too
From forth the loftiest fashion of his sleep
Guesses at Heaven; pity these have not
Trac'd upon vellum or wild Indian leaf
The shadows of melodious utterance.
But bare of laurel they live, dream, and die;
For Poesy alone can tell her dreams,
With the fine spell of words alone can save

Imagination from the sable chain
And dumb enchantment. Who alive can say,
'Thou art no Poet—may'st not tell thy dreams?'
Since every man whose soul is not a clod
Hath visions, and would speak, if he had loved,
And been well nurtured in his mother tongue.
Whether the dream now purpos'd to rehearse
Be poet's or fanatic's will be known
When this warm scribe my hand is in the grave.

(ii)

. . . — 'High Prophetess,' said I, 'purge off,
Benign, if so it please thee, my mind's film.'—
'None can usurp this height,' return'd that shade,
'But those to whom the miseries of the world
Are misery, and will not let them rest.
All else who find a haven in the world,
Where they may thoughtless sleep away their days,
If by a chance into this fane they come,
Rot on the pavement where thou rottedst half.'—
'Are there not thousands in the world,' said I,
Encourag'd by the sooth voice of the shade,
Who love their fellows even to the death,
Who feel the giant agony of the world,
And more, like slaves to poor humanity,
Labour for mortal good? I sure should see
Other men here; but I am here alone.'
'Those whom thou spak'st of are no vision'ries,'
Rejoin'd that voice—'They are no dreamers weak,
They seek no wonder but the human face;

No music but a happy-noted voice—
They come not here, they have no thought to come—
And thou art here, for thou art less than they—
What benefit canst thou, or all thy tribe,
To the great world? Thou art a dreaming thing,
A fever of thyself—think of the Earth;
What bliss even in hope is there for thee?
What haven? every creature hath its home;
Every sole man hath days of joy and pain,
Whether his labours be sublime or low—
The pain alone; the joy alone; distinct;
Only the dreamer venoms all his days,
Bearing more woe than all his sins deserve.
Therefore, that happiness be somewhat shar'd,
Such things as thou art are admitted oft
Into like gardens thou didst pass erewhile,
And suffer'd in these temples: for that cause
Thou standest safe beneath this statue's knees,'
'That I am favour'd for unworthiness,
By such propitious parley medicin'd
In sickness not ignoble, I rejoice,
'Aye, and could weep for love of such award.'
So answer'd I, continuing. 'If it please,
Majestic shadow, tell me: sure nor all
Those melodies sung into the World's ear
Are useless: sure a poet is a sage;
A humanist, physician to all men.
That I am none I feel, as vultures feel
They are no birds when eagles are abroad.
What am I then: Thou spakest of my tribe:
What tribe?' The tall shade veil'd in drooping white

Then spake, so much more earnest, that the breath
Moved the thin linen folds that drooping hung
About a golden censer from the hand
Pendent— 'Art thou not of the dreamer tribe?
The poet and the dreamer are distinct,
Diverse, sheer opposite, antipodes.
The one pours out a balm upon the World,
The other vexes it'. . .

THOMAS LOVELL BEDDOES
(1803—1849)

THE MIGHTY THOUGHTS OF AN OLD WORLD

The mighty thoughts of an old world
Fan, like a dragon's wing unfurled,
   The surface of my yearnings deep;
And solemn shadows then awake,
Like the fish-lizard in the lake,
   Troubling a planet's morning sleep.

My waking is a Titan's dream,
Where a strange sun, long set, doth beam
   Through Montezuma's cypress bough:
Through the fern wilderness forlorn
Glisten the giant harts' great horn
   And serpents vast with helmed brow.

The measureless from caverns rise
With steps of earthquake, thunderous cries,
   And graze upon the lofty wood;

The palmy grove, through which doth gleam
Such antideluvian ocean's stream,
 Haunts shadowy my domestic mood.

LORD TENNYSON
(1809—1892)

SONG OF THE LOTOS-EATERS

There is sweet music here that softer falls
Than petals from blown roses on the grass,
Or night-dews on still waters between walls
Of shadowy granite, in a gleaming pass;
Music that gentlier on the spirit lies,
Than tired eyelids upon tired eyes;
Music that brings sweet sleep down from the blissful skie
Here are cool mosses deep,
And thro' the moss the ivies creep,
And in the stream the long-leaved flowers weep,
And from the craggy ledge the poppy hangs in sleep.

Why are we weigh'd upon with heaviness,
And utterly consumed with sharp distress,
While all things else have rest from weariness?
All things have rest: why should we toil alone,
We only toil, who are the first of things,
And make perpetual moan,
Still from one sorrow to another thrown:
Nor ever fold our wings,
And cease from wanderings,
Nor steep our brows in slumber's holy balm;
Nor harken what the inner spirit sings,

'There is no joy but calm!'—
Why should we only toil, the roof and crown of things?

Lo! in the middle of the wood,
The folded leaf is woo'd from out the bud
With winds upon the branch, and there
Grows green and broad, and takes no care,
Sun-steep'd at noon, and in the moon
Nightly dew-fed; and turning yellow
Falls, and floats adown the air
Lo! sweeten'd with the summer light,
The full-juiced apple, waxing over-mellow,
Drops in a silent autumn night.
All its allotted length of days,
The flower ripens in its place,
Ripens and fades, and falls, and hath no toil,
Fast-rooted in the fruitful soil.

Hateful is the dark-blue sky,
Vaulted o'er the dark-blue sea.
Death is the end of life; ah, why
Should life all labour be?
Let us alone. Time driveth onward fast,
And in a little while our lips are dumb.
Let us alone. What is it that will last?
All things are taken from us, and become
Portions and parcels of the dreadful Past.
Let us alone. What pleasure can we have
To war with evil? Is there any peace
In ever climbing up the climbing wave?
All things have rest, and ripen toward the grave

On silence; ripen, fall and cease:
Give us long rest or death, dark death, or dreamful ea

How sweet it were, hearing the downward stream,
With half-shut eyes ever to seem
Falling asleep in a half-dream!
To dream and dream, like yonder amber light,
Which will not leave the myrrh-bush on the height;
To hear each other's whisper'd speech;
Eating the Lotos day by day,
To watch the crisping ripples on the beach,
And tender curving lines of creamy spray;
To lend our hearts and spirits wholly
To the influence of mild-minded melancholy;
To muse and brood and live again in memory,
With those old faces of our infancy
Heap'd over with a mound of grass,
Two handfuls of white dust, shut in an urn of brass!

Dear is the memory of our wedded lives,
And dear the last embraces of our wives
And their warm tears: but all hath suffer'd change:
For surely now our household hearths are cold:
Our sons inherit us: our looks are strange:
And we should come like ghosts to trouble joy.
Or else the island princes over-bold
Have eat our substance, and the minstrel sings
Before them of the ten years' war in Troy,
And our great deeds, as half-forgotten things.
Is there confusion in the little isle?
Let what is broken so remain.
The Gods are hard to reconcile:

'Tis hard to settle order once again.
There *is* confusion worse than death,
Trouble on trouble, pain on pain,
Long labour unto agèd breath,
Sore task to hearts worn out with many wars
And eyes grown dim with gazing on the pilot-stars.

But propt on beds of amaranth and moly,
How sweet (while warm airs lull us, blowing lowly)
With half-dropt eyelids still,
Beneath a heaven dark and holy,
To watch the long bright river drawing slowly
His waters from the purple hill—
To hear the dewy echoes calling
From cave to cave thro' the thick-twinèd vine
To watch the emerald-colour'd water falling
Thro' many a wov'n acanthus-wreath divine!
Only to hear and see the far-off sparkling brine,
Only to hear were sweet, stretch'd out beneath the pine.

The Lotos blooms below the barren peak:
The Lotos blows by every winding creek:
All day the wind breathes low with mellower tone:
Thro' every hollow cave and alley lone
Round and round the spicy downs the yellow Lotos-dust is blown.
We have had enough of action, and of motion we,
Roll'd to starboard, roll'd to larboard, when the surge was
    seething free,
Where the wallowing monster spouted his foam-fountains in
    the sea.
Let us swear an oath, and keep it with an equal mind,

In the hollow Lotos-land to live and lie reclined
On the hills like Gods together, careless of mankind.
For they lie beside their nectar, and the bolts are hurl'd
Far below them in the valleys, and the clouds are lightly curl'd
Round their golden houses, girdled with the gleaming world:
Where they smile in secret, looking over wasted lands,
Blight and famine, plague and earthquake, roaring deeps and
    fiery sands,
Clanging fights, and flaming towns, and sinking ships, and
    praying hands.
But they smile, they find a music centred in a doleful song
Steaming up, a lamentation and an ancient tale of wrong,
Like a tale of little meaning tho' the words are strong;
Chanted from an ill-used race of men that cleave the soil,
Sow the seed, and reap the harvest with enduring toil,
Storing yearly little dues of wheat, and wine and oil;
Till they perish and they suffer—some, 'tis whisper'd—down in
    hell
Suffer endless anguish, others in Elysian valleys dwell,
Resting weary limbs at last on beds of asphodel.
Surely, surely, slumber is more sweet than toil, the shore
Than labour in the deep mid-ocean, wind and wave and oar;
O rest ye, brother mariners, we will not wander more.

SONG FROM 'THE PRINCESS'

Tears, idle tears, I know not what they mean,
Tears from the depth of some divine despair
Rise in the heart, and gather to the eyes,
In looking on the happy Autumn-fields,
And thinking of the days that are no more.

Fresh as the first beam glittering on a sail,
That brings our friends up from the underworld,
Sad as the last which reddens over one
That sinks with all we love below the verge;
So sad, so fresh, the days that are no more.

Ah, sad and strange as in dark summer dawns
The earliest pipe of half-awaken'd birds
To dying ears, when unto dying eyes
The casement slowly grows a glimmering square;
So sad, so strange, the days that are no more.

Dear as remember'd kisses after death,
And sweet as those by hopeless fancy feign'd
On lips that are for others; deep as love,
Deep as first love, and wild with all regret;
O Death in Life, the days that are no more.

THE EAGLE

He clasps the crag with hookèd hands:
Close to the sun in lonely lands,
Ringed with the azure world, he stands.

The wrinkled sea beneath him crawls;
He watches from his mountain walls,
And like a thunderbolt he falls.

ULYSSES

It little profits that an idle king,
By this still hearth, among these barren crags,
Matched with an aged wife, I mete and dole

Unequal laws unto a savage race,
That hoard, and sleep, and feed, and know not me
I cannot rest from travel: I will drink
Life to the lees: all times I have enjoyed
Greatly, have suffered greatly, both with those
That loved me, and alone; on shore, and when
Thro' scudding drifts the rainy Hyades
Vext the dim sea. I am become a name;
For always roaming with a hungry heart
Much have I seen and known: cities of men
And manners, climates, councils, governments,
Myself not least, but honoured of them all;
And drunk delight of battle with my peers,
Far on the ringing plains of windy Troy.
I am a part of all that I have met;
Yet all experience is an arch wherethro'
Gleams that untravelled world, whose margin fades
For ever and for ever when I move.
How dull it is to pause, to make an end,
To rust unburnished, not to shine in use!
As tho' to breathe were life. Life piled on life
Were all too little, and of one to me
Little remains: but every hour is saved
From that eternal silence, something more,
A bringer of new things; and vile it were
For some three suns to store and hoard myself,
And this grey spirit yearning in desire
To follow knowledge, like a sinking star,
Beyond the utmost bound of human thought.

This is my son, mine own Telemachus,
To whom I leave the sceptre and the isle—
Well-loved of me, discerning to fulfil

This labour, by slow prudence to make mild
A rugged people, and thro' soft degrees
Subdue them to the useful and the good.
Most blameless is he, centred in the sphere
Of common duties, decent not to fail
In offices of tenderness, and pay
Meet adoration to my houshold gods,
When I am gone. He works his work, I mine.
    There lies the port: the vessel puffs her sail:
There gloom the dark broad seas. My mariners,
Souls that have toiled, and wrought, and thought with me—
That ever with a frolic welcome took
The thunder and the sunshine, and opposed
Free hearts, free foreheads—you and I are old;
Old age hath yet his honour and his toil;
Death closes all: but something ere the end,
Some work of noble note, may yet be done,
Not unbecoming men that strove with Gods.
The lights begin to twinkle from the rocks:
The long day wanes: the slow moon climbs: the deep
Moans round with many voices. Come, my friends,
'Tis not too late to seek a newer world.
Push off, and sitting well in order smite
The sounding furrows; for my purpose holds
To sail beyond the sunset, and the paths
Of all the western stars, until I die.
It may be that the gulfs will wash us down:
It may be we shall touch the Happy Isles,
And see the great Achilles, whom we knew.
Tho' much is taken, much abides; and tho'
We are not now that strength which in old days
Moved earth and heaven; that which we are, we are;

One equal temper of heroic hearts,
Made weak by time and fate, but strong in will
To strive, to seek, to find, and not to yield.

STANZAS FROM 'IN MEMORIAM'

(i)

Old Yew, which graspest at the stones
    That name the under-lying dead,
    Thy fibres net the dreamless head,
Thy roots are wrapt about the bones.

The seasons bring the flower again,
    And bring the firstling to the flock;
    And in the dust of thee, the clock
Beats out the little lives of men.

O not for thee the glow, the bloom,
    Who changest not in any gale,
    Nor branding summer suns avail
To touch thy thousand years of gloom:

And gazing on thee, sullen tree,
    Sick for thy stubborn hardihood,
    I seem to fail from out my blood
And grow incorporate into thee.

(ii)

Calm is the morn without a sound,
    Calm as to suit a calmer grief,
    And only thro' the faded leaf
The chestnut pattering to the ground:

Calm and deep peace on this high wold,
　　And on these dews that drench the furze,
　　And all the silvery gossamers
That twinkle into green and gold:

Calm and still light on yon great plain
　　That sweeps with all its autumn bowers,
　　And crowded farms and lessening towers,
To mingle with the bounding main:

Calm and deep peace in this wide air,
　　These leaves that redden to the fall;
　　And in my heart, if calm at all,
If any calm, a calm despair:

Calm on the seas, and silver sleep,
　　And waves that sway themselves in rest,
　　And dead calm in that noble breast
Which heaves but with the heaving deep.

(iii)

To-night the winds begin to rise
　　And roar from yonder dropping day:
　　The last red leaf is whirl'd away,
The rooks are blown about the skies;

The forest crack'd, the waters curl'd,
　　The cattle huddled on the lea;
　　And wildly dash'd on tower and tree
The sunbeam strikes along the world:

And but for fancies, which aver
   That all thy motions gently pass
   Athwart a plane of molten glass,
I scarce could brook the strain and stir

That makes the barren branches loud;
   And but for fear it is not so,
   The wild unrest that lives in woe
Would dote and pore on yonder cloud

That rises upward always higher,
   And onward drags a labouring breast,
   And topples round the dreary west,
A looming bastion fringed with fire.

EDWARD LEAR

(1812—1888)

THE JUMBLIES

I

They went to sea in a Sieve, they did,
   In a Sieve they went to sea:
In spite of all their friends could say,
On a winter's morn, on a stormy day,
   In a Sieve they went to sea!
And when the Sieve turned round and round,
   And every one cried, "You'll all be drowned!'
They called aloud, "Our Sieve ain't big,
But we don't care a button! we don't care a fig!
   In a Sieve we'll go to sea!"

Far and few, far and few,
  Are the lands where the Jumblies live;
  Their heads are green, and their hands are blue,
    And they went to sea in a Sieve.

2

They sailed away in a Sieve, they did,
  In a Sieve they sailed so fast,
With only a beautiful pea-green veil
Tied with a riband by way of a sail,
  To a small tobacco-pipe mast;
And every one said, who saw them go,
"O won't they be soon upset, you know!
For the sky is dark, and the voyage is long,
And happen what may, it's extremely wrong
  In a Sieve to sail so fast!"
    Far and few, far and few,
      Are the lands where the Jumblies live;
      Their heads are green, and their hands are blue,
        And they went to sea in a Sieve.

3

The water it soon came in, it did,
  The water it soon came in;
So to keep them dry, they wrapped their feet
In a pinky paper all folded neat.
  And they fastened it down with a pin.
And they passed the night in a crockery-jar,
And each of them said, "How wise we are!
Though the sky be dark, and the voyage be long,
Yet we never can think we were rash or wrong,
  While round in our Sieve we spin!"

Far and few, far and few,
　Are the lands where the Jumblies live;
Their heads are green, and their hands are blue,
　And they went to sea in a Sieve.

4

And all night long they sailed away;
　And when the sun went down,
They whistled and warbled a moony song
To the echoing sound of a coppery gong,
　In the shade of the mountains brown.
"O Timballo! How happy we are,
When we live in a sieve and a crockery-jar,
And all night long in the moonlight pale,
We sail away with a pea-green sail,
　In the shade of the mountains brown!"
　　Far and few, far and few,
　　　Are the lands where the Jumblies live;
　　Their heads are green, and their hands are blue,
　　　And they went to sea in a Sieve.

5

They sailed to the Western Sea, they did,
　To a land all covered with trees,
And they bought an Owl, and a useful Cart,
And a pound of Rice, and a Cranberry Tart,
　And a hive of silvery Bees.
And they bought a Pig, and some green Jack-daws,
And a lovely Monkey with lollipop paws,
And forty bottles of Ring-Bo-Ree,
　And no end of Stilton Cheese.

Far and few, far and few,
  Are the lands where the Jumblies live;
Their heads are green, and their hands are blue,
  And they went to sea in a Sieve.

6

And in twenty years they all came back,
  In twenty years or more,
And every one said, "How tall they've grown!
For they've been to the Lakes, and the Terrible Zone,
  And the hills of the Chankly Bore";
And they drank their health, and gave them a feast
Of dumplings made of beautiful yeast;
And every one said, "If we only live,
We too will go to sea in a Sieve,—
  To the hills of the Chankly Bore!"
    Far and few, far and few,
      Are the lands where the Jumblies live;
Their heads are green, and their hands are blue,
      And they went to sea in a Sieve.

ROBERT BROWNING
(1812—1889)

MY LAST DUCHESS

FERRARA

That's my last Duchess painted on the wall,
Looking as if she were alive. I call
That piece a wonder, now: Frà Pandolf's hands
Worked busily a day, and there she stands.

Will't please you sit and look at her? I said
"Frà Pandolf" by design, for never read
Strangers like you that pictured countenance,
The depth and passion of its earnest glance,
But to myself they turned (since none puts by
The curtain I have drawn for you, but I)
And seemed as they would ask me, if they durst,
How such a glance came there; so, not the first
Are you to turn and ask thus. Sir, 'twas not
Her husband's presence only, called that spot
Of joy into the Duchess' cheek: perhaps
Frà Pandolf chanced to say "Her mantle laps
"Over my lady's wrist too much," or "Paint
"Must never hope to reproduce the faint
"Half-flush that dies along her throat:" such stuff
Was courtesy, she thought, and cause enough
For calling up that spot of joy. She had
A heart—how shall I say?—too soon made glad,
Too easily impressed; she liked whate'er
She looked on, and her looks went everywhere.
Sir, 'twas all one! My favour at her breast,
The dropping of the daylight in the West,
The bough of cherries some officious fool
Broke in the orchard for her, the white mule
She rode with round the terrace—all and each
Would draw from her alike the approving speech,
Or blush, at least. She thanked men,—good! but thank
Somehow—I know not how—as if she ranked
My gift of a nine-hundred-years-old name
With anybody's gift. Who'd stoop to blame
This sort of trifling? Even had you skill
In speech—(which I have not)—to make your will

Quite clear to such an one, and say, "Just this
"Or that in you disgusts me; here you miss,
"Or there exceed the mark"—and if she let
Herself be lessoned so, nor plainly set
Her wits to yours, forsooth, and made excuse,
—E'en then would be some stooping; and I choose
Never to stoop. Oh sir, she smiled, no doubt,
Whene'er I passed her; but who passed without
Much the same smile? This grew; I gave commands;
Then all smiles stopped together. There she stands
As if alive. Will't please you rise? We'll meet
The company below, then. I repeat,
The Count your master's known munificence
Is ample warrant that no just pretence
Of mine for dowry will be disallowed;
Though his fair daughter's self, as I avowed
At starting, is my object. Nay, we'll go
Together down, sir. Notice Neptune, though,
Taming a sea-horse, thought a rarity,
Which Claus of Innsbruck cast in bronze for me!

THE BISHOP ORDERS HIS TOMB AT SAINT PRAXED'S CHURCH

ROME 15—

Vanity, saith the preacher, vanity!
Draw round my bed: is Anselm keeping back?
Nephews—sons mine ... ah God, I know not! Well—
She, men would have to be your mother once,
Old Gandolf envied me, so fair she was!

What's done is done, and she is dead beside,
Dead long ago, and I am Bishop since,
And as she died so must we die ourselves,
And thence ye may perceive the world's a dream.
Life, how and what is it? As here I lie
In this state-chamber, dying by degrees,
Hours and long hours in the dead night, I ask
"Do I live, am I dead?" Peace, peace seems all.
Saint Praxed's ever was the church for peace;
And so, about this tomb of mine. I fought
With tooth and nail to save my niche, ye know:
—Old Gandolf cozened me, despite my care;
Shrewd was that snatch from out the corner South
He graced his carrion with, God curse the same!
Yet still my niche is not so cramped but thence
One sees the pulpit o' the epistle-side,
And somewhat of the choir, those silent seats,
And up into the aery dome where live
The angels, and a sunbeam's sure to lurk:
And I shall fill my slab of basalt there,
And 'neath my tabernacle take my rest,
With those nine columns round me, two and two,
The odd one at my feet where Anselm stands:
Peach-blossom marble all, the rare, the ripe
As fresh-poured red wine of a mighty pulse.
—Old Gandolf with his paltry onion-stone,
Put me where I may look at him! True peach,
Rosy and flawless: how I earned the prize!
Draw close: that conflagration of my church
—What then? So much was saved if aught were misse
My sons, ye would not be my death? Go dig
The white-grape vineyard where the oil-press stood,

Drop water gently till the surface sink,
And if ye find ... Ah God, I know not, I! ...
Bedded in store of rotten fig-leaves soft,
And corded up in a tight olive-frail,
Some lump, ah God, of *lapis lazuli,*
Big as a Jew's head cut off at the nape,
Blue as a vein o'er the Madonna's breast ...
Sons, all have I bequeathed you, villas, all,
That brave Frascati villa with its bath,
So, let the blue lump poise between my knees,
Like God the Father's globe on both his hands
Ye worship in the Jesu Church so gay,
For Gandolf shall not choose but see and burst!
Swift as a weaver's shuttle fleet our years:
Man goeth to the grave, and where is he?
Did I say basalt for my slab, sons? Black—
'Twas ever antique-black I meant! How else
Shall ye contrast my frieze to come beneath?
The bas-relief in bronze ye promised me,
Those Pans and Nymphs ye wot of, and perchance
Some tripod, thyrsus, with a vase or so,
The Saviour at his sermon on the mount,
Saint Praxed in a glory, and one Pan
Ready to twitch the Nymph's last garment off,
And Moses with the tables ... but I know
Ye mark me not! What do they whisper thee,
Child of my bowels, Anselm? Ah, ye hope
To revel down my villas while I gasp
Bricked o'er with beggar's mouldy travertine
Which Gandolf from his tomb-top chuckles at!
Nay, boys, ye love me—all of jasper, then!
'Tis jasper ye stand pledged to, lest I grieve.

My bath must needs be left behind, alas!
One block, pure green as a pistachio-nut,
There's plenty jasper somewhere in the world—
And have I not Saint Praxed's ear to pray
Horses for ye, and brown Greek manuscripts,
And mistresses with great smooth marbly limbs?
—That's if ye carve my epitaph aright,
Choice Latin, picked phrase, Tully's every word,
No gaudy ware like Gandolf's second line—
Tully, my masters? Ulpian serves his need!
And then how I shall lie through centuries,
And hear the blessed mutter of the mass,
And see God made and eaten all day long,
And feel the steady candle-flame, and taste
Good strong thick stupefying incense-smoke!
For as I lie here, hours of the dead night,
Dying in state and by such slow degrees,
I fold my arms as if they clasped a crook,
And stretch my feet forth straight as stone can point,
And let the bedclothes, for a mortcloth, drop
Into great laps and folds of sculptor's-work:
And as yon tapers dwindle, and strange thoughts
Grow, with a certain humming in my ears,
About the life before I lived this life,
And this life too, popes, cardinals, and priests,
Saint Praxed at his sermon on the mount,
Your tall pale mother with her talking eyes,
And new-found agate urns as fresh as day,
And marble's language, Latin pure, discreet,
—Aha, Elucescebat quoth our friend?
No Tully, said I, Ulpian at the best!
Evil and brief hath been my pilgrimage.

All *lapis*, all, sons! Else I give the Pope
My villas! Will ye ever eat my heart?
Ever your eyes were as a lizard's quick,
They glitter like your mother's for my soul,
Or ye would heighten my impoverished frieze,
Piece out its starved design, and fill my vase
With grapes, and add a vizor and a Term,
And to the tripod ye would tie a lynx
That in his struggle throws the thyrsus down,
To comfort me on my entablature
Whereon I am to lie till I must ask
"Do I live, am I dead?" There, leave me, there!
For ye have stabbed me with ingratitude
To death —ye wish it—God, ye wish it! Stone—
Gritstone, a-crumble! Clammy squares which sweat
As if the corpse they keep were oozing through—
And no more *lapis* to delight the world!
Well go! I bless ye. Fewer tapers there,
But in a row: and, going, turn your backs
—Ay, like departing altar-ministrants,
And leave me in my church, the church for peace,
That I may watch at leisure if he leers—
Old Gandolf, at me, from his onion-stone,
As still he envied me, so fair she was!

TWO IN THE CAMPAGNA

I wonder do you feel to-day
    As I have felt since, hand in hand,
We sat down on the grass, to stray
    In spirit better through the land,
This morn of Rome and May?

For me, I touched a thought, I know,
  Has tantalized me many times,
(Like turns of thread the spiders throw
  Mocking across our path) for rhymes
To catch at and let go.

Help me to hold it! First it left
  The yellowing fennel, run to seed
There, branching from the brickwork's cleft,
  Some old tomb's ruin: yonder weed
Took up the floating weft,

Where one small orange cup amassed
  Five beetles,—blind and green they grope
Among the honey-meal: and last,
  Everywhere on the grassy slope
I traced it. Hold it fast!

The champaign with its endless fleece
  Of feathery grasses everywhere!
Silence and passion, joy and peace,
  An everlasting wash of air—
Rome's ghost since her decease.

Such life here, through such lengths of hours,
  Such miracles performed in play,
Such primal naked forms of flowers,
  Such letting nature have her way
While heaven looks from its towers!

How say you? Let us, O my dove,
  Let us be unashamed of soul,

As earth lies bare to heaven above!
   How is it under our control
To love or not to love?

I would that you were all to me,
   You that are just so much, no more.
Nor yours nor mine, nor slave nor free!
   Where does the fault lie? What the core
O' the wound, since wound must be?

I would I could adopt your will,
   See with your eyes, and set my heart
Beating by yours, and drink my fill
   At your soul's springs,—your part my part
In life, for good and ill.

No. I yearn upward, touch you close,
   Then stand away. I kiss your cheek,
Catch your soul's warmth,—I pluck the rose
   And love it more than tongue can speak—
Then the good minute goes.

Already how am I so far
   Out of that minute? Must I go
Still like the thistle-ball, no bar,
   Onward, whenever light winds blow,
Fixed by no friendly star?

Just when I seemed about to learn!
   Where is the thread now? Off again!
The old trick! Only I discern—
   Infinite passion, and the pain
Of finite hearts that yearn.

EMILY BRONTË
(1818—1848)

REMEMBRANCE

Cold in the earth—and the deep snow piled above thee
Far, far removed, cold in the dreary grave!
Have I forgot, my only Love, to love thee,
Severed at last by Time's all-severing wave?

Now, when alone, do my thoughts no longer hover
Over the mountains, on that northern shore,
Resting their wings where heath and fern-leaves cover
Thy noble heart for ever, ever more?

Cold in the earth—and fifteen wild Decembers,
From those brown hills, have melted into spring:
Faithful, indeed, is the spirit that remembers
After such years of change and suffering!

Sweet Love of youth, forgive, if I forget thee,
While the world's tide is bearing me along;
Other desires and other hopes beset me,
Hopes which obscure, but cannot do thee wrong!

No later light has lightened up my heaven,
No second morn has ever shone for me;
All my life's bliss from thy dear life was given,
All my life's bliss is in the grave with thee.

But, when the days of golden dreams have perished,
And even Despair was powerless to destroy;
Then did I learn how existence could be cherished,
Strengthened, and fed without the aid of joy.

Then did I check the tears of useless passion—
Weaned my young soul from yearning after thine;
Sternly denied its burning wish to hasten
Down to that tomb already more than mine.

And, even yet, I dare not let it languish,
Dare not indulge in memory's rapturous pain;
Once drinking deep of that divinest anguish,
How could I seek the empty world again?

STANZAS

Often rebuked, yet always back returning
    To those first feelings that were born with me,
And leaving busy chase of wealth and learning
    For idle dreams of things which cannot be:

To-day, I will seek not the shadowy region;
    Its unsustaining vastness waxes drear;
And visions rising, legion after legion,
    Bring the unreal world too strangely near.

I'll walk, but not in old heroic traces,
    And not in paths of high morality,
And not among the half-distinguished faces,
    The clouded forms of long-past history.

I'll walk where my own nature would be leading:
It vexes me to choose another guide:
Where the grey flocks in ferny glens are feeding;
Where the wild wind blows on the mountain-side.

What have those lonely mountains worth revealing?
More glory and more grief than I can tell:
The earth that wakes *one* human heart to feeling
Can centre both the worlds of Heaven and Hell.

LAST LINES

No coward soul is mine,
No trembler in the world's storm-troubled sphere:
I see Heaven's glories shine,
And faith shines equal, arming me from fear.

O God within my breast,
Almighty, ever-present Deity!
Life—that in me has rest,
As I—undying Life—have power in Thee!

Vain are the thousand creeds
That move men's hearts: unutterably vain;
Worthless as withered weeds,
Or idle froth amid the boundless main,

To waken doubt in one
Holding so fast by Thine infinity;
So surely anchored on
The steadfast rock of immortality.

With wide-embracing love
Thy spirit animates eternal years,
        Pervades and broods above,
Changes, sustains, dissolves, creates, and rears.

        Though earth and man were gone,
And suns and universes ceased to be,
        And Thou were left alone,
Every existence would exist in Thee.

        There is not room for Death,
Nor atom that his might could render void:
        Thou—thou art being and Breath,
And what thou art may never be destroyed.

ARTHUR HUGH CLOUGH
(1819—1861)

THE LATEST DECALOGUE

Thou shalt have one God only; who
Would be at the expense of two?
No graven images may be
Worshipped, except the currency:
Swear not at all; for, for thy curse
Thine enemy is none the worse:
At church on Sunday to attend
Will serve to keep the world thy friend:
Honour thy parents; that is, all
From whom advancement may befall;

Thou shalt not kill; but need'st not strive
Officiously to keep alive:
Do not adultery commit;
Advantage rarely comes of it:
Thou shalt not steal; an empty feat,
When it's so lucrative to cheat:
Bear not false witness; let the lie
Have time on its own wings to fly:
Thou shalt not covet, but tradition
Approves all forms of competition.

'SAY NOT THE STRUGGLE NOUGHT AVAILETH'

Say not the struggle nought availeth,
  The labour and the wounds are vain,
The enemy faints not, nor faileth,
  And as things have been they remain.

If hopes were dupes, fears may be liars;
  It may be, in yon smoke conceal'd,
Your comrades chase e'en now the fliers,
  And, but for you, possess the field.

For while the tired waves, vainly breaking,
  Seem here no painful inch to gain,
Far back, through creeks and inlets making,
  Comes silent, flooding in, the main.

And not by eastern windows only,
  When daylight comes, comes in the light;
In front, the sun climbs slow, how slowly,
  But westward, look, the land is bright.

MATTHEW ARNOLD
(1822—1888)

THE SCHOLAR GIPSY

Go, for they call you, Shepherd, from the hill;
  Go, Shepherd, and untie the wattled cotes:
    No longer leave thy wistful flock unfed,
  Nor let thy bawling fellows rack their throats,
    Nor the cropp'd grasses shoot another head.
      But when the fields are still,
  And the tired men and dogs all gone to rest,
    And only the white sheep are sometimes seen
    Cross and recross the strips of moon-blanch'd green;
    Come, Shepherd, and again renew the quest.

Here, where the reaper was at work of late,
  In this high field's dark corner, where he leaves
    His coat, his basket, and his earthen cruise,
  And in the sun all morning binds the sheaves,
    Then here, at noon, comes back his stores to use;
      Here will I sit and wait,
  While to my ear from uplands far away
    The bleating of the folded flocks is borne,
    With distant cries of reapers in the corn—
    All the live murmur of a summer's day.

Screen'd is this nook o'er the high, half-reap'd field,
  And here till sun-down, Shepherd, will I be.
    Through the thick corn the scarlet poppies peep,

And round green roots and yellowing stalks I see
   Pale blue convolvulus in tendrils creep:
     And air-swept lindens yield
Their scent, and rustle down their perfum'd showers
   Of bloom on the bent grass where I am laid,
   And bower me from the August sun with shade;
     And the eye travels down to Oxford's towers:

And near me on the grass lies Glanvil's book—
   Come, let me read the oft-read tale again,
     The story of that Oxford scholar poor
Of pregnant parts and quick inventive brain,
   Who, tir'd of knocking at Preferment's door,
     One summer morn forsook
His friends, and went to learn the Gipsy lore,
   And roam'd the world with that wild brotherhood,
   And came, as most men deem'd, to little good,
     But came to Oxford and his friends no more.

But once, years after, in the country lanes,
   Two scholars whom at college erst he knew
     Met him, and of his way of life inquir'd.
Whereat he answer'd, that the Gipsy crew,
   His mates, had arts to rule as they desir'd
     The workings of men's brains;
And they can bind them to what thoughts they will:
   'And I,' he said, 'the secret of their art,
   When fully learn'd, will to the world impart:
     But it needs heaven-sent moments for this skill.'

This said, he left them, and return'd no more,
   But rumours hung about the countryside
     That the lost Scholar long was seen to stray,

Seen by rare glimpses, pensive and tongue-tied,
    In hat of antique shape, and cloak of grey,
        The same the Gipsies wore.
Shepherds had met him on the Hurst in spring;
    At some lone alehouse in the Berkshire moors,
        On the warm ingle bench, the smock-frock'd boors
            Had found him seated at their entering,

But, mid their drink and clatter, he would fly:
    And I myself seem half to know thy looks,
        And put the shepherds, Wanderer, on thy trace;
    And boys who in lone wheatfields scare the rooks
        I ask if thou hast pass'd their quiet place;
            Or in my boat I lie
Moor'd to the cool bank in the summer heats,
    Mid wide grass meadows which the sunshine fills,
    And watch the warm green-muffled Cumner hills,
        And wonder if thou haunt'st their shy retreats.

For most I know, thou lov'st retired ground.
    Thee, at the ferry, Oxford riders blithe,
        Returning home on summer nights, have met
    Crossing the stripling Thames at Bablock-hithe,
        Trailing in the cool stream thy fingers wet,
            As the slow punt swings round:
    And leaning backwards in a pensive dream,
        And fostering in thy lap a heap of flowers
        Pluck'd in shy fields and distant Wychwood bowers,
            And thine eyes resting on the moonlit stream:

And then they land, and thou art seen no more.
    Maidens who from the distant hamlets come
        To dance around the Fyfield elm in May,

Oft through the darkening fields have seen thee roam,
Or cross a stile into the public way.
    Oft thou hast given them store
Of flowers—the frail-leaf'd, white anemone—
    Dark bluebells drench'd with dews of summer eves—
    And purple orchises with spotted leaves—
        But none has words she can report of thee.

And, above Godstow Bridge, when hay-time's here
In June, and many a scythe in sunshine flames,
    Men who through those wide fields of breezy grass
Where black-wing'd swallows haunt the glittering Thames,
    To bathe in the abandon'd lasher pass,
        Have often pass'd thee near
Sitting upon the river bank o'ergrown:
    Mark'd thy outlandish garb, thy figure spare,
    Thy dark vague eyes, and soft abstracted air;
        But, when they came from bathing, thou wert gone.

At some lone homestead in the Cumner hills,
    Where at her open door the housewife darns,
        Thou hast been seen, or hanging on a gate
To watch the threshers in the mossy barns.
    Children, who early range these slopes and late
        For cresses from the rills,
Have known thee watching, all an April day,
    The springing pastures and the feeding kine;
    And mark'd thee, when the stars come out and shine,
        Through the long dewy grass move slow away.

In Autumn, on the skirts of Bagley wood,
    Where most the Gipsies by the turf-edg'd way
        Pitch their smok'd tents, and every bush you see

With scarlet patches tagg'd and shreds of grey,
  Above the forest ground call'd Thessaly—
    The blackbird picking food
Sees thee, nor stops his meal, nor fears at all;
  So often has he known thee past him stray
  Rapt, twirling in thy hand a wither'd spray,
    And waiting for the spark from Heaven to fall.

And once, in winter, on the causeway chill
  Where home through flooded fields foot-travellers go,
  Have I not pass'd thee on the wooden bridge
  Wrapt in thy cloak and battling with the snow,
    Thy face towards Hinksey and its wintry ridge?
      And thou hast climb'd the hill
  And gain'd the white brow of the Cumner range,
    Turn'd once to watch, while thick the snowflakes fall,
    The line of festal light in Christ-Church hall—
      Then sought thy straw in some sequester'd grange . . .

. . . O born in day when wits were fresh and clear,
  And life ran gaily as the sparkling Thames;
  Before this strange disease of modern life,
  With its sick hurry, its divided aims,
    Its heads o'ertax'd, its palsied hearts, was rife—
      Fly hence, our contact fear!
  Still fly, plunge deeper in the bowering wood!
    Averse, as Dido did with gesture stern
    From her false friend's approach in Hades turn,
      Wave us away, and keep thy solitude.

Still nursing the unconquerable hope,
  Still clutching the inviolable shade,
    With a free onward impulse brushing through,

By night, the silver'd branches of the glade—
  Far on the forest skirts, where none pursue,
    On some mild pastoral slope
Emerge, and resting on the moonlit pales,
  Freshen thy flowers, as in former years,
  With dew, or listen with enchanted ears,
    From the dark dingles, to the nightingales.

But fly our paths, our feverish contact fly!
  For strong the infection of our mental strife,
    Which, though it gives no bliss, yet spoils for rest;
  And we should win thee from thy own fair life,
    Like us distracted, and like us unblest.
      Soon, soon thy cheer would die,
  Thy hopes grow timorous, and unfix'd thy powers,
    And thy clear aims be cross and shifting made:
  And then thy glad perennial youth would fade,
    Fade, and grow old at last, and die like ours.

Then fly our greetings, fly our speech and smiles!
  —As some grave Tyrian trader, from the sea,
    Descried at sunrise an emerging prow
  Lifting the cool-hair'd creepers stealthily,
    The fringes of a southward-facing brow
      Among the Ægean isles;
  And saw the merry Grecian coaster come,
    Freighted with amber grapes, and Chian wine,
    Green bursting figs, and tunnies steep'd in brine;
      And knew the intruders on his ancient home,

The young light-hearted Masters of the waves;
  And snatch'd his rudder, and shook out more sail,
    And day and night held on indignantly

O'er the blue Midland waters with the gale,
   Betwixt the Syrtes and soft Sicily,
   To where the Atlantic raves
Outside the Western Straits, and unbent sails
  There, where down cloudy cliffs, through sheets of foam,
  Shy traffickers, the dark Iberians come;
   And on the beach undid his corded bales.

TO MARGUERITE

   Yes: in the sea of life enisl'd,
With echoing straits between us thrown,
   Dotting the shoreless watery wild,
We mortal millions live *alone*.
   The islands feel the enclasping flow,
   And then their endless bounds they know.

   But when the moon their hollows lights
And they are swept by balms of spring,
   And in their glens, on starry nights,
The nightingales divinely sing;
   And lovely notes, from shore to shore,
   Across the sounds and channels pour;

   Oh then a longing like despair
Is to their farthest caverns sent;
   For surely once, they feel, we were
Parts of a single continent.
   Now round us spreads the watery plain—
   Oh might our marges meet again!

   Who order'd, that their longing's fire
Should be, as soon as kindled, cool'd?

Who renders vain their deep desire?—
 A God, a God their severance rul'd;
And bade betwixt their shores to be
The unplumb'd, salt, estranging sea.

DOVER BEACH

The sea is calm to-night,
The tide is full, the moon lies fair
Upon the Straits;—on the French coast, the light
Gleams, and is gone; the cliffs of England stand,
Glimmering and vast, out in the tranquil bay,
Come to the window, sweet is the night air!
Only, from the long line of spray
Where the ebb meets the moon-blanch'd sand,
Listen! you hear the grating roar
Of pebbles which the waves suck back, and fling,
At their return, up the high strand,
Begin, and cease, and then again begin,
With tremulous cadence slow, and bring
The eternal note of sadness in.

 Sophocles long ago
Heard it on the Ægæan, and it brought
Into his mind the turbid ebb and flow
Of human misery; we
Find also in the sound a thought,
Hearing it by this distant northern sea.

The sea of faith
Was once, too, at the full, and round earth's shore
Lay like the folds of a bright girdle furl'd;

But now I only hear
Its melancholy, long, withdrawing roar,
Retreating to the breath
Of the night-wind down the vast edges drear
And naked shingles of the world.

Ah, love, let us be true
To one another! for the world, which seems
To lie before us like a land of dreams,
So various, so beautiful, so new,
Hath really neither joy, nor love, nor light,
Nor certitude, nor peace, nor help for pain;
And we are here as on a darkling plain
Swept with confused alarms of struggle and flight,
Where ignorant armies clash by night.

COVENTRY PATMORE
(1823—1896)

REMEMBERED GRACE

Since succour to the feeblest of the wise
Is charge of nobler weight
Than the security
Of many and many a foolish soul's estate,
This I affirm,
Though fools will fools more confidently be:
Whom God does once with heart to heart befriend,
He does so till the end:
And having planted life's miraculous germ,
One sweet pulsation of responsive love,
He sets him sheer above,

Not sin and bitter shame
And wreck of fame,
But Hell's insidious and more black attempt,
The envy, malice, and pride,
Which men who share so easily condone
That few ev'n list such ills as these to hide.
From these unalterably exempt
Through the remember'd grace
Of that divine embrace,
Of his sad errors none,
Though gross to blame,
Shall cast him lower than the cleansing flame,
Nor make him quite depart
From the small flock named 'after God's own heart,'
And to themselves unknown.
Nor can he quail
In faith, nor flush nor pale
When all the other idiot people spell
How this or that new Prophet's word belies
Their last high oracle;
But constantly his soul
Points to its pole
Ev'n as the needle points, and knows not why;
And, under the ever-changing clouds of doubt,
When others cry,
'The stars, if stars there were,
Are quench'd and out!'
To him, uplooking t'ward the hills for aid,
Appear, at need display'd,
Gaps in the low-hung gloom, and, bright in air
Orion or the Bear.

DANTE GABRIEL ROSSETTI
(1828—1882)

THE BLESSÈD DAMOZEL

The blessèd damozel lean'd out
  From the gold bar of Heaven;
Her eyes were deeper than the depth
  Of waters still'd at even;
She had three lilies in her hand,
  And the stars in her hair were seven.

Her robe, ungirt from clasp to hem,
  No wrought flowers did adorn,
But a white rose of Mary's gift,
  For service meetly worn;
Her hair that lay along her back
  Was yellow like ripe corn.

Herseem'd she scarce had been a day
  One of God's choristers;
The wonder was not yet quite gone
  From that still look of hers;
Albeit, to them she left, her day
  Had counted as ten years.

(To one, it is ten years of years.
  ... Yet now, and in this place,
Surely she lean'd o'er me—her hair
  Fell all about my face ...

Nothing: the autumn-fall of leaves.
   The whole year sets apace.)

It was the rampart of God's house
   That she was standing on;
By God built over the sheer depth
   The which is Space begun;
So high, that looking downward thence
   She scarce could see the sun.

It lies in Heaven, across the flood
   Of ether, as a bridge.
Beneath, the tides of day and night
   With flame and darkness ridge
The void, as low as where this earth
   Spins like a fretful midge.

Around her, lovers, newly met
   'Mid deathless love's acclaims,
Spoke evermore among themselves
   Their heart-remember'd names;
And the souls mounting up to God
   Went by her like thin flames.

And still she bow'd herself and stoop'd
   Out of the circling charm;
Until her bosom must have made
   The bar she lean'd on warm,
And the lilies lay as if asleep
   Along her bended arm.

From the fix'd place of Heaven she saw
   Time like a pulse shake fierce
Through all the worlds. Her gaze still strove
   Within the gulf to pierce
Its path; and now she spoke as when
   The stars sang in their spheres.

The sun was gone now; the curl'd moon
   Was like a little feather
Fluttering far down the gulf; and now
   She spoke through the still weather.
Her voice was like the voice the stars
   Had when they sang together.

(Ah sweet! Even now, in that bird's song,
   Strove not her accents there,
Fain to be hearkened? When those bells
   Possess'd the mid-day air,
Strove not her steps to reach my side
   Down all the echoing stair?)

'I wish that he were come to me:
   For he will come' she said.
'Have I not pray'd in Heaven?—on earth,
   Lord, Lord, has he not pray'd?
Are not two prayers a perfect strength?
   And shall I feel afraid?

'When round his head the aureole clings,
   And he is clothed in white,

I'll take his hand and go with him
　　To the deep wells of light;
As unto a stream we will step down,
　　And bathe there in God's sight.

'We two will stand beside that shrine,
　　Occult, withheld, untrod,
Whose lamps are stirred continually
　　With prayer sent up to God;
And see our old prayers, granted, melt
　　Each like a little cloud.

'We two will lie i' the shadow of
　　That living mystic tree,
Within whose secret growth the Dove
　　Is sometimes felt to be,
While every leaf that His plumes touch
　　Saith His Name audibly.

'And I myself will teach to him,
　　I myself, lying so,
The songs I sing here; which his voice
　　Shall pause in, hush'd and slow,
And find some knowledge at each pause,
Or some new thing to know.'

(Alas! We two, we two, thou say'st!
　　Yea, one wast thou with me
That once of old. But shall God lift
　　To endless unity

The soul whose likeness with thy soul
    Was but its love for thee?

'We two,' she said, 'will seek the groves
    Where the lady Mary is,
With her five handmaidens, whose names
    Are five sweet symphonies,
Cecily, Gertrude, Magdalen,
    Margaret and Rosalys.

'Circlewise sit they, with bound locks
    And foreheads garlanded;
Into the fine cloth white like flame
    Weaving the golden thread,
To fashion the birth-robes for them
    Who are just born, being dead.

'He shall fear, haply, and be dumb:
    Then will I lay my cheek
To his, and tell about our love,
    Not once abash'd or weak:
And the dear Mother will approve
    My pride, and let me speak.

'Herself shall bring us, hand in hand,
    To Him round whom all souls
Kneel, the clear-ranged unnumbered heads
    Bowed with their aureoles:
And angels meeting us shall sing
    To their citherns and citoles.

'There will I ask of Christ the Lord
  Thus much for him and me:—
Only to live as once on earth
  With Love,—only to be,
As then awhile, for ever now
  Together, I and he.'

She gazed and listen'd and then said,
  Less sad of speech than mild.—
'All this is when he comes.' She ceased.
  The light thrill'd towards her, fill'd
With angels in strong level flight.
  Her eyes prayed, and she smiled.

(I saw her smile.) But soon their path
  Was vague in distant spheres:
And then she cast her arms along
  The golden barriers,
And laid her face between her hands,
  And wept. (I heard her tears.)

GEORGE MEREDITH
(1828—1909)

PASSAGES FROM 'MODERN LOVE'

(i)

Mark where the pressing wind shoots javelin-like
Its skeleton shadow on the broad-backed wave!
Here is a fitting spot to dig Love's grave;
Here where the ponderous breakers plunge and strike,

And dart their hissing tongues high up the sand:
In hearing of the ocean, and in sight
Of those ribbed wind-streaks running into white.
If I the death of Love had deeply planned,
I never could have made it half so sure,
As by the unblest kisses which upbraid
The full-waked sense; or failing that, degrade!
'Tis morning: but no morning can restore
What we have forfeited. I see no sin:
The wrong is mixed. In tragic life, God wot,
No villain need be! Passions spin the plot:
We are betrayed by what is false within.

(ii)

We saw the swallows gathering in the sky,
And in the osier-isle we heard them noise.
We had not to look back on summer joys,
Or forward to a summer of bright dye:
But in the largeness of the evening earth
Our spirits grew as we went side by side.
The hour became her husband and my bride.
Love, that had robbed us so, thus blessed our dearth!
The pilgrims of the year waxed very loud
In multitudinous chatterings, as the flood
Full brown came from the West, and like pale blood
Expanded to the upper crimson cloud.
Love, that had robbed us of immortal things,
This little moment mercifully gave,
Where I have seen across the twilight wave
The swan sail with her young beneath her wings.

CHRISTINA GEORGINA ROSSETTI
(1830—1894)

MEMORY

I have a room whereinto no one enters
　　Save I myself alone:
　　There sits a blessed memory on a throne,
There my life centres.

While winter comes and goes—oh tedious comer!—
　　And while its nip-wind blows;
　　While bloom the bloodless lily and warm rose
Of lavish summer.

If any should force entrance he might see there
　　One buried yet not dead,
　　Before whose face I no more bow my head
Or bend my knee there;

But often in my worn life's autumn weather
　　I watch there with clear eyes,
　　And think how it will be in Paradise
When we're together.

REST

O Earth, lie heavily upon her eyes;
　　Seal her sweet eyes weary of watching, Earth;
　　Lie close around her; leave no room for mirth
With its harsh laughter, nor for sound of sighs.

She hath no questions, she hath no replies,
　Hushed in and curtained with a blessed dearth
　Of all that irked her from the hour of birth;
With stillness that is almost Paradise.
Darkness more clear than noonday holdeth her,
　Silence more musical than any song;
Even her very heart has ceased to stir:
Until the morning of Eternity
Her rest shall not begin nor end, but be;
　And when she wakes she will not think it long.

LEWIS CARROLL

(Charles Dodgson)

(1832—1898)

THE AGED AGED MAN

"I'll tell thee everything I can;
　There's little to relate.
I saw an aged aged man,
　A-sitting on a gate.
"Who are you, aged man?" I said.
　"And how is it you live?"
And his answer trickled through my head
　Like water through a sieve.

He said, "I look for butterflies
　That sleep among the wheat:
I make them into mutton-pies,
　And sell them in the street.

I sell them unto men," he said,
　　"Who sail on stormy seas;
And that's the way I get my bread—
　　A trifle, if you please."

But I was thinking of a plan
　　To dye one's whiskers green,
And always use so large a fan
　　That they could not be seen.
So, having no reply to give
　　To what the old man said,
I cried, "Come, tell me how you live!"
　　And thumped him on the head.

His accents mild took up the tale:
　　He said, "I go my ways,
And when I find a mountain-rill,
　　I set it in a blaze;
And thence they make a stuff they call
　　Rowland's Macassar-Oil—
Yet twopence-halfpenny is all
　　They give me for my toil."

But I was thinking of a way
　　To feed oneself on batter,
And so go on from day to day
　　Getting a little fatter.
I shook him well from side to side,
　　Until his face was blue:
"Come, tell me how you live," I cried,
　　"And what it is you do!"

He said, "I hunt for haddocks' eyes
   Among the heather bright,
And work them into waistcoat buttons
   In the silent night.
And these I do not sell for gold
   Or coin of silvery shine,
But for a copper halfpenny,
   And that will purchase nine.

"I sometimes dig for buttered rolls,
   Or set limed twigs for crabs;
I sometimes search the grassy knolls
   For wheels of Hansom-cabs.
And that's the way" (he gave a wink)
   "By which I get my wealth—
And very gladly will I drink
   Your Honour's noble health."

I heard him then, for I had just
   Completed my design
To keep the Menai bridge from rust
   By boiling it in wine.
I thanked him much for telling me
   The way he got his wealth,
But chiefly for his wish that he
   Might drink my noble health.

And now, if e'er by chance I put
   My fingers into glue,
Or madly squeeze a right-hand foot
   Into a left-hand shoe,

Or if I drop upon my toe
A very heavy weight,
I weep, for it reminds me so
Of that old man I used to know—
Whose look was mild, whose speech was slow,
Whose hair was whiter than the snow,
Whose face was very like a crow,
With eyes, like cinders, all aglow,
Who seemed distracted with his woe,
Who rocked his body to and fro,
And muttered mumblingly and low,
As if his mouth were full of dough,
Who snorted like a buffalo—
That summer evening long ago
A-sitting on a gate.

JAMES THOMSON
(1834—1882)

MELANCHOLIA

... Baffled and beaten back she works on still,
   Weary and sick of soul she works the more,
Sustained by her indomitable will:
   The hands shall fashion and the brain shall pore,
And all her sorrow shall be turned to labour,
Till Death the friend-foe piercing with his sabre
   That mighty heart of hearts ends bitter war.

But as if blacker night could dawn on night,
   With tenfold gloom on moonless night unstarred,

A sense more tragic than defeat and blight,
  More desperate than strife with hope debarred,
More fatal than the adamantine Never
Encompassing her passionate endeavour,
  Dawns glooming in her tenebrous regard:

The sense that every struggle brings defeat
  Because Fate holds no prize to crown success;
That all the oracles are dumb or cheat
  Because they have no secret to express;
That none can pierce the vast black veil uncertain
Because there is no light beyond the curtain;
  That all is vanity and nothingness.

Titanic from her high throne in the north,
  That City's sombre Patroness and Queen,
In bronze sublimity she gazes forth
  Over her Capital of teen and threne,
Over the river with its isles and bridges,
The marsh and moorland, to the stern rock-ridges,
  Confronting them with a coëval mien.

The moving moon and stars from east to west
  Circle before her in the sea of air;
Shadows and gleams glide round her solemn rest.
  Her subjects often gaze up to her there:
The strong to drink new strength of iron endurance,
The weak new terrors; all, renewed assurance
  And confirmation of the old despair . . .

                              The City of Dreadful Night.

SIR W. S. GILBERT
(1836—1911)

NIGHTMARE

When you're lying awake with a dismal headache, and repos
is taboo'd by anxiety,

I conceive you may use any language you choose to indulge in
without impropriety;

For your brain is on fire—the bedclothes conspire of usual slumbe
to plunder you:

First your counterpane goes, and uncovers your toes, and you
sheet slips demurely from under you;

Then the blanketing tickles—you feel like mixed pickles—s
terribly sharp is the pricking,

And you're hot, and you're cross, and you tumble and toss ti
there's nothing 'twixt you and the ticking.

Then the bedclothes all creep to the ground in a heap, and yo
pick 'em all up in a tangle;

Next your pillow resigns and politely declines to remain at it
usual angle!

Well, you get some repose in the form of a doze, with hot eye
balls and head ever aching,

But your slumbering teems with such horrible dreams that you'
very much better be waking;

For you dream you are crossing the Channel, and tossing abou
in a steamer from Harwich—

Which is something between a large bathing machine and a ver
small second-class carriage—

And you're giving a treat (penny ice and cold meat) to a part
of friends and relations—

They're a ravenous horde—and they all come on board at Sloane
 Square and South Kensington Stations.

And bound on that journey you find your attorney (who started
 that morning from Devon);

He's a bit undersized, and you don't feel surprised when he tells
 you he's only eleven.

Well, you're driving like mad with this singular lad (by-the-
 bye the ship's now a four-wheeler),

And you're playing round games, and he calls you bad names
 when you tell him that "ties pay the dealer";

But this you can't stand, as you throw up your hand, and you
 find you're as cold as an icicle,

In your shirt and your socks (the black silk with gold clocks),
 crossing Salisbury Plain on a bicycle:

And he and the crew are on bicycles too—which they've somehow
 or other invested in—

And he's telling the tars, all the particulars of a company he's
 interested in—

'S a scheme of devices, to get at low prices all goods from cough
 mixtures to cables

Which tickled the sailors) by treating retailers, as though they
 were all vegetables—

You get a good spadesman to plant a small tradesman (first take
 off his boots with a boot-tree),

And his legs will take root, and his fingers will shoot, and they'll
 blossom and bud like a fruit-tree—

From the greengrocer tree you get grapes and green-pea, cauli-
 flower, pineapple, and cranberries,

While the pastrycook plant, cherry brandy will grant, apple
 puffs, and three-corners, and Banburys—

The shares are a penny, and ever so many are taken by Roth-
 schild and Baring,

And just as a few are allotted to you, you awake with a shudder
   despairing—
You're a regular wreck, with a crick in your neck, and no wonder
   you snore, for your head's on the floor, and you've needles
   and pins from your soles to your shins, and your flesh is
   a-creep, for your left leg's asleep, and you've cramp in your
   toes, and a fly on your nose, and some fluff in your lung,
   and a feverish tongue, and a thirst that's intense, and a
   general sense that you haven't been sleeping in clover;
But the darkness has passed, and it's daylight at last, and the
   night has been long—ditto ditto my song—and thank goodness they're both of them over!

ALGERNON CHARLES SWINBURNE
(1837—1909)

THE SUNDEW

A little marsh-plant, yellow green,
And pricked at lip with tender red.
Tread close, and either way you tread
Some faint black water jets between
Lest you should bruise the curious head.

A live thing maybe; who shall know?
The summer knows and suffers it;
For the cool moss is thick and sweet
Each side, and saves the blossom so
That it lives out the long June heat.

The deep scent of the heather burns
About it; breathless though it be,

Bow down and worship; more than we
Is the least flower whose life returns,
Least weed renascent in the sea.

We are vexed and cumbered in earth's sight
With wants, with many memories;
These see their mother what she is,
Glad-growing, till August leave more bright
The apple-coloured cranberries.

Wind blows and bleaches the strong grass,
Blown all one way to shelter it
From trample of strayed kine, with feet
Felt heavier than the moorhen was,
Strayed up past patches of wild wheat.

You call it sundew: how it grows,
If with its colour it have breath,
If life taste sweet to it, if death
Pain its soft petal, no man knows:
Man has no sight or sense that saith.

My sundew, grown of gentle days,
In these green miles the spring begun
Thy growth ere April had half done
With the soft secret of her ways
Or June made ready for the sun.

O red-lipped mouth of marsh-flower,
I have a secret halved with thee.
The name that is love's name to me
Thou knowest, and the face of her
Who is my festival to see.

The hard sun, as thy petals knew,
Coloured the heavy moss-water:
Thou wert not worth green midsummer
Nor fit to live to August blue,
O sundew, not remembering her.

THE GARDEN OF PROSERPINE

Here, where the world is quiet;
    Here, where all trouble seems
Dead winds' and spent waves' riot
    In doubtful dreams of dreams;
I watch the green field growing
For reaping folk and sowing,
For harvest-time and mowing,
    A sleepy world of streams.

I am tired of tears and laughter,
    And men that laugh and weep;
Of what may come hereafter
    For men that sow to reap:
I am weary of days and hours,
Blown buds of barren flowers,
Desires and dreams and powers
    And everything but sleep.

Here life has death for neighbour,
    And far from eye or ear
Wan waves and wet winds labour,
    Weak ships and spirits steer;

They drive adrift, and whither
They wot not who make thither;
But no such winds blow hither,
   And no such things grow here.

No growth of moor or coppice,
   No heather-flower or vine,
But bloomless buds of poppies,
   Green grapes of Proserpine,
Pale beds of blowing rushes
Where no leaf blooms or blushes
Save this whereout she crushes
   For dead men deadly wine.

Pale, without name or number,
   In fruitless fields of corn,
They bow themselves and slumber
   All night till light is born;
And like a soul belated,
In hell and heaven unmated,
By cloud and mist abated
   Comes out of darkness morn.

Though one were strong as seven,
   He too with death shall dwell,
Nor wake with wings in heaven,
   Nor weep for pains in hell;
Though one were fair as roses,
His beauty clouds and closes;
And well though love reposes,
   In the end it is not well.

Pale, beyond porch and portal,
  Crowned with calm leaves, she stands
Who gathers all things mortal
  With cold immortal hands;
Her languid lips are sweeter
Than love's who fears to greet her
To men that mix and meet her
  From many times and lands.

She waits for each and other,
  She waits for all men born;
Forgets the earth her mother,
  The life of fruits and corn;
And spring and seed and swallow
Take wing for her and follow
Where summer song rings hollow
  And flowers are put to scorn.

There go the loves that wither,
  The old loves with wearier wings;
And all dead years draw thither,
  And all disastrous things;
Dead dreams of days forsaken,
Blind buds that snows have shaken,
Wild leaves that winds have taken,
  Red strays of ruined springs.

We are not sure of sorrow,
  And joy was never sure;
To-day will die to-morrow;
  Time stoops to no man's lure;

And love, grown faint and fretful,
With lips but half regretful
Sighs, and with eyes forgetful
    Weeps that no loves endure.

From too much love of living,
    From hope and fear set free,
We thank with brief thanksgiving
    Whatever gods may be
That no life lives for ever;
That dead men rise up never;
That even the weariest river
    Winds somewhere safe to sea.

Then star nor sun shall waken,
    Nor any change of light:
Nor sound of waters shaken,
    Nor any sound or sight;
Not wintry leaves nor vernal,
Nor days nor things diurnal;
Only the sleep eternal
    In an eternal night.

CHORUS FROM 'ATALANTA'

When the hounds of spring are on winter's traces,
    The mother of months in meadow or plain
Fills the shadows and windy places
    With lisp of leaves and ripple of rain;
And the brown bright nightingale amorous
Is half assuaged for Itylus,
For the Thracian ships and the foreign faces,
    The tongueless vigil, and all the pain.

Come with bows bent and with emptying of quivers,
  Maiden most perfect, lady of light,
With a noise of winds and many rivers,
  With a clamour of waters, and with might;
Bind on thy sandals, O thou most fleet,
Over the splendour and speed of thy feet;
For the faint east quickens, the wan west shivers,
  Round the feet of the day and the feet of the night.

Where shall we find her, how shall we sing to her,
  Fold our hands round her knees, and cling?
O that man's heart were fire and could spring to her,
  Fire, or the strength of the streams that spring!
For the stars and winds are unto her
As raiment, as songs of the harp-player;
For the risen stars and the fallen cling to her,
  And the southwest-wind and the west-wind sing.

For winter's rains and ruins are over,
  And all the season of snows and sins;
The days dividing lover and lover,
  The light that loses, the night that wins;
And time remember'd is grief forgotten,
And frosts are slain and flowers begotten,
And in green underwood and cover
  Blossom by blossom the Spring begins.

The full streams feed on flower of rushes,
  Ripe grasses trammel a travelling foot,
The faint fresh flame of the young year flushes
  From leaf to flower and flower to fruit;

And fruit and leaf are as gold and fire,
And the oat is heard above the lyre,
And the hoofed heel of a satyr crushes
    The chestnut-husk at the chestnut-root.

And Pan by noon and Bacchus by night,
    Fleeter of foot than the fleet-foot kid,
Follows with a dancing and fills with delight
    The Mænad and the Bassarid;
And soft as lips that laugh and hide
The laughing leaves of the trees divide,
And screen from seeing and leave in sight
The god pursuing, the maiden hid.

The ivy falls with the Bacchanal's hair
    Over her eyebrows hiding her eyes;
The wild vine slipping down leaves bare
    Her bright breast shortening into sighs;
The wild vine slips with the weight of its leaves,
But the berried ivy catches and cleaves
To the limbs that glitter, the feet that scare
    The wolf that follows, the fawn that flies.

THOMAS HARDY
(1840—1928)

NEUTRAL TONES

We stood by a pond that winter day,
And the sun was white, as though chidden of God,
And a few leaves lay on the starving sod,
    — They had fallen from an ash, and were gray.

Your eyes on me were as eyes that rove
Over tedious riddles solved years ago;
And words played between us to and fro —
      On which lost the more by our love.

The smile on your mouth was the deadest thing
Alive enough to have strength to die;
And a grin of bitterness swept thereby
      Like an ominous bird a-wing . . .

Since then, keen lessons that love deceives,
And wrings with wrong, have shaped to me
Your face, and the God-curst sun, and a tree,
      And a pond edged with grayish leaves.

A BROKEN APPOINTMENT

      You did not come,
And marching Time drew on and wore me numb. —
Yet less for loss of your dear presence there
Than that I thus found lacking in your make
That high compassion which can overbear
Reluctance for pure lovingkindness' sake
Grieved I, when, as the hope-hour stroked its sum,
      You did not come.

      You love not me,
And love alone can lend you loyalty;
— I know and knew it. But unto the store
Of human deeds divine in all but name,

Was it not worth a little hour or more
To add yet this; Once, you, a woman, came
To soothe a time-torn man; even though it be
   You love not me?

THE VOICE

Woman much missed, how you call to me, call to me,
Saying that now you are not as you were
When you had changed from the one who was all to me,
But as at first, when our day was fair.

Can it be you that I hear? Let me view you, then,
Standing as when I drew near to the town
Where you would wait for me; yes, as I knew you then,
Even to the original air-blue gown!

Or is it only the breeze, in its listlessness
Travelling across the wet mead to me here,
You being ever dissolved to existlessness,
Heard no more again far or near?

   Thus I; faltering forward,
   Leaves around me falling,
Wind oozing thin through the thorn from norward,
   And the woman calling.

AFTER A JOURNEY

Hereto I come to view a voiceless ghost;
   Whither, O whither will its whim now draw me?
Up the cliff, down, till I'm lonely, lost,
   And the unseen waters' ejaculations awe me.

Where you will next be there's no knowing,
　　Facing round about me everywhere,
　　　　With your nut-coloured hair,
And gray eyes, and rose-flush coming and going.

Yes: I have re-entered your olden haunts at last;
　　Through the years, through the dead scenes I have tracked yo
What have you now found to say of our past—
　　Scanned across the dark space wherein I have lacked you?
Summer gave us sweets, but autumn wrought division?
　　Things were not lastly as firstly well
　　　　With us twain, you tell?
But all's closed now, despite Time's derision.

I see what you are doing: you are leading me on
　　To the spots we knew when we haunted here together,
The waterfall, above which the mist-bow shone
　　At the then fair hour in the then fair weather,
And the cave just under, with a voice still so hollow
　　That it seems to call out to me from forty years ago,
　　　　When you were all aglow,
And not the thin ghost that I now frailly follow!

Ignorant of what there is flitting here to see,
　　The waked birds preen and the seals flop lazily,
Soon you will have, Dear, to vanish from me,
　　For the stars close their shutters and the dawn whitens hazi
Trust me, I mind not, though Life lours,
　　The bringing me here; nay, bring me here again!
　　　　I am just the same as when
Our days were a joy, and our paths through flowers.

AT CASTLE BOTEREL

As I drive to the junction of lane and highway,
  And the drizzle bedrenches the waggonette,
I look behind at the fading byway,
  And see on its slope, now glistening wet,
    Distinctly yet

Myself and a girlish form benighted
  In dry March weather. We climb the road
Beside a chaise. We had just alighted
  To ease the sturdy pony's load
    When he sighed and slowed.

What we did as we climbed, and what we talked of
  Matters not much, nor to what it led,—
Something that life will not be balked of
  Without rude reason till hope is dead,
    And feeling fled.

It filled but a minute. But was there ever
  A time of such quality, since or before,
In that hill's story? To one mind never,
  Though it has been climbed, foot-swift, foot-sore,
    By thousands more.

Primæval rocks form the road's steep border,
  And much have they faced there, first and last,
Of the transitory in Earth's long order;
  But what they record in colour and cast
    Is—that we two passed.

And to me, though Time's unflinching rigour,
   In mindless rote, has ruled from sight
The substance now, one plantom figure
   Remains on the slope, as when that night
      Saw us alight.

I look and see it there, shrinking, shrinking,
   I look back at it amid the rain
For the very last time; for my sand is sinking,
   And I shall traverse old love's domain
      Never again.

GERARD MANLEY HOPKINS
(1844—1889)

THE WRECK OF THE DEUTSCHLAND

PART THE FIRST

I

Thou mastering me
   God! giver of breath and bread;
World's strand, sway of the sea;
   Lord of living and dead;
Thou hast bound bones and veins in me, fastened me fl
And after it almost unmade, what with dread,
      Thy doing: and dost thou touch me afresh?
Over again I feel thy finger and find thee.

2

I did say yes
O at lightning and lashed rod;
Thou heardst me truer than tongue confess
Thy terror, O Christ, O God;
Thou knowest the walls, altar and hour and night:
The swoon of a heart that the sweep and the hurl of thee trod
Hard down with a horror of height:
And the midriff astrain with leaning of, laced with fire of stress.

3

The frown of his face
Before me, the hurtle of hell
Behind, where, where was a, where was a place?
I whirled out wings that spell
And fled with a fling of the heart to the heart of the Host.
My heart, but you were dovewinged, I can tell,
Carrier-witted, I am bold to boast,
To flash from the flame to the flame then, tower from the grace
to the grace.

4

I am soft sift
In an hourglass—at the wall
Fast, but mined with a motion, a drift,
And it crowds and it combs to the fall;
I steady as a water in a well, to a poise, to a pane,
But roped with, always, all the way down from the tall
Fells or flanks of the voel, a vein
Of the gospel proffer, a pressure, a principle, Christ's gift.

5

I kiss my hand
To the stars, lovely-asunder
Starlight, wafting him out of it; and
Glow, glory in thunder;
Kiss my hand to the dappled-with-damson west:
Since, tho' he is under the world's splendour and wonder,
His mystery must be instressed, stressed;
For I greet him the days I meet him, and bless when I understand.

6

Not out of his bliss
Springs the stress felt
Nor first from heaven (and few know this)
Swings he stroke dealt—
Stroke and a stress that stars and storms deliver,
That guilt is hushed by, hearts are flushed by and melt—
But it rides time like riding a river
(And here the faithful waver, the faithless fable and miss).

7

It dates from day
Of his going in Galilee;
Warm-laid grave of a womb-life grey;
Manger, maiden's knee;
The dense and the driven Passion, and frightful sweat;
Thence the discharge of it, there its swelling to be,
Though felt before, though in high flood yet—
What none would have known of it, only the heart, being hard
at bay,

8

Is out with it! Oh,
We lash with the best or worst
Word last! How a lush-kept plush-capped sloe
Will, mouthèd to flesh-burst,
Gush!—flush the man, the being with it, sour or sweet,
Brim, in a flash, full!—Hither, then, last or first,
To hero of Calvary, Christ's feet—
Never ask if meaning it, wanting it, warned of it—men go.

9

Be adored among men,
God, three-numberèd form;
Wring thy rebel, dogged in den,
Man's malice, with wrecking and storm.
Beyond saying sweet, past telling of tongue,
Thou art lightning and love, I found it, a winter and warm;
Father and fondler of heart thou hast wrung:
Hast thy dark descending and most art merciful then.

10

With an anvil-ding
And with fire in him forge thy will
Or rather, rather then, stealing as Spring
Through him, melt him but master him still:
Whether at once, as once at a crash Paul,
Or as Austin, a lingering-out sweet skill,
Make mercy in all of us, out of us all
Mastery, but be adored, but be adored King.

THE WINDHOVER

TO CHRIST OUR LORD

I caught this morning morning's minion, king-
   dom of daylight's dauphin, dapple-dawn-drawn Falcon, in h
     riding
  Of the rolling level underneath him steady air, and stridir
High there, how he rung upon the rein of a wimpling wing
In his ecstasy! then off, off forth on swing,
   As a skate's heel sweeps smooth on a bow-bend: the hurl ar
     gliding
Rebuffed the big wind. My heart in hiding
Stirred for a bird,—the achieve of, the mastery of the thing!

Brute beauty and valour and act, oh, air, pride, plume, he
  Buckle! AND the fire that breaks from thee then, a billion
Times told lovelier, more dangerous, O my chevalier!
  No wonder of it: shéer plód makes plough down sillion
Shine, and blue-bleak embers, ah my dear,
  Fall, gall themselves, and gash gold-vermilion.

PIED BEAUTY

Glory be to God for dappled things—
   For skies of couple-colour as a brinded cow;
     For rose-moles all in stipple upon trout that swim;
Fresh-firecoal chestnut-falls; finches' wings;
     Landscape plotted and pieced—fold, fallow, and plougl
     And áll trádes, their gear and tackle and trim.

All things counter, original, spare, strange;
   Whatever is fickle, freckled (who knows how?)

With swift, slow; sweet, sour; adazzle, dim;
He fathers-forth whose beauty is past change:
Praise him.

THE CANDLE INDOORS

Some candle clear burns somewhere I come by.
I muse at how its being puts blissful back
With yellowy moisture mild night's blear-all black,
Or to-fro tender trambeams truckle at the eye.
By that window what task what fingers ply,
I plod wondering, a-wanting, just for lack
Of answer the eagerer a-wanting Jessy or Jack
There God to aggrándise, God to glorify.—

Come you indoors, come home; your fading fire
Mend first and vital candle in close heart's vault:
You there are master, do your own desire;
What hinders? Are you beam-blind, yet to a fault
In a neighbour deft-handed? are you that liar
And, cast by conscience out, spendsavour salt?

SPRING AND FALL

TO A YOUNG CHILD

Márgarét, are you gríeving
Over Goldengrove unleaving?
Leáves, líke the things of man, you
With your fresh thoughts care for, can you?
Áh! ás the heart grows older
It will come to such sights colder

By and by, nor spare a sigh
Though worlds of wanwood leafmeal lie;
And yet you wíll weep and know why.
Now no matter, child, the name:
Sórrow's spríngs áre the same.
Nor mouth had, no nor mind, expressed
What heart heard of, ghost guessed:
It ís the blight man was born for,
It is Margaret you mourn for.

SPELT FROM SIBYL'S LEAVES

Earnest, earthless, equal, attuneable, | vaulty, voluminous, . .
    stupendous
Evening strains to be tíme's vást, | womb-of-all, home-of-all
    hearse-of-all night.
Her fond yellow hornlight wound to the west, | her wild hollow
    hoarlight hung to the height
Waste; her earliest stars, earl-stars, | stárs principal, overbend us.
Fíre-féaturing heaven. For earth | her being has unbound, her
    dapple is at an end, as-
tray or aswarm, all throughther, in throngs; | self ín self steepèd
    and páshed—qúite
Disremembering, dísmémbering | áll now. Heart, you round me
    right
With: Óur évening is over us; óur night | whélms, whélms, ánd
    will end us.
Only the beak-leaved boughs dragonish | damask the tool-smooth
    bleak light; black,
Ever so black on it. Óur tale, O óur oracle! | Lét life, wáned,
    ah lét life wind

Off hér once skéined stained véined varíety | upon, áll on twó
    spools; párt, pen, páck
Now her áll in twó flocks, twó folds—black, white; | right,
    wrong; reckon but, reck but, mind
But thése two; wáre of a wórld where bút these | twó tell, each
    off the óther; of a rack
Where, selfwrung, selfstrung, sheathe- and shelterless, | thóughts
    agaínst thoughts ín groans grínd.

SONNETS

(i)

Not, I'll not, carrion comfort, Despair, not feast on thee;
Not untwist— slack they may be—these last strands of man
In me ór, most weary, cry *I can no more.* I can;
Can something, hope, wish day come, not choose not to be.
But ah, but O thou terrible, why wouldst thou rude on me
Thy wring-world right foot rock? lay a lionlimb against me?
                        scan
With darksome devouring eyes my bruisèd bones? and fan,
O in turns of tempest, me heaped there; me frantic to avoid
                        thee and flee?
  Why? That my chaff might fly; my grain lie, sheer and clear.
Nay all that toil, that coil, since (seems) I kissed the rod,
Hand rather, my heart lo! lapped strength, stole joy, would,
                        laugh, chéer.
Cheer whom though? the hero whose heaven-handling flung me,
                        fóot tród
Me? or me that fought him? O which one? is it each one? That
                        night, that year
Of now done darkness I wretch lay wrestling with (my God!)
                        my God.

(ii)

No worst, there is none. Pitched past pitch of grief,
More pangs will, schooled at forepangs, wilder wring.
Comforter, where, where is your comforting?
Mary, mother of us, where is your relief?
My cries heave, herds-long; huddle in a main, a chief
Woe, world-sorrow; on an age-old anvil wince and sing—
Then lull, then leave off. Fury had shrieked 'No ling·
ering! Let me be fell: force I must be brief'.

O the mind, mind has mountains; cliffs of fall
Frightful, sheer, no-man-fathomed. Hold them cheap
May who ne'er hung there. Nor does long our small
Durance deal with that steep or deep. Here! creep,
Wretch, under a comfort serves in a whirlwind: all
Life death does end and each day dies with sleep.

(iii)

I wake and feel the fell of dark, not day.
What hours, O what black hours we have spent
This night! what sights you, heart, saw; ways you went!
And more must, in yet longer light's delay.

With witness I speak this. But where I say
Hours I mean years, mean life. And my lament
Is cries countless, cries like dead letters sent
To dearest him that lives alas! away.

I am gall, I am heartburn. God's most deep decree
Bitter would have me taste: my taste was me;
Bones built in me, flesh filled, blood brimmed the curse.

Selfyeast of spirit a dull dough sours. I see
The lost are like this, and their scourge to be
As I am mine, their sweating selves; but worse.

(iv)

Thou art indeed just, Lord, if I contend
With thee; but, sir, so what I plead is just.
Why do sinners' ways prosper? and why must
Disappointment all I endeavour end?
  Wert thou my enemy, O thou my friend,
How wouldst thou worse, I wonder, than thou dost
Defeat, thwart me? Oh, the sots and thralls of lust
Do in spare hours more thrive than I that spend,
Sir, life upon thy cause. See, banks and brakes
Now, leavèd how thick! lacèd they are again
With fretty chervil, look, and fresh wind shakes
Them; birds build—but not I build; no, but strain,
Time's eunuch, and not breed one work that wakes.
Mine, O thou lord of life, send my roots rain.

ROBERT BRIDGES
(1844—1930)

A PASSER-BY

Whither, O splendid ship, thy white sails crowding,
  Leaning across the bosom of the urgent West,
That fearest nor sea rising, nor sky clouding,
  Whither away, fair rover, and what thy quest?
  Ah! soon, when Winter has all our vales opprest,
When skies are cold and misty, and hail is hurling,

Wilt thoù glide on the blue Pacific, or rest
In a summer haven asleep, thy white sails furling.

I there before thee, in the country that well thou knowes
   Already arrived am inhaling the odorous air:
I watch thee enter unerringly where thou goest,
   And anchor queen of the strange shipping there,
   Thy sails for awnings spread, thy masts bare:
Nor is aught from the foaming reef to the snow-capp'd
                            grandest
   Peak, that is over the feathery palms, more fair
Than thou, so upright, so stately and still thou standest

And yet, O splendid ship, unhail'd and nameless,
   I know not if, aiming a fancy, I rightly divine
That thou hast a purpose joyful, a courage blameless,
   Thy port assured in a happier land than mine.
   But for all I have given thee, beauty enough is thine
As thou, aslant with trim tackle and shrouding,
   From the proud nostril curve of a prow's line
In the offing scatterest foam, thy white sails crowding.

FRANCIS THOMPSON
(1859—1907)

IN NO STRANGE LAND
'THE KINGDOM OF GOD IS WITHIN YOU'

   O world invisible, we view thee,
   O world intangible, we touch thee,
   O world unknowable, we know thee,
   Inapprehensible, we clutch thee!

Does the fish soar to find the ocean,
The eagle plunge to find the air—
That we ask of the stars in motion
If they have rumour of thee there?

Not where the wheeling systems darken,
And our benumb'd conceiving soars!—
The drift of pinions, would we hearken,
Beats at our own clay-shutter'd doors.

The angels keep their ancient places;—
Turn but a stone, and start a wing!
'Tis ye, 'tis your estrangèd faces,
That miss the many-splendour'd thing.

But (when so sad thou canst not sadder)
Cry;—and upon thy so sore loss
Shall shine the traffic of Jacob's ladder
Pitched betwixt Heaven and Charing Cross.

Yea, in the night, my Soul, my daughter,
Cry,—clinging Heaven by the hems;
And lo, Christ walking on the water,
Not of Gennesareth, but Thames!

ALFRED EDWARD HOUSMAN
(1860—1936)

WENLOCK EDGE

On Wenlock Edge the wood's in trouble;
　His forest fleece the Wrekin heaves;
The gale, it plies the saplings double,
　And thick on Severn snow the leaves.

'Twould blow like this through holt and hanger
  When Uricon the city stood:
'Tis the old wind in the old anger,
  But then it threshed another wood.

Then, 'twas before my time, the Roman
  At yonder heaving hill would stare:
The blood that warms an English yeoman,
  The thoughts that hurt him, they were there.

There, like the wind through woods in riot,
  Through him the gale of life blew high;
The tree of man was never quiet:
  Then 'twas the Roman, now 'tis I.

The gale, it plies the saplings double,
  It blows so hard, 'twill soon be gone:
To-day the Roman and his trouble
  Are ashes under Uricon.

EPITAPH ON AN ARMY OF MERCENARIES

These, in the day when heaven was falling,
  The hour when earth's foundations fled,
Follow'd their mercenary calling
  And took their wages and are dead.

Their shoulders held the sky suspended;
  They stood, and earth's foundations stay;
What God abandon'd, these defended,
  And saved the sum of things for pay.

'HER STRONG ENCHANTMENTS FAILING'

Her strong enchantments failing,
    Her towers of fear in wreck,
Her limbecks dried of poisons
    And the knife at her neck,

The Queen of air and darkness
    Begins to shrill and cry,
"O young man, O my slayer,
    To-morrow you shall die."

O Queen of air and darkness,
    I think 'tis truth you say,
And I shall die to-morrow;
    But you will die to-day.

RUDYARD KIPLING
(1865—1936)

DANNY DEEVER

'What are the bugles blowin' for?' said Files-on-Parade.
'To turn you out, to turn you out,' the Colour-Sergeant said.
'What makes you look so white, so white?' said Files-on-Parade.
'I'm dreadin' what I've got to watch,' the Colour-Sergeant said.
    For they're hangin' Danny Deever, you can hear the Dead
                                    March play,
    The Regiment's in 'ollow square—they're hangin' him to-day;
    They've taken of his buttons off an' cut his stripes away,
    An' they're hangin' Danny Deever in the mornin'.

'What makes the rear-rank breathe so 'ard?' said Files-on-Parade.
'It's bitter cold, it's bitter cold,' the Colour-Sergeant said.
'What makes that front-rank man fall down?' said Files-on-
Parade.
'A touch o' sun, a touch o' sun,' the Colour-Sergeant said.
    They are hangin' Danny Deever, they are marchin' of 'im
round,
    They 'ave 'alted Danny Deever by 'is coffin on the ground,
    An' 'e'll swing in 'arf a minute for a sneakin' shootin' hound-
    O they're hangin' Danny Deever in the mornin'!'

' 'Is cot was right-'and cot to mine,' said Files-on-Parade.
' 'E's sleepin' out an' far to-night,' the Colour-Sergeant said.
' 'I've drunk 'is beer a score o' times,' said Files-on-Parade.
' 'E's drinkin' bitter beer alone,' the Colour-Sergeant said.
    They are hangin' Danny Deever, you must mark 'im to
place,
    For 'e shot a comrade sleepin'—you must look 'im in the face,
    Nine 'undred of 'is county an' the Regiment's disgrace,
    While they're hangin' Danny Deever in the mornin'.

'What's that so black agin the sun?' said Files-on-Parade.
'It's Danny fightin' 'ard for life,' the Colour-Sergeant said.
'What's that that whimpers over'ead?' said Files-on-Parade.
'It's Danny's soul that's passin' now,' the Colour-Sergeant said.
    For they're done with Danny Deever, you can 'ear the quick
step play,
    The Regiment's in column, an' they're marchin' us away;
    Ho! the young recruits are shakin', an' they'll want their
beer to-day,
    After hangin' Danny Deever in the mornin'!

'CITIES AND THRONES AND POWERS'

Cities and Thrones and Powers
  Stand in Time's eye,
Almost as long as flowers,
  Which daily die:
But, as new buds put forth
  To glad new men,
Out of the spent and unconsidered Earth
  The Cities rise again.

This season's Daffodil,
  She never hears
What change, what chance, what chill,
  Cut down last year's;
But with bold countenance,
  And knowledge small,
Esteems her seven days' continuance
  To be perpetual.

So Time that is o'er-kind
  To all that be,
Ordains us e'en as blind,
  As bold as she:
That in our very death,
  And burial sure,
Shadow to shadow, well persuaded, saith,
  'See how our works endure!'

W. B. YEATS
(1865—1940)

WHO GOES WITH FERGUS?

Who will go drive with Fergus now,
And pierce the deep wood's woven shade,
And dance upon the level shore?
Young man, lift up your russet brow,
And lift your tender eyelids, maid,
And brood on hopes and fear no more.

And no more turn aside and brood
Upon love's bitter mystery;
For Fergus rules the brazen cars,
And rules the shadows of the wood,
And the white breast of the dim sea
And all dishevelled wandering stars.

MEN IMPROVE WITH THE YEARS

I am worn out with dreams;
A weather-worn, marble triton
Among the streams;
And all day long I look
Upon this lady's beauty
As though I had found in a book
A pictured beauty,
Pleased to have filled the eyes
Or the discerning ears,

Delighted to be but wise,
For men improve with the years;
And yet, and yet,
Is this my dream, or the truth?
O would that we had met
When I had my burning youth!
But I grow old among dreams,
A weather-worn, marble triton
Among the streams.

EASTER, 1916

I have met them at close of day
Coming with vivid faces
From counter or desk among grey
Eighteenth-century houses.
I have passed with a nod of the head
Or polite meaningless words,
Or have lingered awhile and said
Polite meaningless words,
And thought before I had done
Of a mocking tale or a gibe
To please a companion
Around the fire at the club,
Being certain that they and I
But lived where motley is worn:
All changed, changed utterly:
A terrible beauty is born.

That woman's days were spent
In ignorant good will,

Her nights in argument
Until her voice grew shrill.
What voice more sweet than hers
When young and beautiful,
She rode to harriers?
This man had kept a school
And rode our winged horse;
This other his helper and friend
Was coming into his force;
He might have won fame in the end,
So sensitive his nature seemed,
So daring and sweet his thought.
This other man I had dreamed
A drunken, vain-glorious lout.
He had done most bitter wrong
To some who are near my heart,
Yet I number him in the song;
He, too, has resigned his part
In the casual comedy;
He, too, has been changed in his turn,
Transformed utterly:
A terrible beauty is born.

Hearts with one purpose alone
Through summer and winter seem
Enchanted to a stone
To trouble the living stream.
The horse that comes from the road,
The rider, the birds that range
From cloud to tumbling cloud,
Minute by minute they change;

A shadow of cloud on the stream
Changes minute by minute;
A horse-hoof slides on the brim,
And a horse plashes within it
Where long-legged moor-hens dive,
And hens to moor-cocks call.
Minute by minute they live:
The stone's in the midst of all.

Too long a sacrifice
Can make a stone of the heart.
O when may it suffice?
That is heaven's part, our part
To murmur name upon name,
As a mother names her child
When sleep at last has come
On limbs that had run wild.
What is it but nightfall?
No, no, not night but death;
Was it needless death after all?
For England may keep faith
For all that is done and said.
We know their dream; enough
To know they dreamed and are dead;
And what if excess of love
Bewildered them till they died?
I write it out in a verse—
MacDonagh and MacBride
And Connolly and Pearse
Now and in time to be,

Wherever green is worn,
Are changed, changed utterly:
A terrible beauty is born.

THE SECOND COMING

Turning and turning in the widening gyre
The falcon cannot hear the falconer;
Things fall apart; the centre cannot hold;
Mere anarchy is loosed upon the world,
The blood-dimmed tide is loosed, and everywhere
The ceremony of innocence is drowned;
The best lack all conviction, while the worst
Are full of passionate intensity.

Surely some revelation is at hand;
Surely the Second Coming is at hand.
The Second Coming! Hardly are those words out
When a vast image out of *Spiritus Mundi*
Troubles my sight: somewhere in sands of the desert
A shape with lion body and the head of a man,
A gaze blank and pitiless as the sun,
Is moving its slow thighs, while all about it
Reel shadows of the indignant desert birds.
The darkness drops again; but now I know
That twenty centuries of stony sleep
Were vexed to nightmare by a rocking cradle,
And what rough beast, its hour come round at last,
Slouches towards Bethlehem to be born?

SAILING TO BYZANTIUM

I

That is no country for old men. The young
In one another's arms, birds in the trees,
—Those dying generations—at their song,
The salmon-falls, the mackerel-crowded seas,
Fish, flesh, or fowl, commend all summer long
Whatever is begotten, born, and dies.
Caught in that sensual music all neglect
Monuments of unageing intellect.

II

An aged man is but a paltry thing,
A tattered coat upon a stick, unless
Soul clap its hands and sing, and louder sing
For every tatter in its mortal dress,
Nor is there singing school but studying
Monuments of its own magnificence;
And therefore I have sailed the seas and come
To the holy city of Byzantium.

III

O sages standing in God's holy fire
As in the gold mosaic of a wall,
Come from the holy fire, perne in a gyre,
And be the singing-masters of my soul.
Consume my heart away; sick with desire
And fastened to a dying animal
It knows not what it is; and gather me
Into the artifice of eternity.

IV

Once out of nature I shall never take
My bodily form from any natural thing,
But such a form as Grecian goldsmiths make
Of hammered gold and gold enamelling
To keep a drowsy Emperor awake;
Or set upon a golden bough to sing
To lords and ladies of Byzantium
Of what is past, or passing, or to come.

LEDA AND THE SWAN

A sudden blow: the great wings beating still
Above the staggering girl, her thighs caressed
By the dark webs, her nape caught in his bill,
He holds her helpless breast upon his breast.

How can those terrified vague fingers push
The feathered glory from her loosening thighs?
And how can body, laid in that white rush,
But feel the strange heart beating where it lies?

A shudder in the loins engenders there
The broken wall, the burning roof and tower
And Agamemnon dead.
                              Being so caught up,
So mastered by the brute blood of the air,
Did she put on his knowledge with his power
Before the indifferent beak could let her drop?

AMONG SCHOOL CHILDREN

I

I walk through the long schoolroom questioning;
A kind old nun in a white hood replies;
The children learn to cipher and to sing,
To study reading-books and history,
To cut and sew, be neat in everything
In the best modern way—the children's eyes
In momentary wonder stare upon
A sixty-year old smiling public man.

II

I dream of a Ledaean body, bent
Above a sinking fire, a tale that she
Told of a harsh reproof, or trivial event
That changed some childish day to tragedy—
Told, and it seemed that our two natures blent
Into a sphere from youthful sympathy,
Or else, to alter Plato's parable,
Into the yolk and white of the one shell.

III

And thinking of that fit of grief or rage
I look upon one child or t'other there
And wonder if she stood so at that age—
For even daughters of the swan can share
Something of every paddler's heritage—
And had that colour upon cheek or hair,

And thereupon my heart is driven wild:
She stands before me as a living child.

IV

Her present image floats into the mind—
Did Quattrocento finger fashion it
Hollow of cheek as though it drank the wind
And took a mess of shadows for its meat?
And I though never of Ledaean kind
Had pretty plumage once—enough of that,
Better to smile on all that smile, and show
There is a comfortable kind of old scarecrow.

V

What youthful mother, a shape upon her lap
Honey of generation had betrayed,
And that must sleep, shriek, struggle to escape
As recollection or the drug decide,
Would think her son, did she but see that shape
With sixty or more winters on its head,
A compensation for the pang of his birth,
Or the uncertainty of his setting forth?

VI

Plato thought nature but a spume that plays
Upon a ghostly paradigm of things;
Solider Aristotle played the taws
Upon the bottom of a king of kings;

World-famous golden-thighed Pythagoras
Fingered upon a fiddle-stick or strings
What a star sang and careless Muses heard:
Old clothes upon old sticks to scare a bird.

VII

Both nuns and mothers worship images,
But those the candles light are not as those
That animate a mother's reveries,
But keep a marble or a bronze repose.
And yet they too break hearts—O Presences
That passion, piety or affection knows,
And that all heavenly glory symbolise—
O self-born mockers of man's enterprise;

VIII

Labour is blossoming or dancing where
The body is not bruised to pleasure soul,
Nor beauty born out of its own despair,
Nor blear-eyed wisdom out of midnight oil.
O chestnut tree, great rooted blossomer,
Are you the leaf, the blossom or the bole?
O body swayed to music, O brightening glance,
How can we know the dancer from the dance?

BYZANTIUM

The unpurged images of day recede;
The Emperor's drunken soldiery are abed;
Night resonance recedes, night-walkers' song
After great cathedral gong;

A starlit or a moonlit dome disdains
All that man is,
All mere complexities,
The fury and the mire of human veins.

Before me floats an image, man or shade,
Shade more than man, more image than a shade;
For Hades' bobbin bound in mummy-cloth
May unwind the winding path;
A mouth that has no moisture and no breath
Breathless mouths may summon;
I hail the superhuman;
I call it death-in-life and life-in-death.

Miracle, bird or golden handiwork,
More miracle than bird or handiwork,
Planted on the starlit golden bough,
Can like the cocks of Hades crow,
Or, by the moon embittered, scorn aloud
In glory of changeless metal
Common bird or petal
And all complexities of mire or blood.

At midnight on the Emperor's pavement flit
Flames that no faggot feeds, nor steel has lit
Nor storm disturbs, flames begotten of flame,
Where blood-begotten spirits come
And all complexities of fury leave,
Dying into a dance,
An agony of trance,
An agony of flame that cannot singe a sleeve.

Astraddle on the dolphin's mire and blood,
Spirit after spirit! The smithies break the flood,
The golden smithies of the Emperor!
Marbles of the dancing floor
Break bitter furies of complexity,
Those images that yet
Fresh images beget,
That dolphin-torn, that gong-tormented sea.

CRAZY JANE TALKS WITH THE BISHOP

I met the Bishop on the road
And much said he and I.
'Those breasts are flat and fallen now,
Those veins must soon be dry;
Live in a heavenly mansion,
Not in some foul sty.'

'Fair and foul are near of kin,
And fair needs foul,' I cried.
'My friends are gone, but that's a truth
Nor grave nor bed denied,
Learned in bodily lowliness
And in the heart's pride.

'A woman can be proud and stiff
When on love intent;
But Love has pitched his mansion in
The place of excrement;
For nothing can be sole or whole
That has not been rent.'

WALTER DE LA MARE
(1873—   )

THE LISTENERS

'Is there anybody there?' said the Traveller,
   Knocking on the moonlit door;
And his horse in the silence champed the grasses
   Of the forest's ferny floor:
And a bird flew up out of the turret,
   Above the Traveller's head:
And he smote upon the door again a second time;
   'Is there anybody there?' he said.
But no one descended to the Traveller;
   No head from the leaf-fringed sill
Leaned over and looked into his grey eyes,
   Where he stood perplexed and still.
But only a host of phantom listeners
   That dwelt in the lone house then
Stood listening in the quiet of the moonlight
   To that voice from the world of men:
Stood thronging the faint moonbeams on the dark stair,
   That goes down to the empty hall,
Hearkening in an air stirred and shaken
   By the lonely Traveller's call.
And he felt in his heart their strangeness,
   Their stillness answering his cry,
While his horse moved, cropping the dark turf,
   'Neath the starred and leafy sky;
For he suddenly smote on the door, even
   Louder, and lifted his head:—

'Tell them I came, and no one answered,
　　That I kept my word,' he said.
Never the least stir made the listeners,
　　Though every word he spake
Fell echoing through the shadowiness of the still house
　　From the one man left awake:
Ay, they heard his foot upon the stirrup,
　　And the sound of iron on stone,
And how the silence surged softly backward,
　　When the plunging hoofs were gone.

ALL THAT'S PAST

Very old are the woods;
　　And the buds that break
Out of the brier's boughs,
　　When March winds wake,
So old with their beauty are—
　　Oh, no man knows
Through what wild centuries
　　Roves back the rose.

Very old are the brooks;
　　And the rills that rise
Where snow sleeps cold beneath
　　The azure skies
Sing such a history
　　Of come and gone,
Their every drop is as wise
　　As Solomon.

Very old are we men;
Our dreams are tales
Told in dim Eden
By Eve's nightingales;
We wake and whisper awhile,
But, the day gone by,
Silence and sleep like fields
Of amaranth lie.

THE GHOST

'Who knocks?' 'I, who was beautiful,
Beyond all dreams to restore,
I, from the roots of the dark thorn am hither
And knock on the door.'

'Who speaks?' 'I—once was my speech
Sweet as the bird's on the air,
When echo lurks by the waters to heed;
'Tis I speak thee fair.'

'Dark is the hour!' 'Ay, and cold.'
'Lone is my house.' 'Ah, but mine?'
'Sight, touch, lips, eyes yearned in vain.'
'Long dead these to thine...'

Silence. Still faint on the porch
Brake the flames of the stars.
In gloom groped a hope-wearied hand
Over keys, bolts, and bars.

A face peered. All the grey night
  In chaos of vacancy shone;
Nought but vast sorrow was there—
  The sweet cheat gone.

JOHN MASEFIELD
(1876—   )

THE FOX HUNT

... From the Gallows Hill to the Tineton Copse
There were ten ploughed fields, like ten fullstops.
All wet red clay, where a horse's foot
Would be swathed, feet thick, like an ash-tree root.
The fox raced on, on the headlands firm,
Where his swift feet scared the coupling worm;
The rooks rose raving to curse him raw,
He snarled a sneer at their swoop and caw.
Then on, then on, down a half-ploughed field
Where a ship-like plough drove glitter-keeled.
With a bay horse near and a white horse leading.
And a man saying "Zook", and the red earth bleeding.
He gasped as he saw the ploughman drop
The stilts and swear at the team to stop.
The ploughman ran in his red clay clogs.
Crying, "Zick un, Towzer; zick, good dogs!"
A couple of wire-haired lurchers lean
Arose from his wallet, nosing keen;
With a rushing swoop they were on his track,
Putting chest to stubble to bite his back.
He swerved from his line with the curs at heel,
The teeth as they missed him clicked like steel.

With a worrying snarl, they quartered on him,
While the ploughman shouted, "Zick; upon him".

The lurcher dogs soon shot their bolt,
And the fox raced on by the Hazel Holt,
Down the dead grass tilt to the sandstone gash
Of the Pattry Brook at Tineton Ash.
The loitering water, flooded full,
Had yeast on its lip like raddled wool,
It was wrinkled over with Arab script
Of eddies that twisted up and slipt.
The stepping-stones had a rush about them.
So the fox plunged in and swam without them.

He crossed to the cattle's drinking shallow,
Firmed up with rush and roots of mallow;
He wrung his coat from his draggled bones
And romped away for the Sarsen Stones.

The fox raced on, up the Barton Balks,
With a crackle of kex in the nettle stalks,
Over Hammond's grass to the dark green line
Of the larch-wood smelling of turpentine.
Scratch Steven Larches, black to the sky,
A sadness breathing with one long sigh,
Grey ghosts of trees under funeral plumes,
A mist of twig over soft brown glooms.
As he entered the wood he heard the smacks,
Chip-jag, of the fir-pole feller's axe.
He swerved to the left to a broad green ride,
Where a boy made him rush for the farther side.
He swerved to the left, to the Barton Road,

Like a rocket shot to a ship ashore
The lean red bolt of his body tore,
Like a ripple of wind running swift on grass;
Like a shadow on wheat a cloud blows past,
Like a turn at the buoy in a cutter sailing
When the bright green gleam lips white at the railing,
Like the April snake whipping back to sheath,
Like the gannets' hurtle on fish beneath,
Like a kestrel chasing, like a sickle reaping,
Like all things swooping, like all things sweeping,
Like a hound for stay, like a stag for swift,
With his shadow beside like spinning drift.

On he went with a galloping rally
Past Maesbury Clump for Wan Brook Valley
The blood in his veins went romping high,
"Get on, on on, to the earth or die."
The air of the downs went purely past
Till he felt the glory of going fast,
Till the terror of death, though there indeed,
Was lulled for a while by his pride of speed.
He was romping away from hounds and hunt,
He had Wan Dyke Hill and his earth in front,
In a one mile more when his point was made
He would rest in safety from dog or spade;
Nose between paws he would hear the shout
Of the "Gone to earth!" to the hounds without,
The whine of the hounds, and their cat-feet gadding.
Scratching the earth, and their breath pad-padding;
He would hear the horn call hounds away,
And rest in peace till another day...

Reynard the Fox.

EDWARD THOMAS
(1878—1917)

OLD MAN

Old Man, or Lad's-love,—in the name there's nothing
To one that knows not Lad's-love, or Old Man,
The hoar-green feathery herb, almost a tree,
Growing with rosemary and lavender.
Even to one that knows it well, the names
Half decorate, half perplex, the thing it is:
At least, what that is clings not to the names
In spite of time. And yet I like the names.

The herb itself I like not, but for certain
I love it, as some day the child will love it
Who plucks a feather from the door-side bush
Whenever she goes in or out of the house.
Often she waits there, snipping the tips and shrivelling
The shreds at last on to the path, perhaps
Thinking, perhaps of nothing, till she sniffs
Her fingers and runs off. The bush is still
But half as tall as she, though it is as old;
So well she clips it. Not a word she says;
And I can only wonder how much hereafter
She will remember, with that bitter scent,
Of garden rows, and ancient damson trees
Topping a hedge, a bent path to a door,
A low thick bush beside the door, and me
Forbidding her to pick.

As for myself,
Where first I met the bitter scent is lost.
I, too, often shrivel the grey shreds,
Sniff them and think and sniff again and try
Once more to think what it is I am remembering,
Always in vain. I cannot like the scent,
Yet I would rather give up others more sweet,
With no meaning, than this bitter one.
I have mislaid the key. I sniff the spray
And think of nothing; I see and I hear nothing;
Yet seem, too, to be listening, lying in wait
For what I should, yet never can, remember:
No garden appears, no path, no hoar-green bush
Of Lad's-love, or Old Man, no child beside,
Neither father nor mother, nor any playmate;
Only an avenue, dark, nameless, without end.

LIGHTS OUT

I have come to the borders of sleep,
The unfathomable deep
Forest where all must lose
Their way, however straight,
Or winding, soon or late;
They cannot choose.

Many a road and track
That, since the dawn's first crack,
Up to the forest brink,
Deceived the travellers,
Suddenly now blurs,
And in they sink.

Here love ends,
Despair, ambition ends;
All pleasure and all trouble,
Although most sweet or bitter,
Here ends in sleep that is sweeter
Than tasks most noble.

There is not any book
Or face of dearest look
That I would not turn from now
To go into the unknown
I must enter and leave alone
I know not how.

The tall forest towers;
Its cloudy foliage lowers
Ahead, shelf above shelf;
Its silence I hear and obey
That I may lose my way
And myself.

HAROLD MONRO
(1879—1932)

TOO NEAR THE SEA

No foam;
A trippling shallow tread;
The pebbles tingle on the beach,
While, disentangled over head
From clouds, the moonlight, carefully spread,
Lays whiter sheets on my white bed.

From haunted sleeplessness, in quivering dread,
I wander through the sea-sound-empty-full
Large sleeping room above that sea. My bed
Felt like a raft; but now there is the pull
Of dreary sea, toward the window drawing,
Of every slight wave with its itch and drag
Upward toward the tall lean windows clawing,
And, sea-bemysteried, my senses flag.
Yesterday and tomorrow will be waves
Breaking in calm succession on to-day.
Earth-life pales down to sea-foam. Flesh behaves
Like sifted ashes.
Cold slow ocean washes
All round, and then it washes me away.

D. H. LAWRENCE
(1885—1930)

SNAKE

snake came to my water-trough
a hot, hot day, and I in pyjamas for the heat,
drink there.

the deep, strange-scented shade of the great dark carob-tree
ame down the steps with my pitcher
d must wait, must stand and wait, for there he was at the
                                    trough before me.

reached down from a fissure in the earth-wall in the gloom
d trailed his yellow-brown slackness soft-bellied down, over
                                    the edge of the stone trough

And rested his throat upon the stone bottom,
And where the water had dripped from the tap, in a smal
clearness,
He sipped with his straight mouth,
Softly drinking through his straight gums, into his slack lon
body,
Silently.

Someone was before me at my water-trough,
And I, like a second comer, waiting.

He lifted his head from his drinking, as cattle do,
And looked at me vaguely, as drinking cattle do,
And flickered his two-forked tongue from his lips, and muse
a moment,
And stooped and drank a little more,
Being earth-brown, earth-golden from the burning bowels of th
earth
On the day of Sicilian July, with Etna smoking.
The voice of my education said to me
He must be killed,
For in Sicily the black, black snakes are innocent, the gold a
venomous.

And voices in me said, If you were a man
You would take a stick and break him now, and finish him of

But must I confess how I liked him,
How glad I was he had come like a guest in quiet, to drink
my water-trough
And depart peaceful, pacified, and thankless,
Into the burning bowels of this earth?

Was it cowardice, that I dared not kill him?
Was it perversity, that I longed to talk to him?
Was it humility, to feel so honoured?
I felt so honoured.

And yet those voices:
If you were not afraid, you would kill him!

And truly I was afraid, I was most afraid,
But even so, honoured still more
That he should seek my hospitality
From out the dark door of the secret earth.

He drank enough
And lifted his head, dreamily, as one who has drunken,
And flickered his tongue like a forked night on the air, so black,
Seeming to lick his lips,
And looked around like a god, unseeing, into the air,
And slowly turned his head,
And slowly, very slowly, as if thrice adream,
Proceeded to draw his slow length curving round
And climb again the broken bank of my wall-face.
And as he put his head into that dreadful hole,
And as he slowly drew up, snake-easing his shoulders, and
                                    entered farther,
A sort of horror, a sort of protest against his withdrawing into
                                    that horrid black hole,
Deliberately going into the blackness, and slowly drawing him-
                                    self after,
Overcame me now his back was turned.

I looked round, I put down my pitcher,
I picked up a clumsy log,
And threw it at the water-trough with a clatter.

I think it did not hit him,
But suddenly that part of him that was left behind convuls
                              in undignified haste,
Writhed like lightning, and was gone
Into the black hole, the earth-lipped fissure in the wall-fro
At which, in the intense still noon, I stared with fascination.

And immediately I regretted it.
I thought how paltry, how vulgar, what a mean act!
I despised myself and the voices of my accursed human educatic

And I thought of the albatross,
And I wished he would come back, my snake.

For he seemed to me again like a king,
Like a king in exile, uncrowned in the underworld,
Now due to be crowned again.
And so, I missed my chance with one of the lords
Of life.
And I have something to expiate;
A pettiness.

PIANO

Softly, in the dusk, a woman is singing to me;
Taking me back down the vista of years, till I see
A child sitting under a piano, in the boom of the tingling stri
And pressing the small, poised feet of a mother who smiles
                              she sings.

spite of myself the insidious mastery of song
trays me back, till the heart of me weeps to belong
o the old Sunday evenings at home, with winter outside
nd hymns in the cosy parlour, the tinkling piano our guide.

o now it is vain for the singer to burst into clamour
ith the great black piano appasionato. The glamour
f childish days is upon me, my manhood is cast
own in the flood of remembrance, I weep like a child for
the past.

SIEGFRIED SASSOON
(1886—   )

THE HEART'S JOURNEY

(XXXIV)

A flower has opened in my heart . . .
What flower is this, what flower of spring,
What simple, secret thing?
It is the peace that shines apart,
The peace of daybreak skies that bring
Clear song and wild swift wing.

Heart's miracle of inward light,
What powers unknown have sown your seed
And your perfection freed? . . .
O flower within me wondrous white,
I know you only as my need
And my unsealèd sight.

EDITH SITWELL
(1887—   )

HEART AND MIND

Said the Lion to the Lioness— 'When you are amber dust,-
No more a raging fire like the heat of the Sun
(No liking but all lust)—
Remember still the flowering of the amber blood and bone
The rippling of bright muscles like a sea,
Remember the rose-prickles of bright paws
Though we shall mate no more
Till the fire of that sun the heart and the moon-cold bone are on

Said the Skeleton lying upon the sands of Time —
'The great gold planet that is the mourning heat of the S
Is greater than all gold, more powerful
Than the tawny body of a Lion that fire consumes
Like all that grows or leaps ... so is the heart
More powerful than all dust. Once I was Hercules
Or Samson, strong as the pillars of the seas:
But the flames of the heart consumed me, and the mind
Is but a foolish wind.'

Said the Sun to the Moon — 'When you are but a lonely wh:
                                                      crone,
And I, a dead King in my golden armour somewhere in a da
                                                      wood,
Remember only this of our hopeless love
That never till Time is done
Will the fire of the heart and the fire of the mind be one.'

HOLIDAY

O you, all life, and you, the primal Cause—
The Sun and Planets to the husbandman,
The kernel and the sap, the life-blood, flower
Of all that lives, the Power
That holds the Golden Rainers in the heaven,

The wasteful Gardener Who to grow one flower—
Your life, like a long-petalled Sun, has strewn the infinite
Meadow of space with calyxes that die
Like dew, has sown the seed of this hour that comes no more—
Growing in Time, too thin as an abstraction
Yet holding in the end our bones like winter.

Come, we will leave the grey life, the half light
Where we are like the blind, live but in Time
When Toil, the arithmetician, rules the beat
Of blood and heart.
                         Beneath the flowering boughs of heaven
The country roads are made of thickest gold—
They stretch beyond the world, and light like snow
Falls where we go, the Intelligible Light
Turns all to gold, the apple, the dust, the unripe wheat-ear.
Young winds and people have winged feet like Mercury,
And distance is dead, the world ends in the heart.

On this great holiday
Dives and Lazarus are brothers again:
They seem of gold as they come up from the city

Casting aside the grave-clothes of their lives
Where the ragged dust is nobly born as the Sun.
Now Atlas lays aside his dying world,
The clerk, the papers in the dusty office;
And lovers meet their bright Antipodes
To whom they are borne by the young siren seas
Of blood ... he finds no more his dark night is her noon,
For they forget their minds' polarity,
The jarring atoms ... The least ore of gold
And quality of dust
Holds a vein of holiness ... the laws that lie
In the irrefutable dust are Fate's decrees.
No more is Man
The noonday hope of the worm that is his brother —
He who begins with the shape of that eyeless one
Then changes to the world in the mother's side:
For the heart of Man is yet unwearied by Chaos,
And the hands grown thumbless from unuse, the workless hand
Where the needs of famine have grown the claws of the lio
Bear on their palms the wounds of the Crucified.

For now the unborn God in the human heart
Knows for a moment all sublimities ...
Old people at evening sitting in the doorways
See in a broken window of the slum
The Burning Bush reflected, and the crumb
For the starving bird is part of the broken Body
Of Christ Who forgives us — He with the bright Hair —
— The Sun Whose Body was spilt on our fields to bring us
                                                    harvest.

T. S. ELIOT
(1888—   )

THE LOVE SONG OF J. ALFRED PRUFROCK

> S'io credesse che mia risposta fosse
> A persona che mai tornasse al mondo,
> Questa fiamma staria senza piu scosse.
> Ma perciocche giammai di questo fondo
> Non torno vivo alcun, s' i' odo il vero,
> Senza tema d'infamia ti rispondo.

Let us go then, you and I,
When the evening is spread out against the sky
Like a patient etherised upon a table;
Let us go, through certain half-deserted streets,
The muttering retreats
Of restless nights in one-night cheap hotels
And sawdust restaurants with oyster-shells:
Streets that follow like a tedious argument
Of insidious intent
To lead you to an overwhelming question . . .
Oh, do not ask, 'What is it?'
Let us go and make our visit.

In the room the women come and go
Talking of Michelangelo.

The yellow fog that rubs its back upon the window-panes,
The yellow smoke that rubs its muzzle on the window-panes
Licked its tongue into the corners of the evening,
Lingered upon the pools that stand in drains,
Let fall upon its back the soot that falls from chimneys,

Slipped by the terrace, made a sudden leap,
And seeing that it was a soft October night,
Curled once about the house, and fell asleep.
And indeed there will be time
For the yellow smoke that slides along the street
Rubbing its back upon the window-panes;
There will be time, there will be time
To prepare a face to meet the faces that you meet;
There will be time to murder and create,
And time for all the works and days of hands
That lift and drop a question on your plate;
Time for you and time for me,
And time yet for a hundred indecisions,
And for a hundred visions and revisions,
Before the taking of a toast and tea.

In the room the women come and go
Talking of Michelangelo.

And indeed there will be time
To wonder, 'Do I dare?' and, 'Do I dare?'

Time to turn back and descend the stair,
With a bald spot in the middle of my hair—
(They will say: 'How his hair is growing thin!')
My morning coat, my collar mounting firmly to the ch
My necktie rich and modest, but asserted by a simple p
(They will say: 'But how his arms and legs are thin!')
Do I dare
Disturb the universe?
In a minute there is time
For decisions and revisions which a minute will reverse.

For I have known them all already, known them all—
Have known the evenings, mornings, afternoons,
I have measured out my life with coffee spoons;
I know the voices dying with a dying fall
Beneath the music from a farther room.
  So how should I presume?

And I have known the eyes already, known them all—
The eyes that fix you in a formulated phrase,
And when I am formulated, sprawling on a pin,
When I am pinned and wriggling on the wall,
Then how should I begin
To spit out all the butt-ends of my days and ways?
  And how should I presume?

And I have known the arms already, known them all—
Arms that are braceleted and white and bare
(But in the lamplight, downed with light brown hair!)
Is it perfume from a dress
That makes me so digress?
Arms that lie along a table, or wrap about a shawl.
  And should I then presume?
  And how should I begin?

*

Shall I say, I have gone at dusk through narrow streets
And watched the smoke that rises from the pipes
Of lonely men in shirt-sleeves, leaning out of windows? ...

I should have been a pair of ragged claws
Scuttling across the floors of silent seas.

*

And the afternoon, the evening, sleeps so peacefully!
Smoothed by long fingers,
Asleep ... tired ... or it malingers,
Stretched on the floor, here beside you and me.
Should I, after tea and cakes and ices,
Have the strength to force the moment to its crisis?
But though I have wept and fasted, wept and prayed,
Though I have seen my head (grown slightly bald)
                                brought in upon a platter,
I am no prophet—and here's no great matter;
I have seen the moment of my greatness flicker,
And I have seen the eternal Footman hold my coat,
                                and snicker.
And in short, I was afraid.

And would it have been worth it, after all,
After the cups, the marmalade, the tea,
Among the porcelain, among some talk of you and me,
Would it have been worth while,
To have bitten off the matter with a smile,
To have squeezed the universe into a ball
To roll it toward some overwhelming question,
To say: 'I am Lazarus, come from the dead,
Come back to tell you all, I shall tell you all'—
If one, settling a pillow by her head,
    Should say: 'That is not what I meant at all.
    That is not it, at all.'

And would it have been worth it, after all,
Would it have been worth while,
After the sunsets and the dooryards and the sprinkled
                                streets,

After the novels, after the teacups, after the skirts that
                              trail along the floor—
And this, and so much more?—
It is impossible to say just what I mean!
But as if a magic lantern threw the nerves in patterns
                              on a screen:
Would it have been worth while
If one, settling a pillow or throwing off a shawl,
And turning toward the window, should say:
  'That is not it at all,
  That is not what I meant, at all.'

                    *

No! I am not Prince Hamlet, nor was meant to be;
Am an attendant lord, one that will do
To swell a progress, start a scene or two,
Advise the prince; no doubt, an easy tool,
Deferential, glad to be of use,
Politic, cautious, and meticulous;
Full of high sentence, but a bit obtuse;
At times, indeed, almost ridiculous —
Almost, at times, the Fool.

I grow old ... I grow old ...
I shall wear the bottoms of my trousers rolled.

Shall I part my hair behind? Do I dare to eat a peach?
I shall wear white flannel trousers, and walk upon
                              the beach.
I have heard the mermaids singing, each to each.

I do not think that they will sing to me.

I have seen them riding seaward on the waves
Combing the white hair of the waves blown back
When the wind blows the water white and black.

We have lingered in the chambers of the sea
By sea-girls wreathed with seaweed red and brown
Till human voices wake us, and we drown.

SWEENEY AMONG THE NIGHTINGALES

ὤμοι, πέπληγμαι καιρίαν πληγὴν ἔσω.

Apeneck Sweeney spreads his knees
Letting his arms hang down to laugh,
The zebra stripes along his jaw
Swelling to maculate giraffe.

The circles of the stormy moon
Slide westward toward the River Plate,
Death and the Raven drift above
And Sweeney guards the hornèd gate.

Gloomy Orion and the Dog
Are veiled; and hushed the shrunken seas;
The person in the Spanish cape
Tries to sit on Sweeney's knees

Slips and pulls the table cloth
Overturns a coffee-cup,
Reorganised upon the floor
She yawns and draws a stocking up;

The silent man in mocha brown
Sprawls at the window-sill and gapes;
The waiter brings in oranges
Bananas figs and hothouse grapes;

The silent vertebrate in brown
Contracts and concentrates, withdraws;
Rachel *née* Rabinovitch
Tears at the grapes with murderous paws;

She and the lady in the cape
Are suspect, thought to be in league;
Therefore the man with heavy eyes
Declines the gambit, shows fatigue,

Leaves the room and reappears
Outside the window, leaning in,
Branches of wistaria
Circumscribe a golden grin;

The host with someone indistinct
Converses at the door apart,
The nightingales are singing near
The Convent of the Sacred Heart,

And sang within the bloody wood
When Agamemnon cried aloud,
And let their liquid siftings fall
To stain the stiff dishonoured shroud.

WHISPERS OF IMMORTALITY

Webster was much possessed by death
And saw the skull beneath the skin;
And breastless creatures under ground
Leaned backward with a lipless grin.

Daffodil bulbs instead of balls
Stared from the sockets of the eyes!
He knew that thought clings round dead limbs
Tightening its lusts and luxuries.

Donne, I suppose, was such another
Who found no substitute for sense,
To seize and clutch and penetrate;
Expert beyond experience,

He knew the anguish of the marrow
The ague of the skeleton;
No contact possible to flesh
Allayed the fever of the bone.

*

Grishkin is nice: her Russian eye
Is underlined for emphasis;
Uncorseted, her friendly bust
Gives promise of pneumatic bliss.

The couched Brazilian jaguar
Compels the scampering marmoset

With subtle effluence of cat;
Grishkin has a maisonnette;

The sleek Brazilian jaguar
Does not in its arboreal gloom
Distil so rank a feline smell
As Grishkin in a drawing-room.

And even the Abstract Entities
Circumambulate her charm;
But our lot crawls between dry ribs
To keep our metaphysics warm.

GERONTION

> Thou hast nor youth nor age
> But as it were an after dinner sleep
> Dreaming of both.

Here I am, an old man in a dry month,
Being read to by a boy, waiting for rain.
I was neither at the hot gates
Nor fought in the warm rain
Nor knee deep in the salt marsh, heaving a cutlass,
Bitten by flies, fought.
My house is a decayed house,
And the jew squats on the window sill, the owner,
Spawned in some estaminet of Antwerp,
Blistered in Brussels, patched and peeled in London.
The goat coughs at night in the field overhead;
Rocks, moss, stonecrop, iron, merds.

The woman keeps the kitchen, makes tea,
Sneezes at evening, poking the peevish gutter.
                              I an old man,
A dull head among windy spaces.

Signs are taken for wonders. 'We would see a sign!'
The word within a word, unable to speak a word,
Swaddled with darkness. In the juvescence of the year
Came Christ the tiger

In depraved May, dogwood and chestnut, flowering jud:
To be eaten, to be divided, to be drunk
Among whispers; by Mr. Silvero
With caressing hands, at Limoges
Who walked all night in the next room;
By Hakagawa, bowing among the Titians;
By Madame de Tornquist, in the dark room
Shifting the candles; Fräulein von Kulp
Who turned in the hall, one hand on the door. Vacant
                                                  shuttles
Weave the wind. I have no ghosts,
An old man in a draughty house
Under a windy knob.

After such knowledge, what forgiveness? Think now
History has many cunning passages, contrived corridors
And issues, deceives with whispering ambitions,
Guides us by vanities. Think now
She gives when our attention is distracted
And what she gives, gives with such supple confusions
That the giving famishes the craving. Gives too late
What's not believed in, or if still believed,

In memory only, reconsidered passion. Gives too soon
Into weak hands, what's thought can be dispensed with
Till the refusal propagates a fear. Think
Neither fear nor courage saves us. Unnatural vices
Are fathered by our heroism. Virtues
Are forced upon us by our impudent crimes.
These tears are shaken from the wrath-bearing tree.

The tiger springs in the new year. Us he devours. Think
                                              at last
We have not reached conclusion, when I
Stiffen in a rented house. Think at last
I have not made this show purposelessly
And it is not by any concitation
Of the backward devils.
I would meet you upon this honestly.
I that was near your heart was removed therefrom
To lose beauty in terror, terror in inquisition.
I have lost my passion: why should I need to keep it
Since what is kept must be adulterated?
I have lost my sight, smell, hearing, taste and touch:
How should I use them for your closer contact?

These with a thousand small deliberations
Protract the profit of their chilled delirium,
Excite the membrane, when the sense has cooled,
With pungent sauces, multiply variety
In a wilderness of mirrors. What will the spider do,
Suspend its operations, will the weevil
Delay? De Bailhache, Fresca, Mrs. Cammel, whirled
Beyond the circuit of the shuddering Bear

In fractured atoms. Gull against the wind, in the windy
                          straits
Of Belle Isle, or running on the Horn,
White feathers in the snow, the Gulf claims,
And an old man driven by the Trades
To a sleepy corner.

                          Tenants of the house,
Thoughts of a dry brain in a dry season.

MARINA

                        Quis hic locus, quae
                        regio, quae mundi pla

What seas what shores what grey rocks and what islands
What water lapping the bow
And scent of pine and the woodthrush singing through the f
What images return
O my daughter.

Those who sharpen the tooth of the dog, meaning
Death
Those who glitter with the glory of the hummingbird, mean
Death
Those who sit in the stye of contentment, meaning
Death
Those who suffer the ecstasy of the animals, meaning
Death

Are become unsubstantial, reduced by a wind,
A breath of pine, and the woodsong fog
By this grace dissolved in place

hat is this face, less clear and clearer
ae pulse in the arm, less strong and stronger—
ven or lent? more distant than stars and nearer than the eye

hispers and small laughter between leaves and hurrying feet
ader sleep, where all the waters meet.
wsprit cracked with ice and paint cracked with heat.
made this, I have forgotten
ad remember.
ae rigging weak and the canvas rotten
tween one June and another September.
ade this unknowing, half conscious, unknown, my own.
e garboard strake leaks, the seams need caulking.
is form, this face, this life
ring to live in a world of time beyond me; let me
sign my life for this life, my speech for that unspoken,
e awakened, lips parted, the hope, the new ships.

aat seas what shores what granite islands towards my timbers
d woodthrush calling through the fog
   daughter.

ISAAC ROSENBERG
(1890—1918)

BREAK OF DAY IN THE TRENCHES

The darkness crumbles away—
It is the same old druid Time as ever.
Only a live thing leaps my hand—
A queer sardonic rat—
As I pull the parapet's poppy
To stick behind my ear.

Droll rat, they would shoot you if they knew
Your cosmopolitan sympathies.
(And God knows what antipathies.)
Now you have touched this English hand
You will do the same to a German—
Soon, no doubt, if it be your pleasure
To cross the sleeping green between.
It seems you inwardly grin as you pass
Strong yes, fine limbs, haughty athletes
Less chanced than you for life,
Bonds to the whims of murder,
Sprawled in the bowels of the earth,
The torn fields of France.
What do you see in our eyes
At the shrieking iron and flame
Hurled through still heavens?
What quaver—what heart aghast?
Poppies whose roots are in man's veins
Drop, and are ever dropping;
But mine in my ear is safe,
Just a little white with the dust.

WILFRED OWEN
(1893—1918)

STRANGE MEETING

It seemed that out of battle I escaped
Down some profound dull tunnel, long since scooped
Through granites which titanic wars had groined.

Yet also there encumbered sleepers groaned,
Too fast in thought or death to be bestirred.
Then, as I probed them, one sprang up, and stared
With piteous recognition in fixed eyes,
Lifting distressful hands as if to bless.
And by his smile, I knew that sullen hall,
By his dead smile I knew we stood in Hell.
With a thousand pains that vision's face was grained;
Yet no blood reached there from the upper ground,
And no guns thumped, or down the flues made moan.
"Strange friend," I said, "here is no cause to mourn.'
"None," said the other, "save the undone years,
The hopelessness. Whatever hope is yours,
Was my life also; I went hunting wild
After the wildest beauty in the world,
Which lies not calm in eyes, or braided hair,
But mocks the steady running of the hour,
And if it grieves, grieves richlier than here.
For by my glee might many men have laughed,
And of my weeping something had been left,
Which must die now. I mean the truth untold,
The pity of war, the pity war distilled.
Now men will go content with what we spoiled.
Or, discontent, boil bloody, and be spilled.
They will be swift with swiftness of the tigress,
None will break ranks, though nations trek from progress.
Courage was mine, and I had mystery,
Wisdom was mine, and I had mastery;
To miss the march of this retreating world
Into vain citadels that are not walled.
Then, when much blood had clogged their chariot-wheels

I would go up and wash them from sweet wells,
Even with truths that lie too deep for taint.
I would have poured my spirit without stint
But not through wounds; not on the cess of war.
Foreheads of men have bled where no wounds were.
I am the enemy you killed, my friend.
I knew you in this dark; for so you frowned
Yesterday through me as you jabbed and killed.
I parried; but my hands were loath and cold.
Let us sleep now...."

INSENSIBILITY

Happy are men who yet before they are killed
Can let their veins run cold.
Whom no compassion fleers
Or makes their feet
Sore on the alleys cobbled with their brothers.
The front line withers,
But they are troops who fade, not flowers
For poets' tearful fooling:
Men, gaps for filling
Losses who might have fought
Longer; but no one bothers.

And some cease feeling
Even themselves or for themselves.
Dullness best solves
The tease and doubt of shelling,
And Chance's strange arithmetic
Comes simpler than the reckoning of their shilling.
They keep no check on Armies' decimation.

Happy are these who lose imagination:
They have enough to carry with ammunition.
Their spirit drags no pack.
Their old wounds save with cold can not more ache.
Having seen all things red,
Their eyes are rid
Of the hurt of the colour of blood for ever.
And terror's first constriction over
Their hearts remain small drawn.
Their senses in some scorching cautery of battle
Now long since ironed,
Can laugh among the dying, unconcerned.

Happy the soldier home, with not a notion
How somewhere, every dawn, some men attack,
And many sighs are drained.
Happy the lad whose mind was never trained:
His days are worth forgetting more than not.
He sings along the march
Which we march taciturn, because of dusk,
The long, forlorn, relentless trend
From larger day to huger night.

We wise, who with a thought besmirch
Blood over all our soul,
How should we see our task
But through his blunt and lashless eyes?
Alive, he is not vital overmuch;
Dying, not mortal overmuch;
Nor sad, nor proud,
Nor curious at all.

He cannot tell
Old men's placidity from his.

But cursed are dullards whom no cannon stuns,
That they should be as stones.
Wretched are they, and mean
With paucity that never was simplicity.
By choice they made themselves immune
To pity and whatever mourns in man
Before the last sea and the hapless stars;
Whatever mourns when many leave these shores;
Whatever shares
The eternal reciprocity of tears.

THE SEND-OFF

Down the close, darkening lanes they sang their way
To the siding-shed,
And lined the train with faces grimly gay.

Their breasts were stuck all white with wreath and spr
As men's are, dead.

Dull porters watched them, and a casual tramp
Stood staring hard,
Sorry to miss them from the upland camp.
Then, unmoved, signals nodded, and a lamp
Winked to the guard.

So secretly, like wrongs hushed-up, they went.
They were not ours:
We never heard to which front these were sent.

Nor there if they yet mock what women meant
Who gave them flowers.

Shall they return to beatings of great bells
In wild train-loads?
A few, a few, too few for drums and yells,
May creep back, silent, to village wells
Up half-known roads.

ROBERT GRAVES
(1895—)

IN BROKEN IMAGES

He is quick, thinking in clear images;
I am slow, thinking in broken images.

He becomes dull, trusting to his clear images;
I become sharp, mistrusting my broken images,

Trusting his images, he assumes their relevance;
Mistrusting my images, I question their relevance.

Assuming their relevance, he assumes the fact,
Questioning their relevance, I question the fact.

When the fact fails him, he questions his senses;
When the fact fails me, I approve my senses.

He continues quick and dull in his clear images;
I continue slow and sharp in my broken images.

He in a new confusion of his understanding;
I in a new understanding of my confusion.

TIME

The vague sea thuds against the marble cliffs
And from their fragments age-long grinds
Pebbles like flowers.

Or the vague weather wanders in the fields,
When up spring flowers with coloured buds
Like marble pebbles.

The beauty of the flowers is Time, death-grieved;
The pebbles' beauty too is Time,
Life-weary.

It is all too easy to admire a flower
Or a smooth pebble flower-like freaked
By Time and vagueness.

Time is Time's ease and the sweet oil that coaxes
All obstinate locks and rusty hinges
To loving-kindness.

What monster's proof against that lovesome pair,
Old age and childhood, seals of Time,
His sorrowful vagueness?

Or will not render him the accustomed thanks:
Humouring age with filial flowers,
Childhood with pebbles?

SICK LOVE

O Love, be fed with apples while you may,
And feel the sun and go in royal array,
A smiling innocent on the heavenly causeway,

Though in what listening horror for the cry
That soars in outer blackness dismally,
The dumb blind beast, the paranoiac fury:

Be warm, enjoy the season, lift your head,
Exquisite in the pulse of tainted blood,
That infirm passion not to be despised.

Take your delight in momentariness,
Walk between dark and dark — a shining space
With the grave's narrowness, though not its peace.

MID-WINTER WAKING

Stirring suddenly from long hibernation
I knew myself once more a poet
Guarded by timeless principalities
Against the worm of death, this hillside haunting;
And presently dared open both my eyes.

O gracious, lofty, shone against from under,
Back-of-the-mind-far clouds like towers;
And you, sudden warm airs that blow
Before the expected season of new blossom,
While sheep still gnaw at roots and lambless go —

Be witness that on waking, this mid-winter,
I found her hand in mine laid closely
Who shall watch out the Spring with me.
We stared in silence all around us
But found no winter anywhere to see.

VANITY

Be assured, the Dragon is not dead
But once more from the pools of peace
Shall rear his fabulous green head.

The flowers of innocence shall cease
And like a harp the wind shall roar
And the clouds shake an angry fleece.

'Here, here is certitude,' you swore,
'Below this lightning-blasted tree.
Where once it struck, it strikes no more.

'Two lovers in one house agree.
The roof is tight, the walls unshaken.
As now, so must it always be.'

Such prophecies of joy awaken
The toad who dreams away the past
Under your hearth-stone, light-forsaken.

Who knows that certitude at last
Must fall away in vanity —
No gate is fast, no door is fast.

That thunder bursts from the blue sky,
That gardens of the mind fall waste,
That fountains of the heart go dry.

EDMUND BLUNDEN
(1896—   )

THE POOR MAN'S PIG

Already fallen plum-bloom stars the green,
   And apple-boughs as knarred as old toads' backs
Wear their small roses ere a rose is seen;
   The building thrush watches old Job who stacks
The fresh-peeled osiers on the sunny fence,
   The pent sow grunts to hear him stumping by,
And tries to push the bolt and scamper thence,
   But her ringed snout still keeps her to the sty.

Then out he lets her run; away she snorts
   In bundling gallop for the cottage door,
With hungry hubbub begging crusts and orts,
   Then like the whirlwind bumping round once more;
Nuzzling the dog, making the pullets run,
And sulky as a child when her play's done.

THE MIDNIGHT SKATERS

The hop-poles stand in cones,
   The icy pond lurks under,
The pole-tops steeple to the thrones
   Of stars, sound gulfs of wonder;

But not the tallest there, 'tis said,
Could fathom to this pond's black bed.

Then is not death at watch
    Within those secret waters?
What wants he but to catch
    Earth's heedless sons and daughters?
With but a crystal parapet
Between, he has his engines set.

Then on, blood shouts, on, on,
    Twirl, wheel and whip above him,
Dance on this ball-floor thin and wan,
    Use him as though you love him;
Court him, elude him, reel and pass,
And let him hate you through the glass.

ROY CAMPBELL
(1902—   )

TRISTAN DA CUNHA

Snore in the foam: the night is vast and blind,
The blanket of the mist around your shoulders,
Sleep your old sleep of rock, snore in the wind,
Snore in the spray! The storm your slumber lulls,
His wings are folded on your nest of boulders
As on their eggs the grey wings of your gulls.

No more as when, ten thousand years ago,
You hissed a giant cinder from the ocean—
Around your rocks you furl the shawling snow,

Half sunk in your own darkness, vast and grim,
And round you on the deep with surly motion
Pivot your league-long shadow as you swim.

Why should you haunt me thus but that I know
My surly heart is in your own displayed,
Round whom such wastes in endless circuit flow,
Whose hours in such a gloomy compass run—
A dial with its league-long arm of shade
Slowly revolving to the moon and sun.

My heart has sunk, like your grey fissured crags,
By its own strength o'ertoppled and betrayed:
I too have burned the wind with fiery flags,
Who now am but a roost for empty words—
An island of the sea whose only trade
Is in the voyages of its wandering birds.

Did you not, when your strength became your pyre,
Deposed and tumbled from your flaming tower,
Awake in gloom from whence you sank in fire
To find Antaeus-like, more vastly grown,
A throne in your own darkness, and a power
Sheathed in the very coldness of your stone?

Your strength is that you have no hope or fear,
You march before the world without a crown:
The nations call you back, you do not hear:
The cities of the earth grow grey behind you,
You will be there when their great flames go down
And still the morning in the van will find you.

You march before the continents: you scout
In front of all the earth: alone you scale
The masthead of the world, a lorn look-out,
Waving the snowy flutter of your spray
And gazing back in infinite farewell
To suns that sink, and shores that fade away.

From your grey tower what long regrets you fling
To where, along the low horizon burning,
The great swan-breasted seraphs soar and sing,
And suns go down, and trailing splendours dwindle,
And sails on lonely errands unreturning,
Glow with a gold no sunrise can rekindle.

Turn to the Night, these flames are not for you
Whose steeple for the thunder swings its bells:
Grey Memnon, to the tempest only true,
Turn to the night, turn to the shadowing foam,
And let your voice, the saddest of farewells,
With sullen curfew toll the grey wings home.

The wind your mournful syren haunts the gloom:
The rocks, spray-clouded, are your signal-guns
Whose stony nitre, puffed with flying spume,
Rolls forth in grim salute your broadside hollow,
Over the gorgeous burials of suns,
To sound the tocsin of the storms that follow.

Plunge forward; like a ship to battle hurled,
Slip the long cables of the failing light,
The level rays that moor you to the world:

Sheathed in your armour of eternal frost,
Plunge forward, in the thunder of the fight
To lose yourself as I would fain be lost.

Exiled, like you, and severed from my race
By the cold ocean of my own disdain,
Do I not freeze in such a wintry space,
Do I not travel through a storm as vast
And rise at times, victorious from the main,
To fly the sunrise at my shattered mast?

Your path is but a desert where you reap
Only the bitter knowledge of your soul,
You fish with nets of seaweed in the deep
As fruitlessly as I with nets of rhyme,
Yet forth you stride: yourself the way, the goal,
The surges are your strides, your path is time.

Hurled by what aim to what tremendous range!
A missile from the great sling of the past
Your passage leaves its track of death and change
And ruin on the world: you fly beyond,
Leaping the current of the ages vast
As lightly as a pebble skims a pond.

The years are undulations in your flight
Whose awful motion we can only guess:
Too swift for sense, too terrible for sight,
We only know how fast behind you darken
Our days like lonely beacons of distress:
We know that you stride on and will not harken.

Now in the eastern sky the fairest planet
Pierces the dying wave with dangled spear,
And in the whirring hollows of your granite
That vaster Sea, to which you are a shell,
Sighs with a ghostly rumour like the drear
Moan of the nightwind in a hollow cell.

We shall not meet again: over the wave
Our ways divide, and yours is straight and endless—
But mine is short and crooked to the grave:
Yet what of these dark crowds, amid whose flow
I battle like a rock, aloof and friendless—
Are not their generations, vague and endless,
The waves, the strides, the feet on which I go?

CECIL DAY LEWIS
(1904—   )

FROM FEATHERS TO IRON

Suppose that we, to-morrow or the next day,
Came to an end—in storm the shafting broken,
Or a mistaken signal, the flange lifting—
Would that be premature, a text for sorrow?

Say what endurance gives or death denies us.
Love's proved in its creation, not eternity:
Like leaf or linnet the true heart's affection
Is born, dies later, asks no reassurance.

Over dark wood rises one dawn felicitous,
Bright through awakened shadows fall her crystal
Cadenzas, and once for all the woods is quickened.
So our joys visit us, and it suffices.

Nor fear we now to live who in the valley
Of the shadow of life have found a causeway;
For love restores the nerve and love is under
Our feet resilient. Shall we be weary?

Some say we walk out of Time altogether
This way into a region where the primrose
Shows an immortal dew, sun at meridian
Stands up for ever and in scent the lime tree.

This is a land which later we may tell of.
Here-now we know, what death cannot diminish
Needs no replenishing; yet certain are, though
Dying were well enough, to live is better.

Passion has grown full man by his first birthday.
Running across the bean-fields in a south wind,
Fording the river mouth to feel the tide-race—
Child's play that was, though proof of our possessions.

Now our research is done, measured the shadow,
The plains mapped out, the hills a natural bound'ry.
Such and such is our country. There remains to
Plough up the meadowland, reclaim the marshes.

RONALD BOTTRALL
(1906—   )

ARION ANADYOMENOS
(Storm on a Sunday Evening)

We are sitting in a swimming air
Swept by the rain phalanx, talking drily
Of Noah in the flood season. "Repair
The beams and rafters, let the light lie
Heavy on our roofs provided we may rest unhaunte
By threats of entombment
Being yet unhouseled, unwanted."

Within, the toothless beldam purrs applause
At the nice posture of our slippered feet
Uneager to exert her adept jaws
On the stringy unsubstantial meat
Or her brain on the mould of a remainder biscuit.
Outside a black row of sycamores
Re-rank their tops from out the mist
Saddled, however, by no Zaccheus
To invite attention from the Paraclete,
A dove content, assuredly, with his olive branch
And sworn foe to the syllogist.

"We are three of us here and the passing
Of day, the sight of a spider
Walking the wall, or the patter of ashes
As they drop on the hearth have,

For our palates, a varied piquancy,
Objects angled from three compass points
And thus irreconcilable. Nor do these alone
Move through contraries, for often
Our delights are childed on our fears
And we sin from an excess
Of righteousness."

Implications of our pedigree
Cleave this whirl of light and shade,
No room to allot the praise here or agree
Upon an exegesis of the crime. The horoscope
Our fathers cast has set our teeth on edge;
See, they have shortened this man's scope,
Crippled him for private ends
And sent him down the wind, a pledge
To be redeemed in the Greek Kalends.

"Is it worth while to make lips smile again,
To transmit that uneasiness in us which craves
A moment's mouthing, craves to bully the pain
The pain and pity of it into staves
Of crabbed pothooks, filling the breadth
Of tile-page to colophon?
Is it worth while to debate upon
The automatic sense which forces us
To circumvent our quietus
And put instead on record
Reactions to the vibrations of a vocal cord?"

The waters are lifting at length, and stand revealed
The shoddy roofs steeled,

Even silvered, by reflected light, quite rent
From their cadaverous cerement,
While the final passacaglia of Brahms
Weaves itself point by point
Into the shuddering waves of rain,
Assertive, affirmative, triumphant...
Perchance, after all, living within
And for ourselves, exhaling our entity
In our perceptions, yet not altogether bent
With our breaths to petrify and eternize
Some stony replica, we have tracked
What song the sirens sang. So may the disjoint
Time resolve itself and raise up dolphins backed
Like whales to waft us where a confident sea
Is ever breaking, never spent.

GENESIS

The child quickens the coy light of a candle
With faint voices and echoing alleys,
Fathers a world in nooks, thoroughfares in an angle.
But we have lost the transmuting eye that sees
Heaven in a sapphire light, or in a seared face hell.

The fisherman gleaming with salt pilchard scales,
Blackcocks burring on the wing, are taken
From our blood, and slatted prison walls
Fracture the fringes of our winter sun.

Time was, in the days of pilgrimage,
When the equinox leapt as a ram, green

As an emerald at the moment of its cleavage,
When the world ran rippling in a rune.

Now, constricted in an agony of labour,
We retch our hearts out, teasing the sublime
To intricate motives, adequate to the hour,
And envy no man's pedestal of rhyme.

But the desert moth waits, dormant for years, to fertilize
The yucca blossom on its one night of flower,
And the listener patient with attuned ear
Will catch, at length, in the dead house infant cries.

WILLIAM EMPSON
(1907—   )

TO AN OLD LADY

Ripeness is all; her in her cooling planet
Revere; do not presume to think her wasted.
Project her no projectile, plan nor man it;
Gods cool in turn, by the sun long outlasted.

Our earth alone given no name of god
Gives, too, no hold for such a leap to aid her;
Landing, you break some palace and seem odd;
Bees sting their need, the keeper's queen invader.

No, to your telescope; spy out the land;
Watch while her ritual is still to see,
Still stand her temples emptying in the sand
Whose waves o'erthrow their crumbled tracery;

Still stands uncalled-on her soul's appanage;
Much social detail whose successor fades,
Wit used to run a house and to play Bridge,
And tragic fervour, to dismiss her maids.

Years her precession do not throw from gear.
She reads a compass certain of her pole;
Confident, finds no confines on her sphere,
Whose failing crops are in her sole control.

Stars how much further from me fill my night,
Strange that she too should be inaccessible,
Who shares my sun. He curtains her from sight,
And but in darkness is she visible.

LEGAL FICTION

Law makes long spokes of the short stakes of men.
Your well fenced out real estate of mind
No high flat of the nomad citizen
Looks over, or train leaves behind.

Your rights extend under and above your claim
Without bound; you own land in Heaven and Hell;
Your part of earth's surface and mass the same,
Of all cosmos' volume, and all stars as well.

Your rights reach down where all owners meet, in Hel
Pointed exclusive conclave, at earth's centre
(Your spun farm's root still on that axis dwells);
And up, through galaxies, a growing sector.

You are nomad yet; the lighthouse beam you own
Flashes, like Lucifer, through the firmament.
Earth's axis varies; your dark central cone
Wavers, a candle's shadow, at the end.

W. H. AUDEN
(1907—   )

CHORUS FROM 'PAID ON BOTH SIDES'

Though he believe it, no man is strong
He thinks to be called the fortunate,
To bring home a wife, to live long.

But he is defeated; let the son
Sell the farm lest the mountain fall;
His mother and her mother won.

His fields are used up where the moles visit,
The contours worn flat; if there show
Passage for water he will miss it:

Give up his breath, his woman, his team;
No life to touch, though later there be
Big fruit, eagles above the stream.

'SIR, NO MAN'S ENEMY'

Sir, no man's enemy, forgiving all
But will his negative inversion, be prodigal:
Send to us power and light, a sovereign touch
Curing the intolerable neural itch,

The exhaustion of weaning, the liar's quinsy,
And the distortions of ingrown virginity.
Prohibit sharply the rehearsed response
And gradually correct the coward's stance;
Cover in time with beams those in retreat
That, spotted, they turn though the reverse were great;
Publish each healer that in city lives
Or country houses at the end of drives;
Harrow the house of the dead; look shining at
New styles of architecture, a change of heart.

'O WHERE ARE YOU GOING'

'O where are you going?' said reader to rider,
'That valley is fatal when furnaces burn,
Yonder's the midden whose odours will madden,
That gap is the grave where the tall return.'

'O do you imagine', said fearer to farer,
'That dusk will delay on your path to the pass,
Your diligent looking discover the lacking
Your footsteps feel from granite to grass?'

'O what was that bird,' said horror to hearer,
'Did you see that shape in the twisted trees?
Behind you swiftly the figure comes softly,
The spot on your skin is a shocking disease?'

'Out of this house'—said rider to reader
'Yours never will'—said farer to fearer
'They're looking for you'—said hearer to horror
As he left them there, as he left them there.

O LOVE, THE INTEREST ITSELF IN THOUGHTLESS HEAVEN'

O love, the interest itself in thoughtless Heaven,
Make simpler daily the beating of man's heart; within,
There in the ring where name and image meet,

Inspire them with such a longing as will make his thought
Alive like patterns a murmuration of starlings
Rising in joy over wolds unwittingly weave;

Here too on our little reef display your power,
This fortress perched on the edge of the Atlantic scarp,
The mole between all Europe and the exile-crowded sea;

And make us as Newton was, who in his garden watching
The apple falling towards England, became aware
Between himself and her of an eternal tie.

For now that dream which so long has contented our will,
I mean, of uniting the dead into a splendid empire,
Under whose fertilising flood the Lancashire moss

Sprouted up chimneys, and Glamorgan hid a life
Grim as a tidal rock-pool's in its glove-shaped valleys,
Is already retreating into her maternal shadow;

Leaving the furnaces gasping in the impossible air,
The flotsam at which Dumbarton gapes and hungers;
While upon wind-loved Rowley no hammer shakes

The cluster of mounds like a midget golf course, graves
Of some who created these intelligible dangerous marvels;
Affectionate people, but crude their sense of glory.

Far-sighted as falcons, they looked down another future;
For the seed in their loins were hostile, though afraid of their
                                      pride,
And, tall with a shadow now, inertly wait.

In bar, in netted chicken-farm, in lighthouse,
Standing on these impoverished constricting acres,
The ladies and gentlemen apart, too much alone,

Consider the years of the measured world begun,
The barren spiritual marriage of stone and water.
Yet, O, at this very moment of our hopeless sigh

When inland they are thinking their thoughts but are watching
                                     these islands,
As children in Chester look to Moel Fammau to decide
On picnics by the clearness or withdrawal of her treeless crown

Some possible dream, long coiled in the ammonite's slumber
Is uncurling, prepared to lay on our talk and comfort
Its military silence, its surgeon's idea of pain;

And out of the Future into actual History,
As when Merlin, tamer of horses, and his lords to whom
Stonehenge was still a thought, the Pillars passed

And into the undared ocean swung north their prow,
Drives through the night and star-concealing dawn
For the virgin roadsteads of our hearts an unwavering keel.

STEPHEN SPENDER
(1909—   )

I THINK CONTINUALLY...

I think continually of those who were truly great.
Who, from the womb, remembered the soul's history
Through corridors of light where the hours are suns
Endless and singing. Whose lovely ambition
Was that their lips, still touched with fire,
Should tell of the Spirit clothed from head to foot in song.
And who hoarded from the Spring branches
The desires falling across their bodies like blossoms.

What is precious is never to forget
The essential delight of the blood drawn from ageless springs
Breaking through rocks in worlds before our earth
Never to deny its pleasure in the morning simple light
Nor its grave evening demand for love.
Never to allow gradually the traffic to smother
With noise and fog the flowering of the spirit.

Near the snow, near the sun, in the highest fields
See how these names are fêted by the waving grass
And by streamers of white cloud
And whispers of wind in the listening sky.
The names of those who in their lives fought for life
Who wore at their hearts the fire's centre.
Born of the sun they travelled a short while towards the sun,
And left the vivid air signed with their honour.

DYLAN THOMAS
(1914—   )

POEM FIVE

The force that through the green fuse drives the flower
Drives my green age; that blasts the roots of trees
Is my destroyer.
And I am dumb to tell the crooked rose
My youth is bent by the same wintry fever.

The force that drives the water through the rocks
Drives my red blood; that dries the mouthing streams
Turns mine to wax.
And I am dumb to mouth unto my veins
How at the mountain spring the same mouth sucks.

The hand that whirls the water in the pool
Stirs the quicksand; that ropes the blowing wind
Hauls my shroud sail.
And I am dumb to tell the hanging man
How of my clay is made the hangman's lime.

The lips of time leech to the fountain head;
Love drips and gathers, but the fallen blood
Shall calm her sores.
And I am dumb to tell a weather's wind
How time has ticked a heaven round the stars.

And I am dumb to tell the lover's tomb
How at my sheet goes the same crooked worm.

IN MEMORY OF ANN JONES

After the funeral, mule praises, brays,
Windshake of sailshaped ears, muffle-toed tap
Tap happily of one peg in the thick
Grave's foot, blinds down the lids, the teeth in black,
The spittled eyes, the salt ponds in the sleeves,
Morning smack of the spade that wakes up sleep,
Shakes a desolate boy who slits his throat
In the dark of the coffin and sheds dry leaves,
That breaks one bone to light with a judgment clout,
After the feast of tear-stuffed time and thistles
In a room with a stuffed fox and a stale fern,
I stand, for this memorial's sake, alone
In the snivelling hours with dead, humped Ann
Whose hooded, fountain heart once fell in puddles
Round the parched worlds of Wales and drowned each sun
(Though this for her is a monstrous image blindly
Magnified out of praise; her death was a still drop;
She would not have me sinking in the holy
Flood of her heart's fame; she would lie dumb and deep
And need no druid of her broken body).
But I, Ann's bard on a raised hearth, call all
The seas to service that her wood-tongued virtue
Babble like a bellbuoy over the hymning heads,
Bow down the walls of the ferned and foxy woods
That her love sing and swing through a brown chapel,
Bless her bent spirit with four, crossing birds.
Her flesh was meek as milk, but this skyward statue
With the wild breast and blessed and giant skull
Is carved from her in a room with a wet window
In a fiercely mourning house in a crooked year.

I know her scrubbed and sour humble hands
Lie with religion in their cramp, her threadbare
Whisper in a damp word, her wits drilled hollow,
Her fist of a face died clenched on a round pain;
And sculptured Ann is seventy years of stone.
These cloud-sopped, marble hands, this monumental
Argument of the hewn voice, gesture and psalm
Storm me forever over her grave until
The stuffed lung of the fox twitch and cry Love
And the strutting fern lay seeds on the black sill.